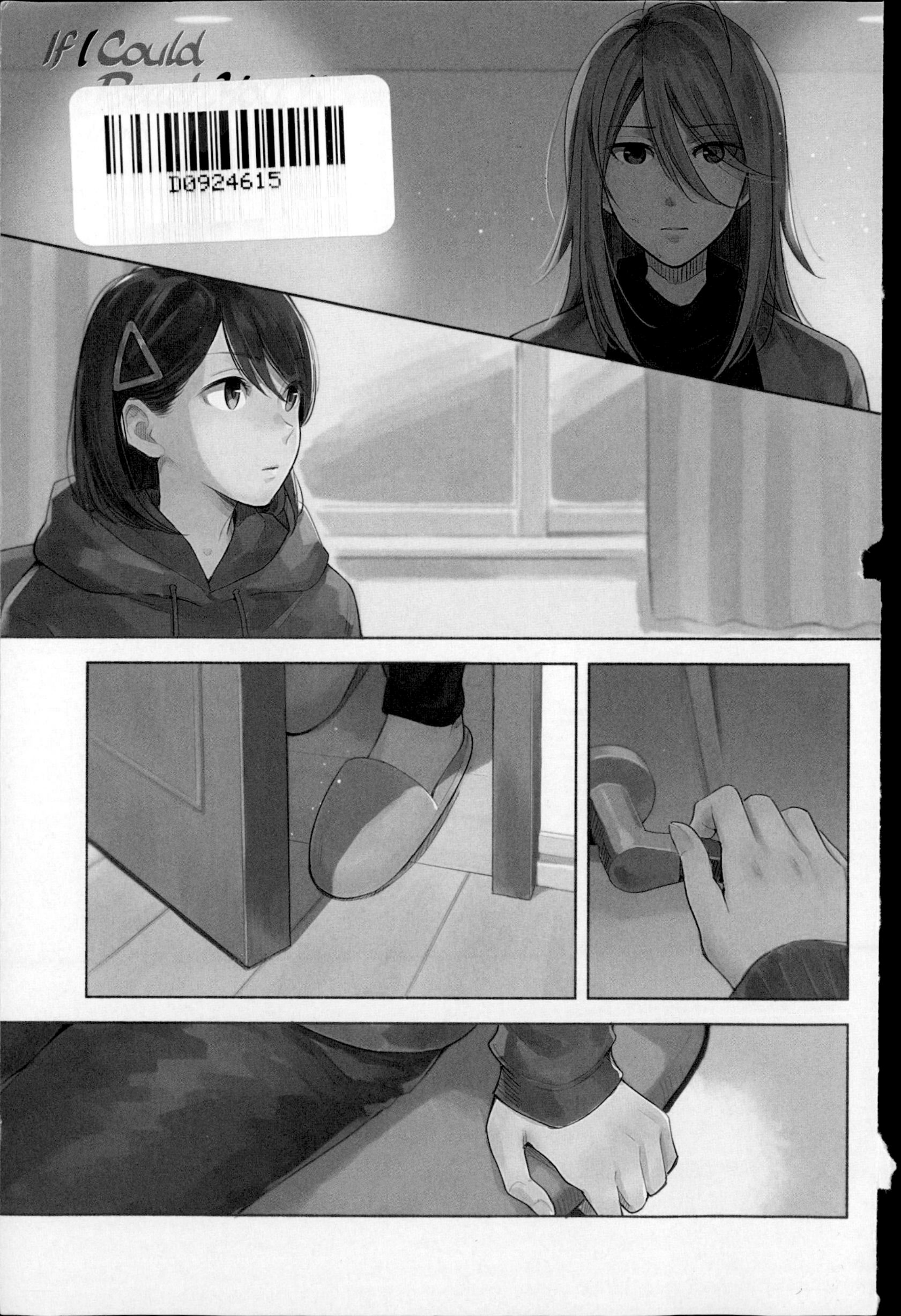
If I Could

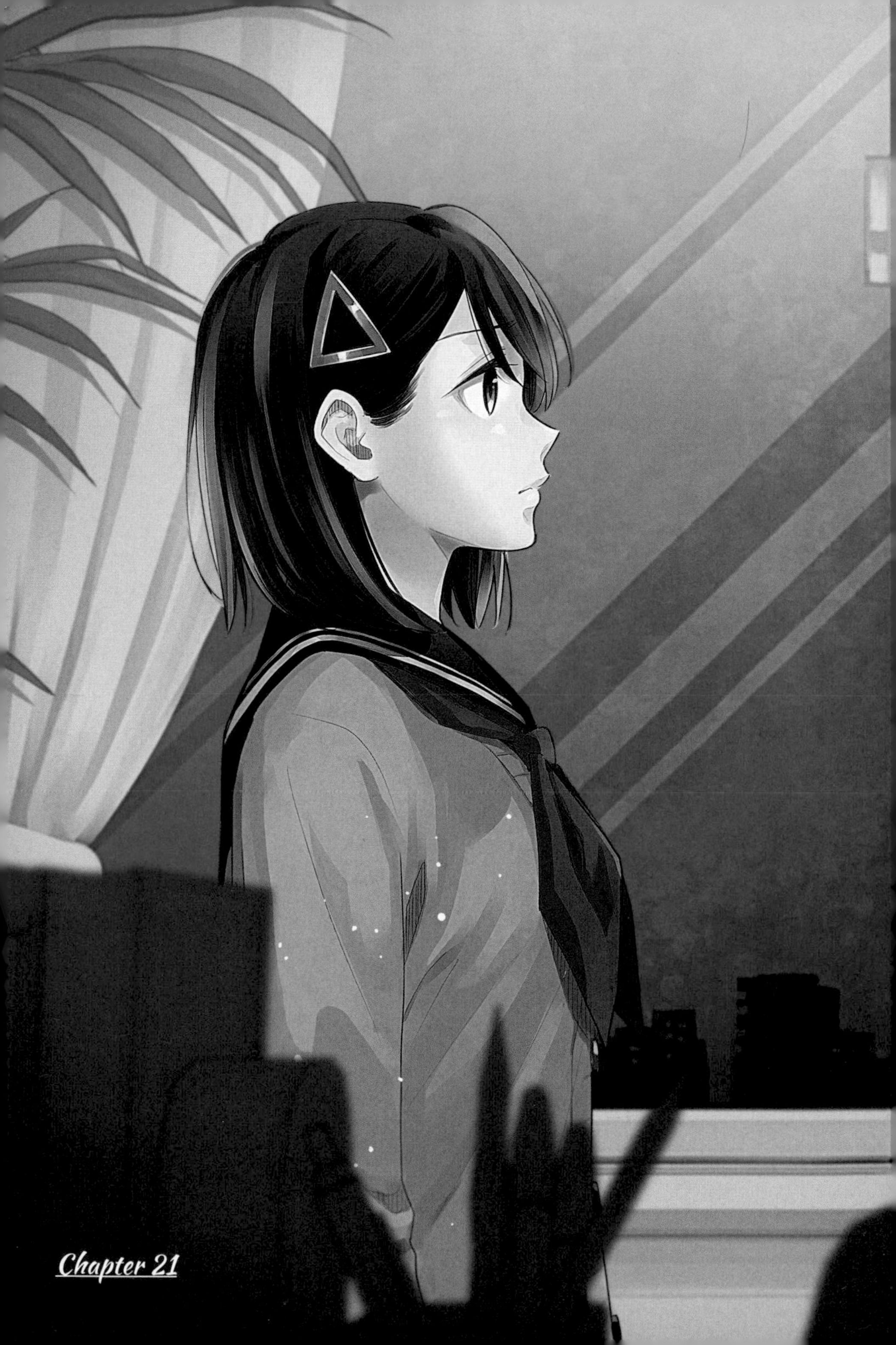
Chapter 21

If I Could Reach You

5

CONTENTS

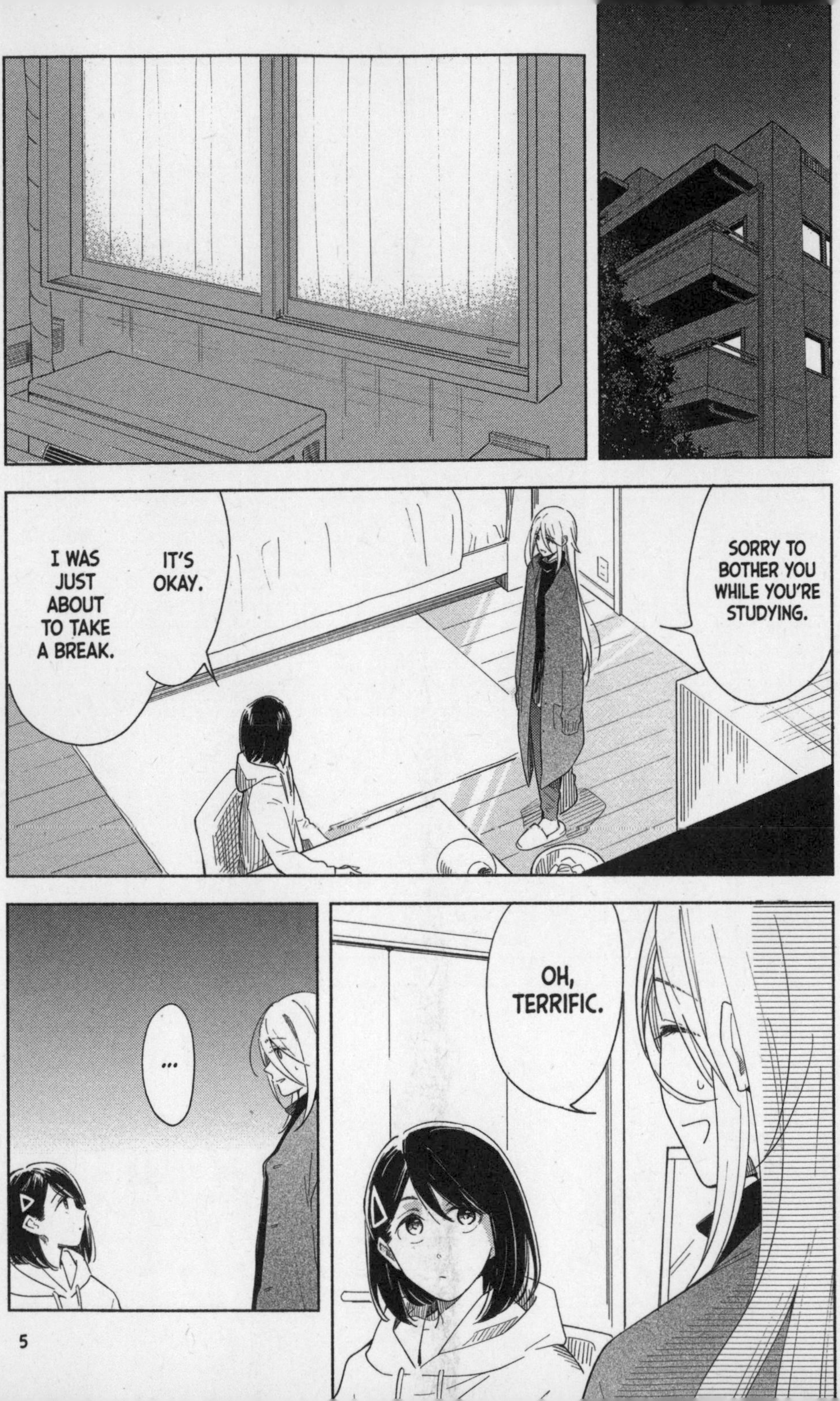
SORRY TO BOTHER YOU WHILE YOU'RE STUDYING.
IT'S OKAY.
I WAS JUST ABOUT TO TAKE A BREAK.
OH, TERRIFIC.
...

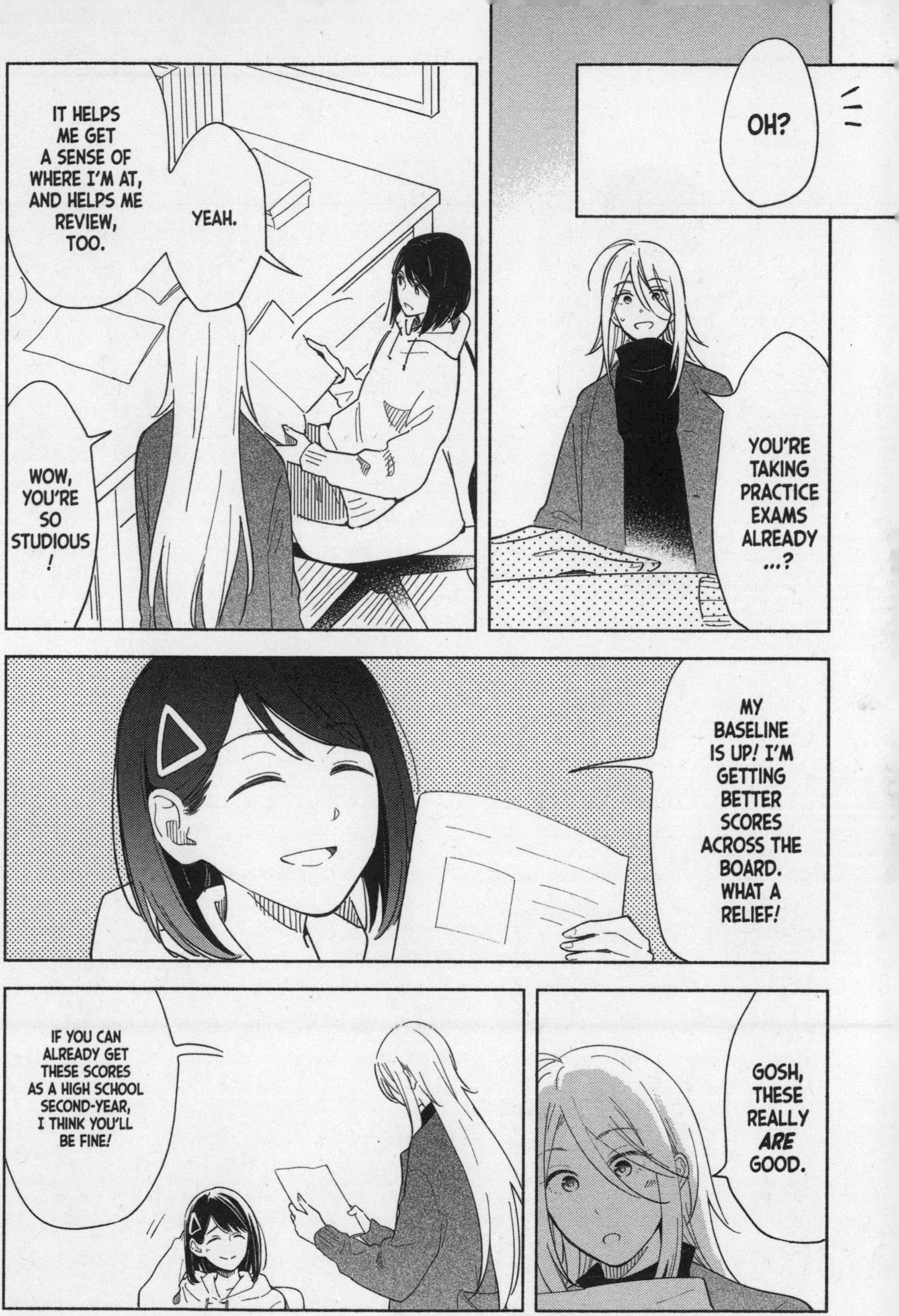
OH?
YOU'RE TAKING PRACTICE EXAMS ALREADY ...?
YEAH.
IT HELPS ME GET A SENSE OF WHERE I'M AT, AND HELPS ME REVIEW, TOO.
WOW, YOU'RE SO STUDIOUS!
MY BASELINE IS UP! I'M GETTING BETTER SCORES ACROSS THE BOARD. WHAT A RELIEF!
GOSH, THESE REALLY *ARE* GOOD.
IF YOU CAN ALREADY GET THESE SCORES AS A HIGH SCHOOL SECOND-YEAR, I THINK YOU'LL BE FINE!

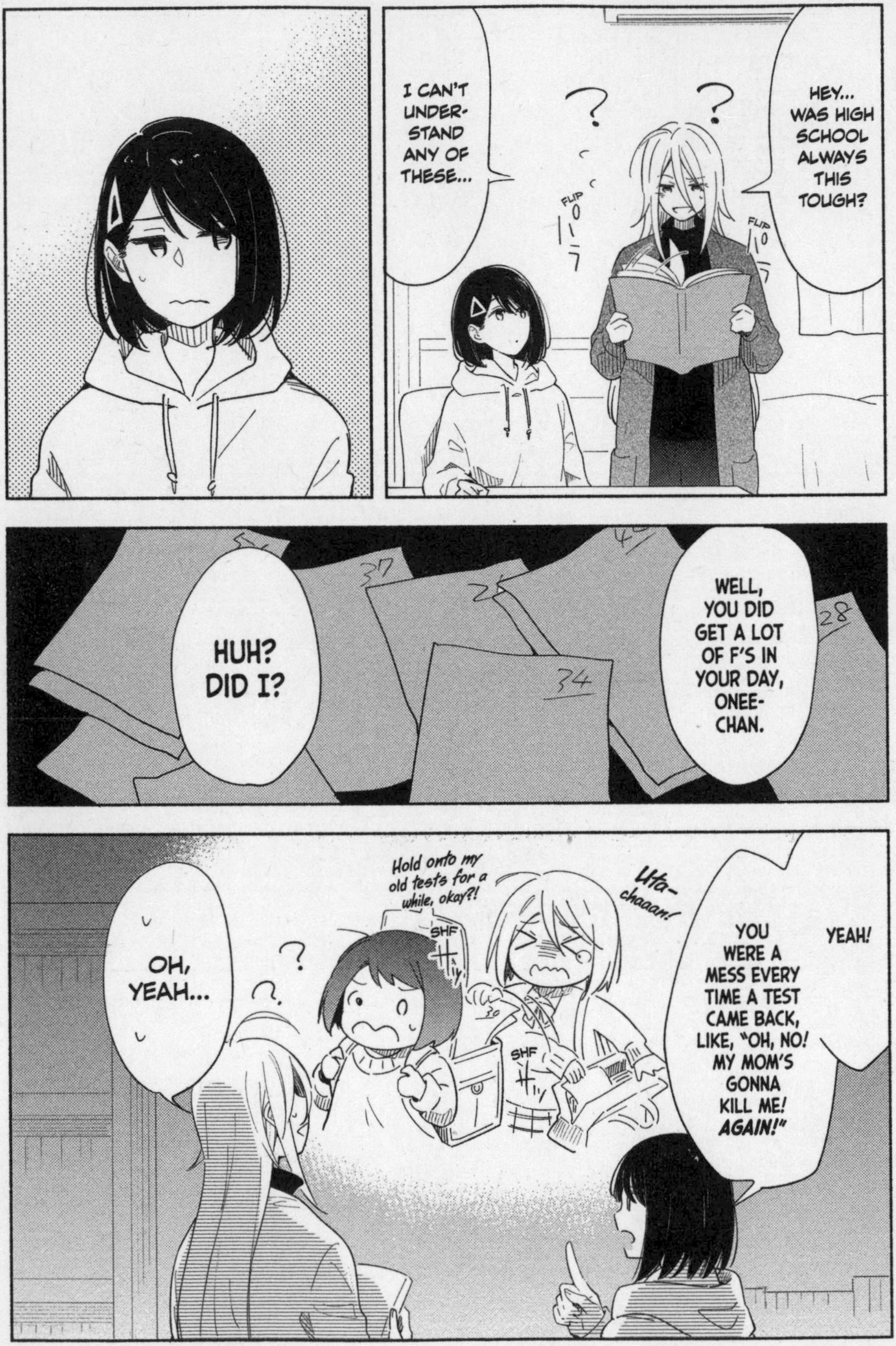
HEY... WAS HIGH SCHOOL ALWAYS THIS TOUGH?
FLIP
FLIP
I CAN'T UNDER-STAND ANY OF THESE...
WELL, YOU DID GET A LOT OF F'S IN YOUR DAY, ONEE-CHAN.
28
34
37
HUH? DID I?
YOU WERE A MESS EVERY TIME A TEST CAME BACK, LIKE, "OH, NO! MY MOM'S GONNA KILL ME! *AGAIN!*"
YEAH!
Uta-chaaan!
Hold onto my old tests for a while, okay?!
SHF
SHF
OH, YEAH...

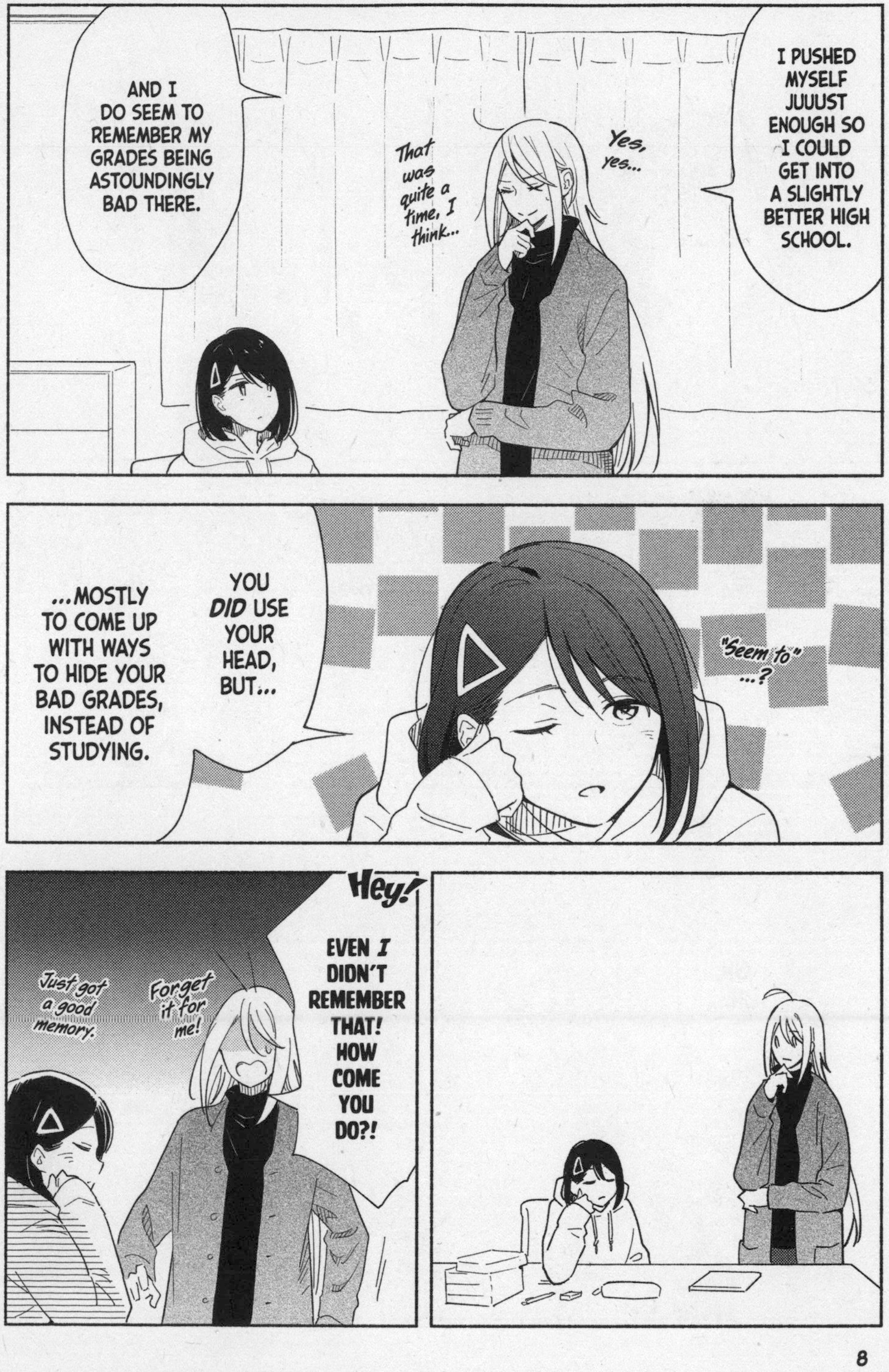
I PUSHED MYSELF JUUUST ENOUGH SO I COULD GET INTO A SLIGHTLY BETTER HIGH SCHOOL.
Yes, yes...
That was quite a time, I think...
AND I DO SEEM TO REMEMBER MY GRADES BEING ASTOUNDINGLY BAD THERE.
"Seem to" ...?
YOU DID USE YOUR HEAD, BUT...
...MOSTLY TO COME UP WITH WAYS TO HIDE YOUR BAD GRADES, INSTEAD OF STUDYING.
Hey!
EVEN I DIDN'T REMEMBER THAT! HOW COME YOU DO?!
Forget it for me!
Just got a good memory.

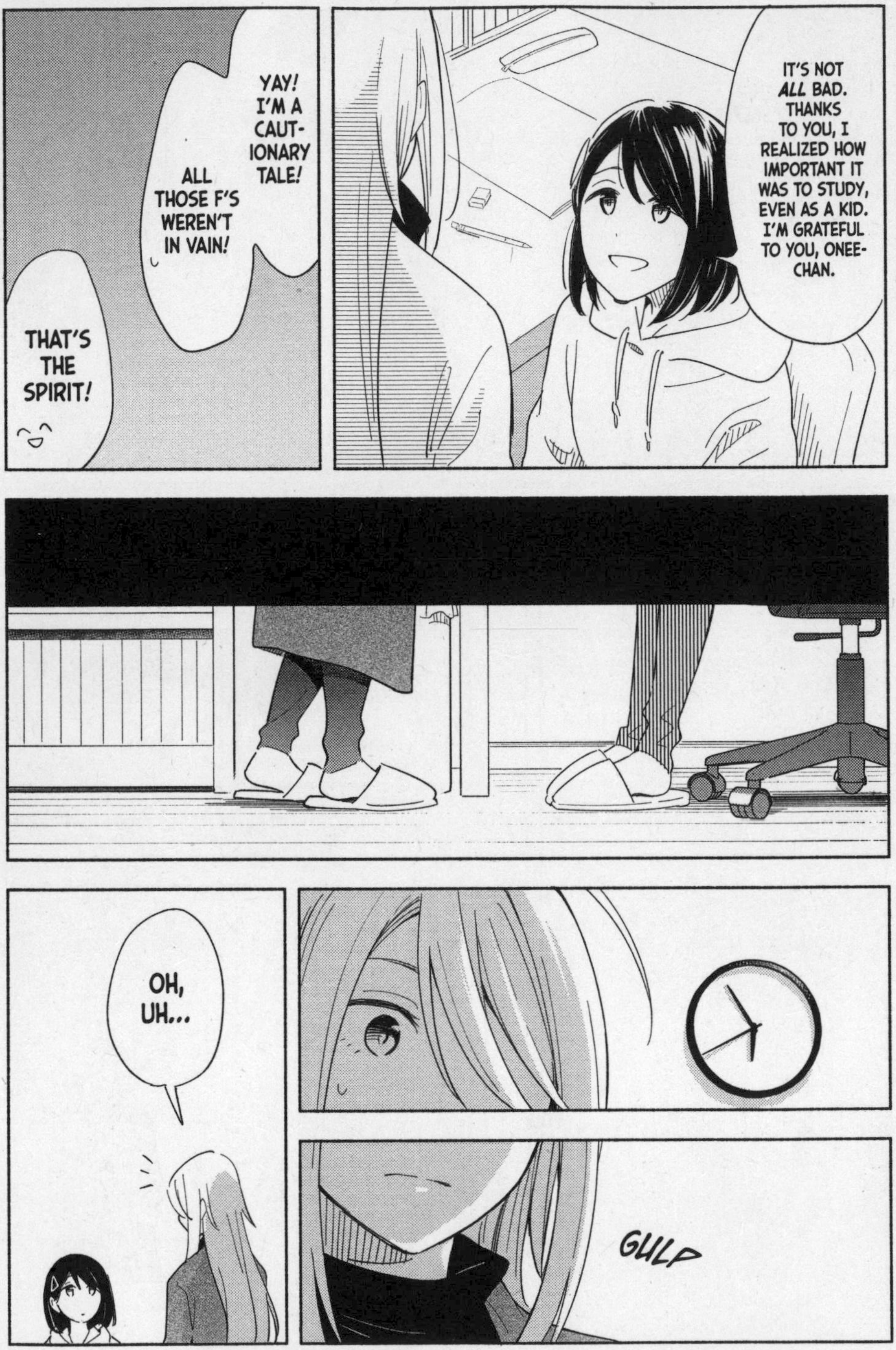
IT'S NOT *ALL* BAD. THANKS TO YOU, I REALIZED HOW IMPORTANT IT WAS TO STUDY, EVEN AS A KID. I'M GRATEFUL TO YOU, ONEE-CHAN.
YAY! I'M A CAUTIONARY TALE!
ALL THOSE F'S WEREN'T IN VAIN!
THAT'S THE SPIRIT!
GULP
OH, UH...

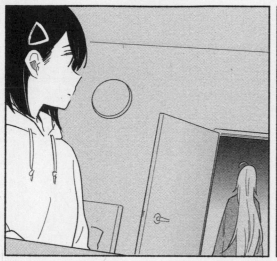

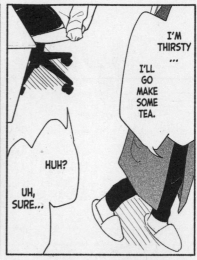

I'M
THIRSTY
...

I'LL
GO
MAKE
SOME
TEA.

HUH?

UH,
SURE...

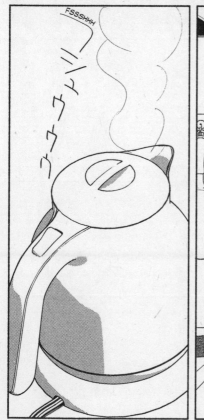

FSSSHHH

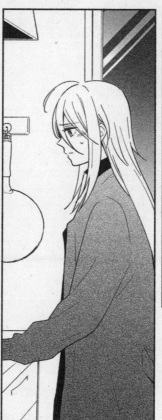

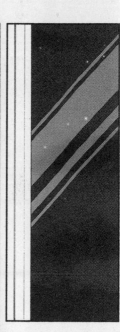

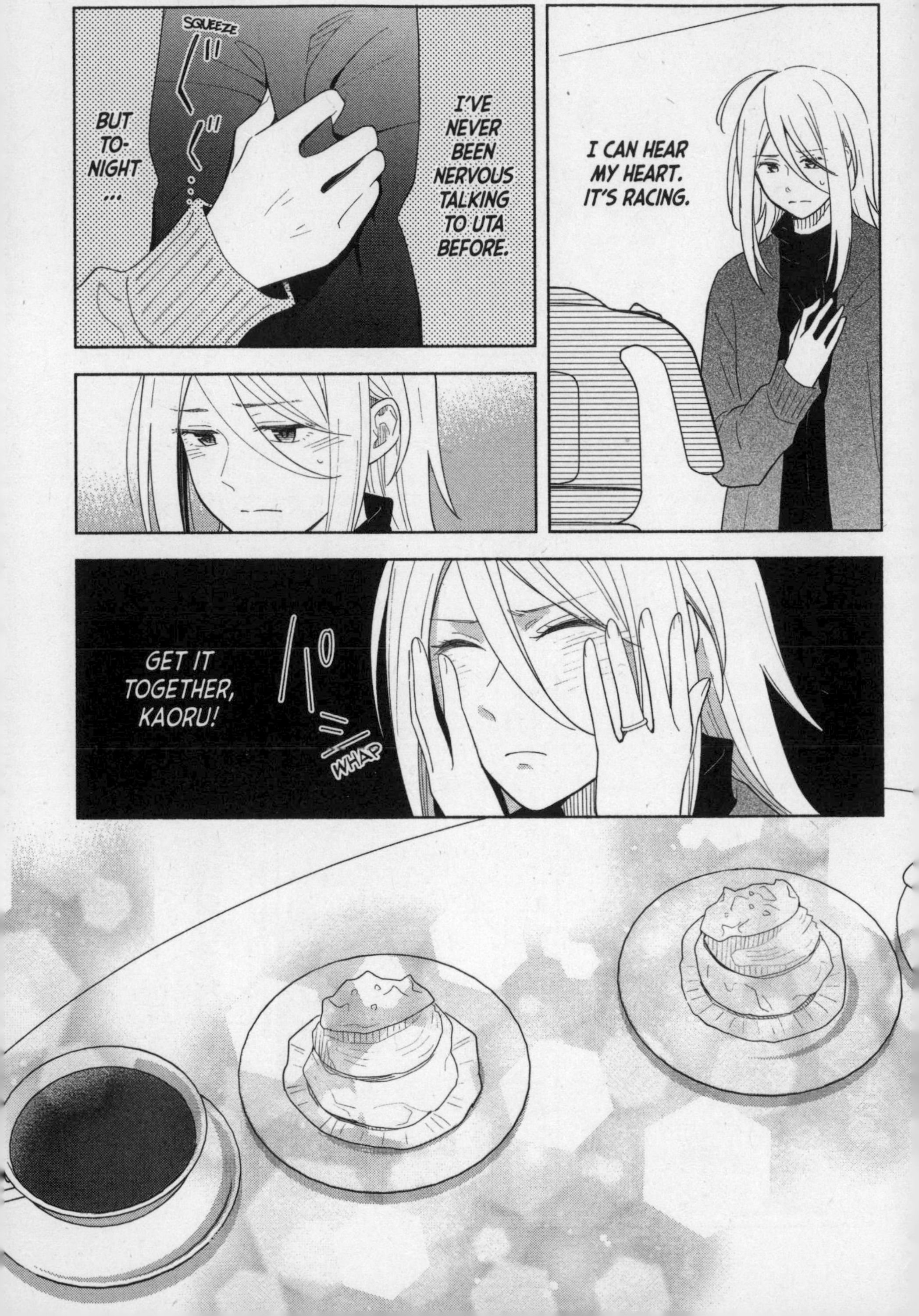
I CAN HEAR MY HEART. IT'S RACING.
SQUEEZE
I'VE NEVER BEEN NERVOUS TALKING TO UTA BEFORE.
BUT TO-NIGHT...
GET IT TOGETHER, KAORU!
WHAP

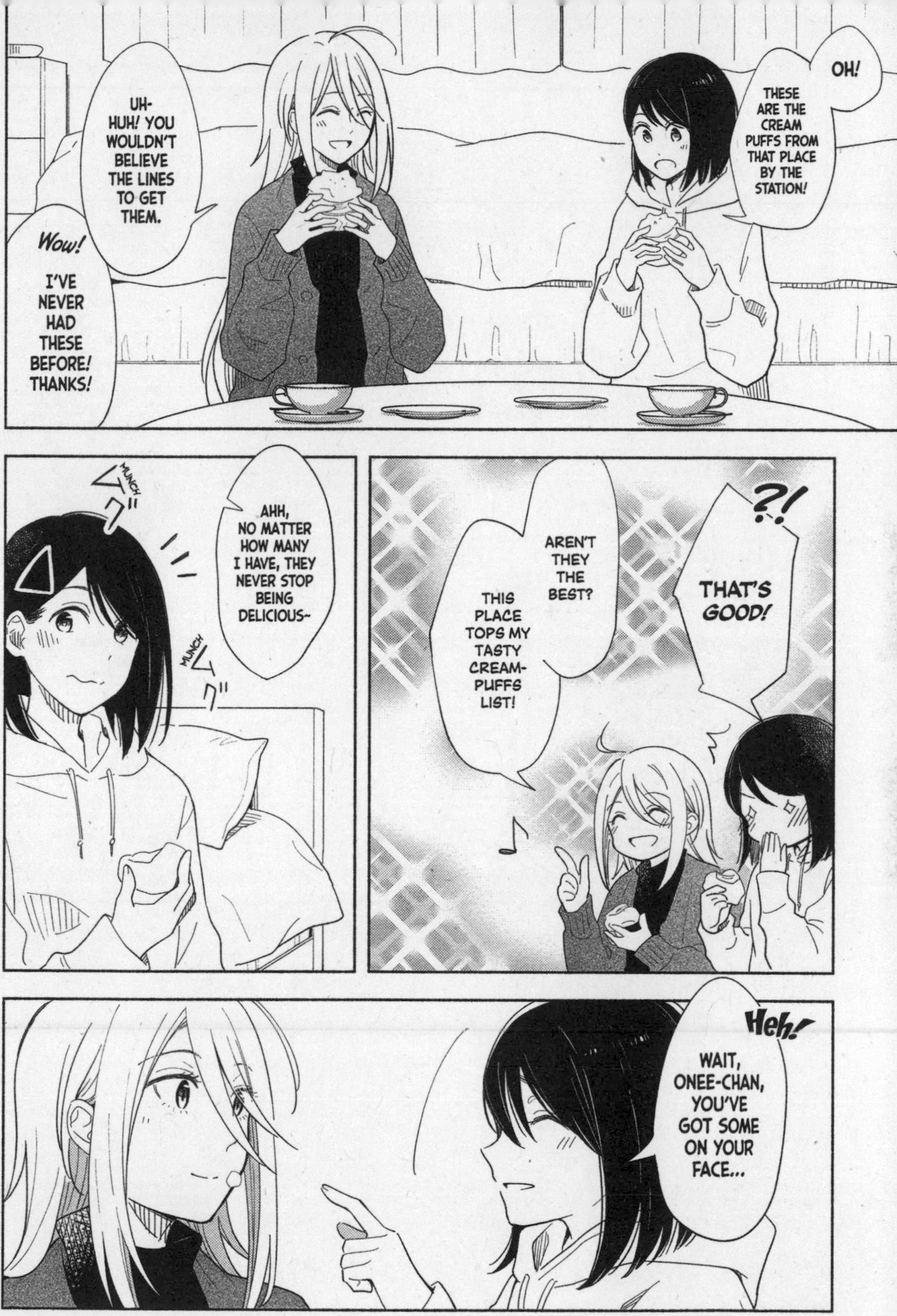
OH!
THESE ARE THE CREAM PUFFS FROM THAT PLACE BY THE STATION!
UH-HUH! YOU WOULDN'T BELIEVE THE LINES TO GET THEM.
Wow!
I'VE NEVER HAD THESE BEFORE! THANKS!
?!
THAT'S GOOD!
AREN'T THEY THE BEST?
THIS PLACE TOPS MY TASTY CREAM-PUFFS LIST!
AHH, NO MATTER HOW MANY I HAVE, THEY NEVER STOP BEING DELICIOUS~
MUNCH
MUNCH
Heh!
WAIT, ONEE-CHAN, YOU'VE GOT SOME ON YOUR FACE...

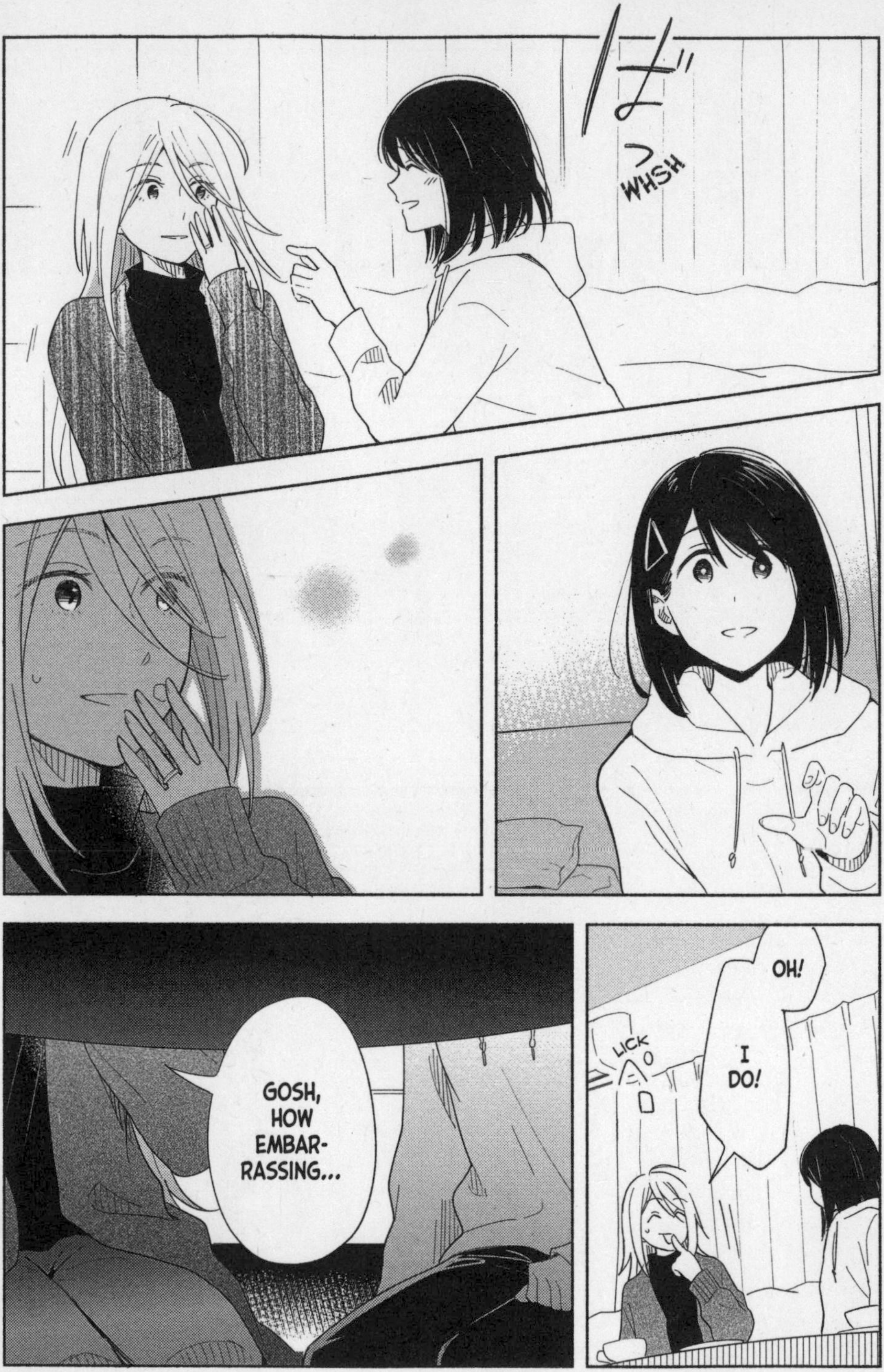
ぱっ
WHSH
OH! I DO!
LICK
GOSH, HOW EMBARRASSING...

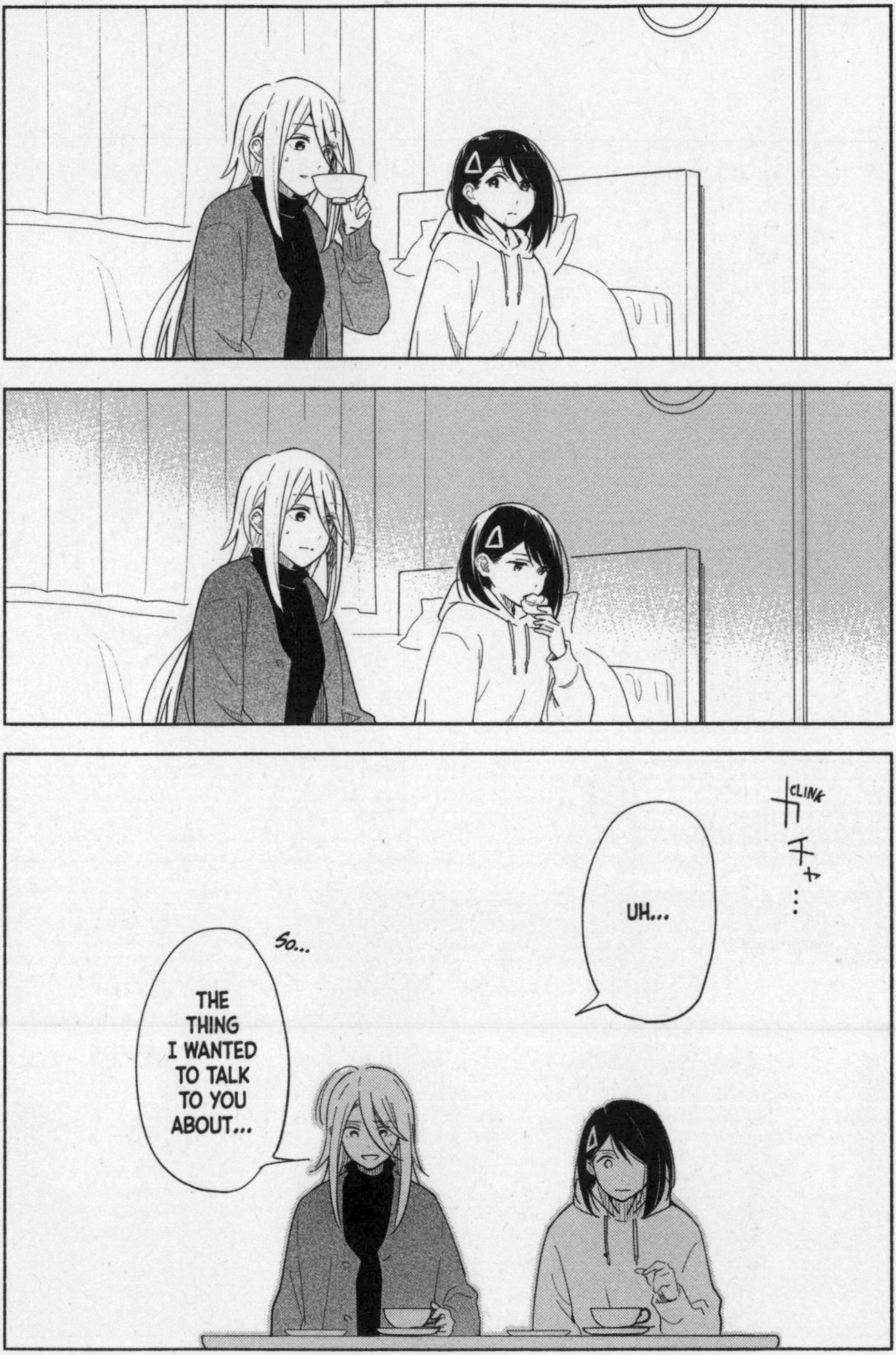
ガチャ…
CLINK
UH...
SO...
THE THING I WANTED TO TALK TO YOU ABOUT...

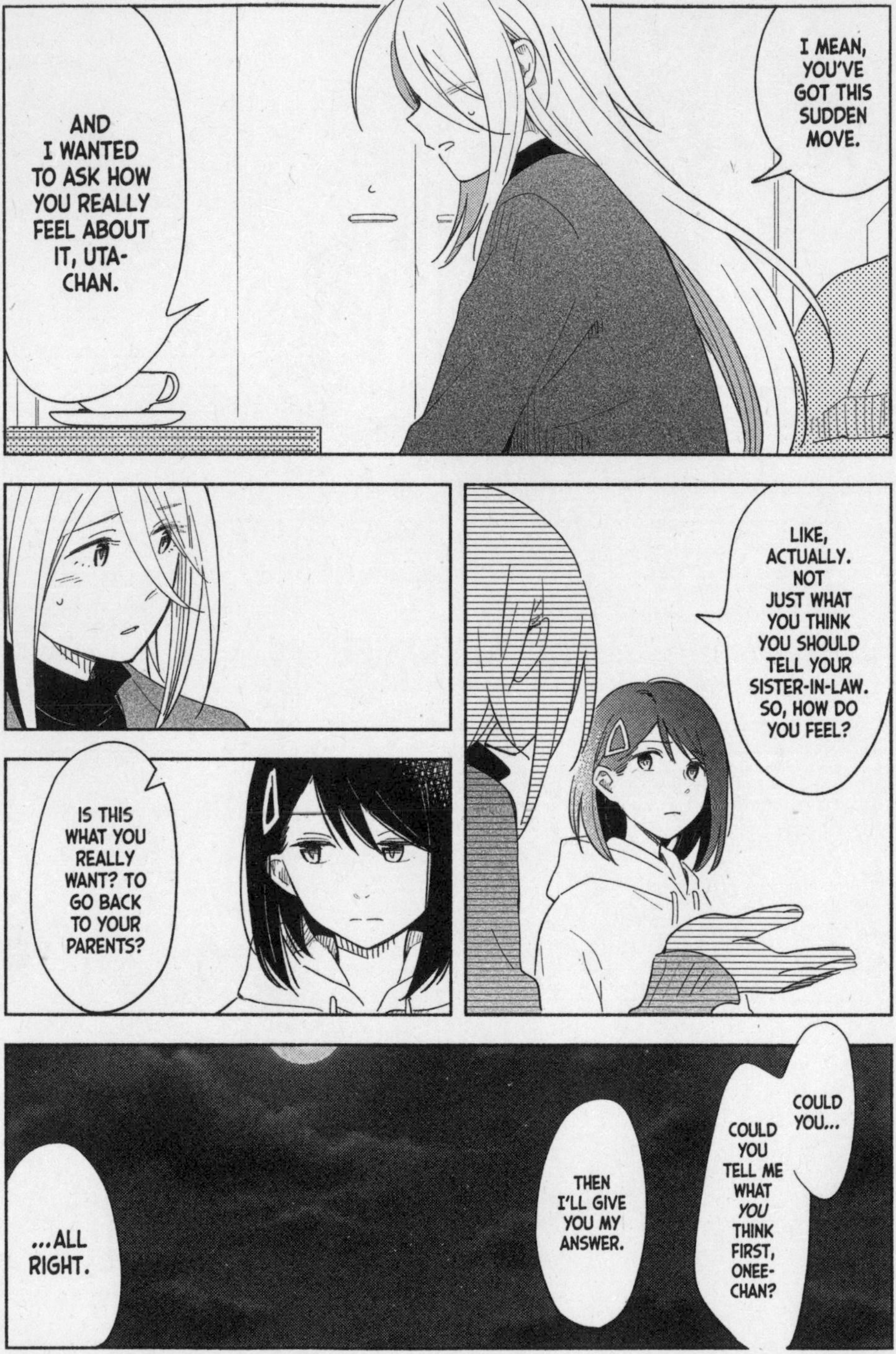
I MEAN, YOU'VE GOT THIS SUDDEN MOVE.
AND I WANTED TO ASK HOW YOU REALLY FEEL ABOUT IT, UTA-CHAN.
LIKE, ACTUALLY. NOT JUST WHAT YOU THINK YOU SHOULD TELL YOUR SISTER-IN-LAW. SO, HOW DO YOU FEEL?
IS THIS WHAT YOU REALLY WANT? TO GO BACK TO YOUR PARENTS?
COULD YOU...
COULD YOU TELL ME WHAT *YOU* THINK FIRST, ONEE-CHAN?
THEN I'LL GIVE YOU MY ANSWER.
...ALL RIGHT.

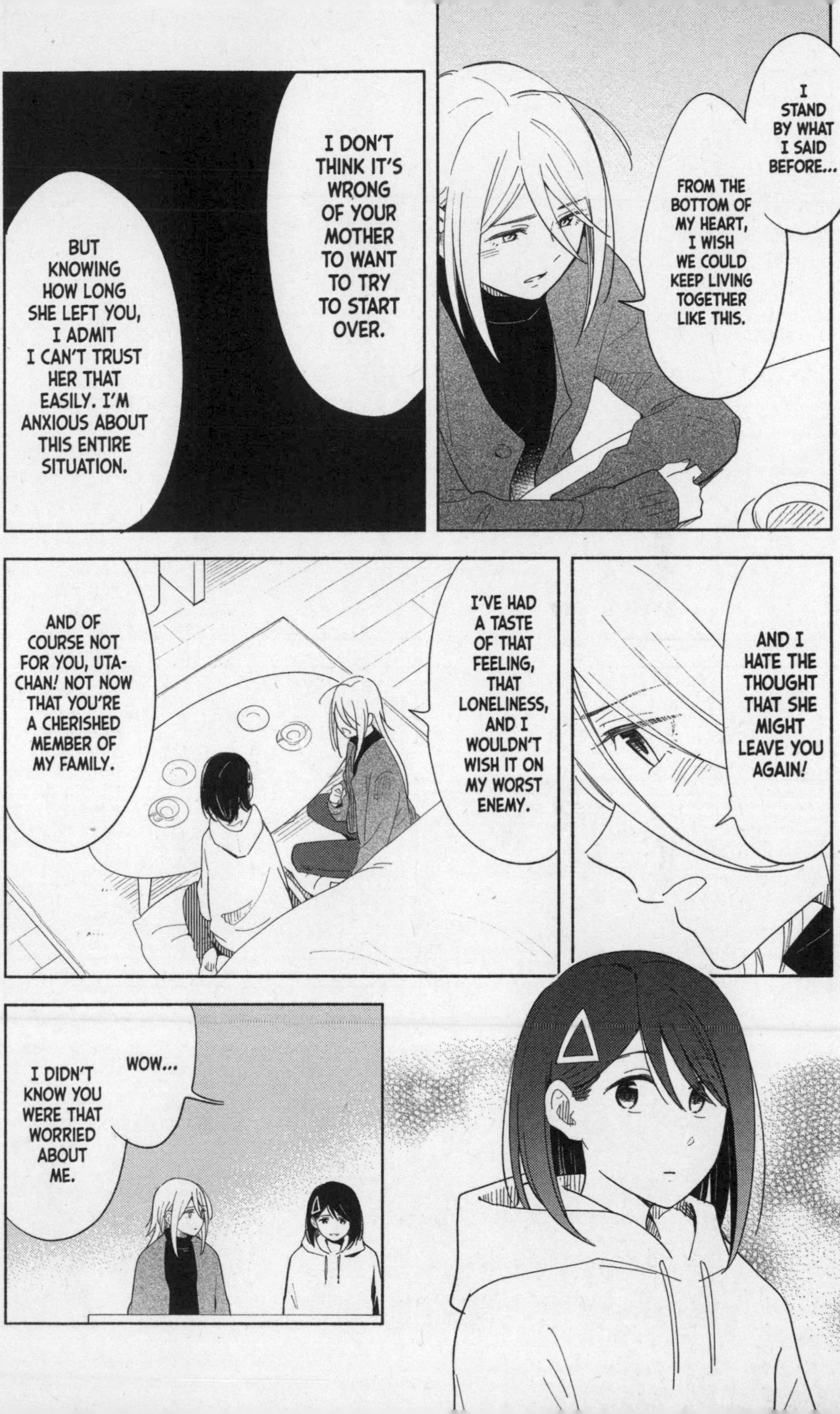
I STAND BY WHAT I SAID BEFORE...
FROM THE BOTTOM OF MY HEART, I WISH WE COULD KEEP LIVING TOGETHER LIKE THIS.
I DON'T THINK IT'S WRONG OF YOUR MOTHER TO WANT TO TRY TO START OVER.
BUT KNOWING HOW LONG SHE LEFT YOU, I ADMIT I CAN'T TRUST HER THAT EASILY. I'M ANXIOUS ABOUT THIS ENTIRE SITUATION.
AND I HATE THE THOUGHT THAT SHE MIGHT LEAVE YOU AGAIN!
I'VE HAD A TASTE OF THAT FEELING, THAT LONELINESS, AND I WOULDN'T WISH IT ON MY WORST ENEMY.
AND OF COURSE NOT FOR YOU, UTA-CHAN! NOT NOW THAT YOU'RE A CHERISHED MEMBER OF MY FAMILY.
WOW...
I DIDN'T KNOW YOU WERE THAT WORRIED ABOUT ME.

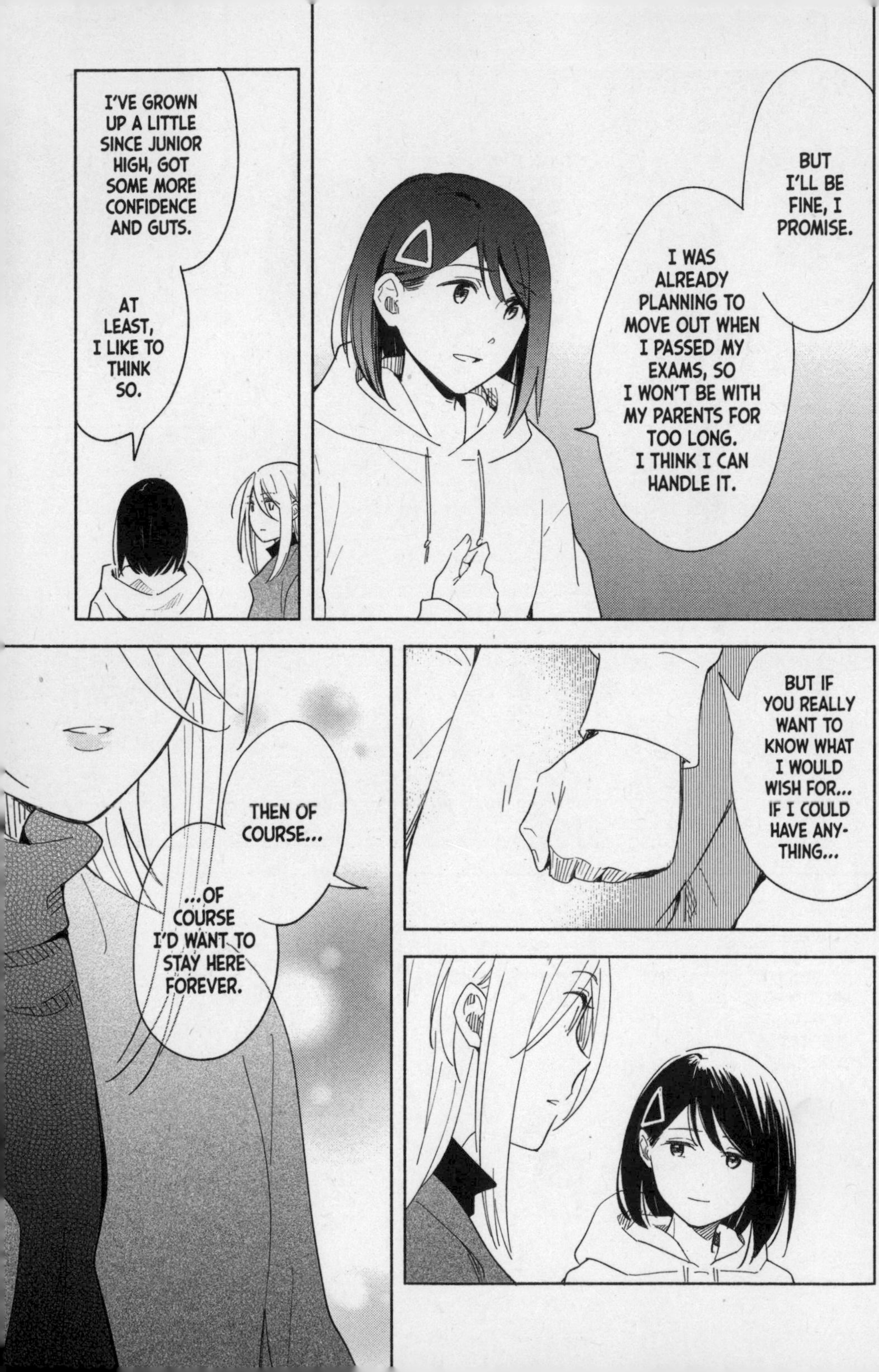
BUT I'LL BE FINE, I PROMISE.
I WAS ALREADY PLANNING TO MOVE OUT WHEN I PASSED MY EXAMS, SO I WON'T BE WITH MY PARENTS FOR TOO LONG. I THINK I CAN HANDLE IT.
I'VE GROWN UP A LITTLE SINCE JUNIOR HIGH, GOT SOME MORE CONFIDENCE AND GUTS.
AT LEAST, I LIKE TO THINK SO.
BUT IF YOU REALLY WANT TO KNOW WHAT I WOULD WISH FOR... IF I COULD HAVE ANY-THING...
THEN OF COURSE...
...OF COURSE I'D WANT TO STAY HERE FOREVER.

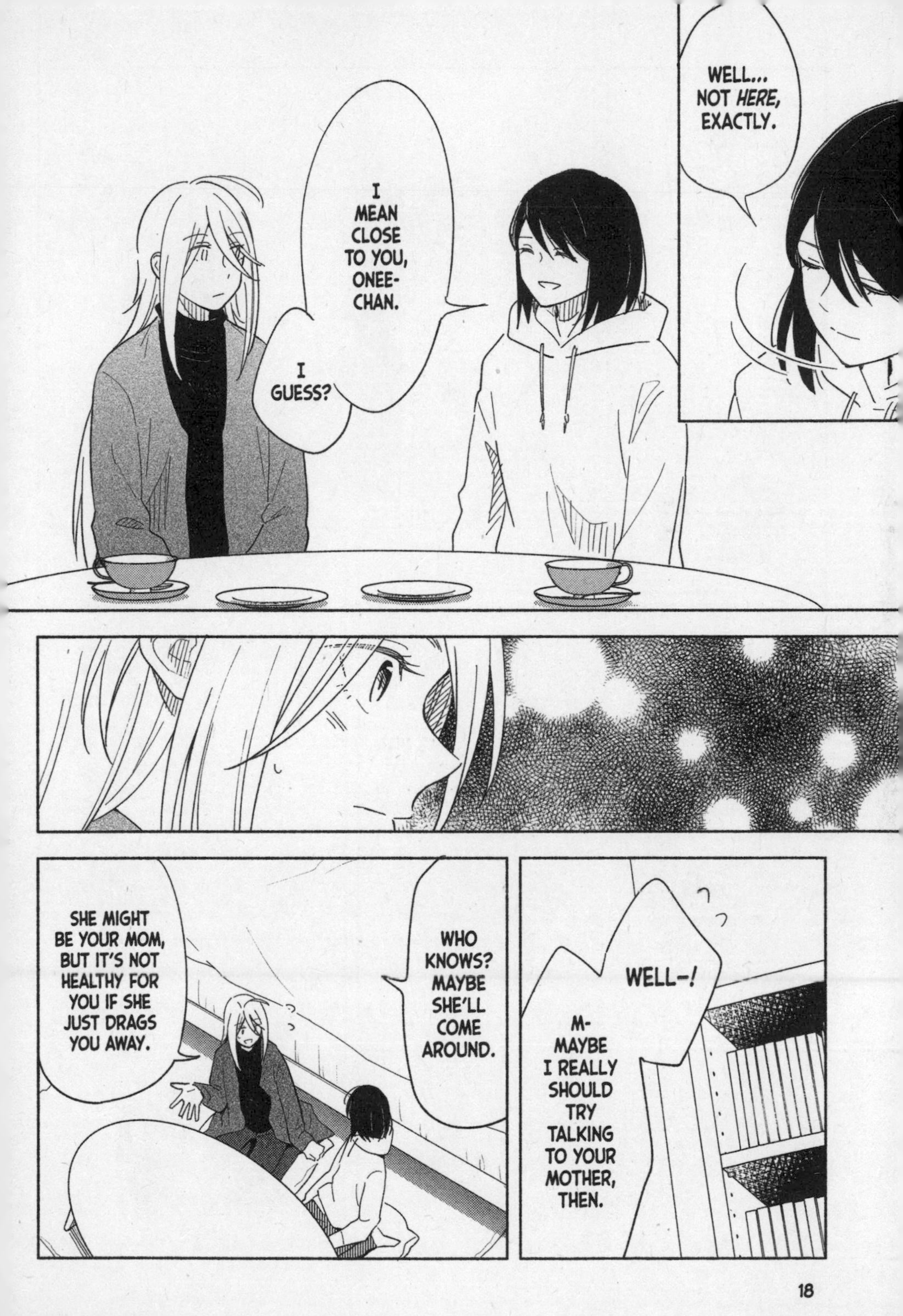
WELL... NOT *HERE*, EXACTLY.
I MEAN CLOSE TO YOU, ONEE-CHAN.
I GUESS?
WELL-!
M-MAYBE I REALLY SHOULD TRY TALKING TO YOUR MOTHER, THEN.
WHO KNOWS? MAYBE SHE'LL COME AROUND.
SHE MIGHT BE YOUR MOM, BUT IT'S NOT HEALTHY FOR YOU IF SHE JUST DRAGS YOU AWAY.

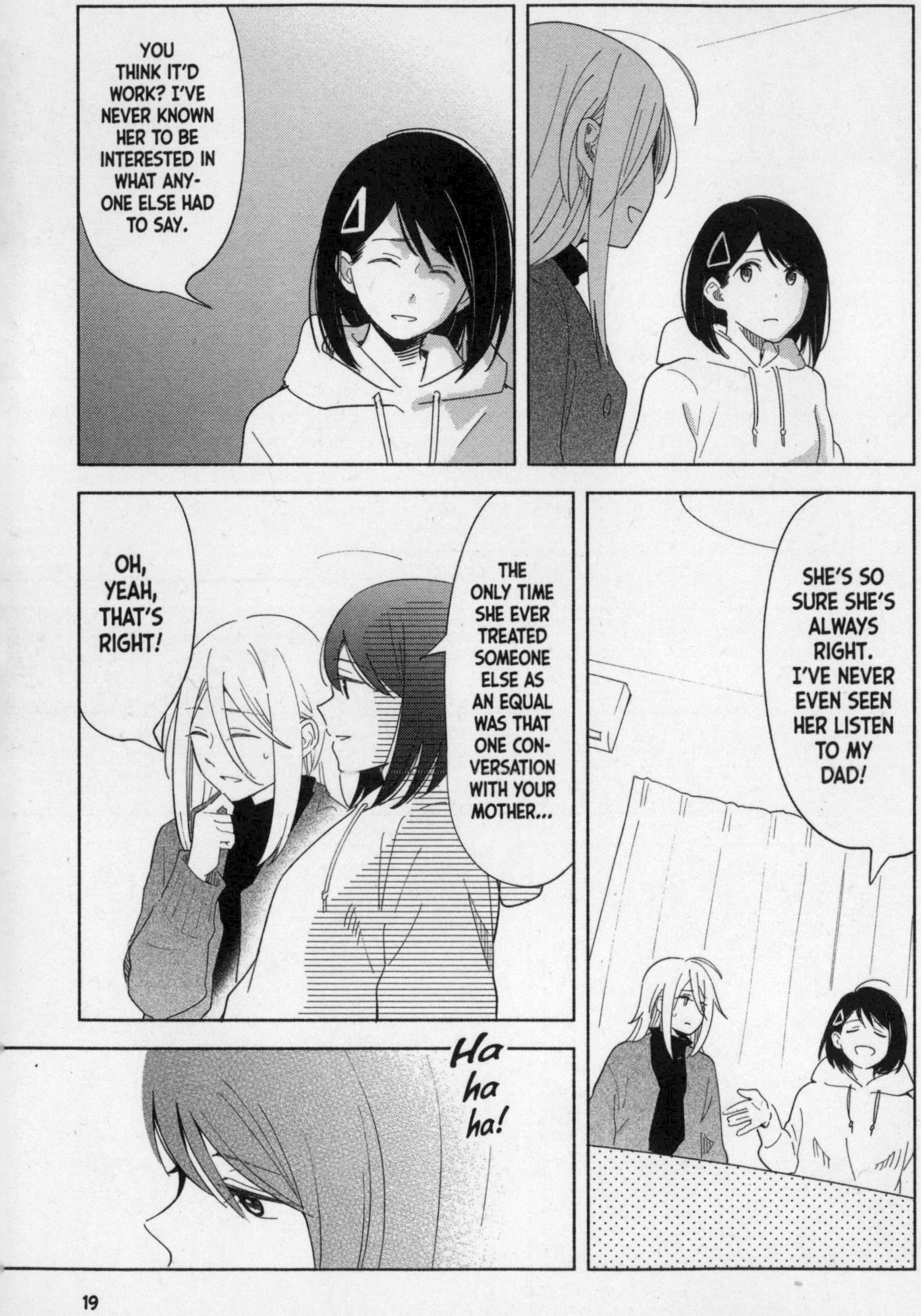
YOU THINK IT'D WORK? I'VE NEVER KNOWN HER TO BE INTERESTED IN WHAT ANY-ONE ELSE HAD TO SAY.
SHE'S SO SURE SHE'S ALWAYS RIGHT. I'VE NEVER EVEN SEEN HER LISTEN TO MY DAD!
THE ONLY TIME SHE EVER TREATED SOMEONE ELSE AS AN EQUAL WAS THAT ONE CON-VERSATION WITH YOUR MOTHER...
OH, YEAH, THAT'S RIGHT!
Ha ha ha!

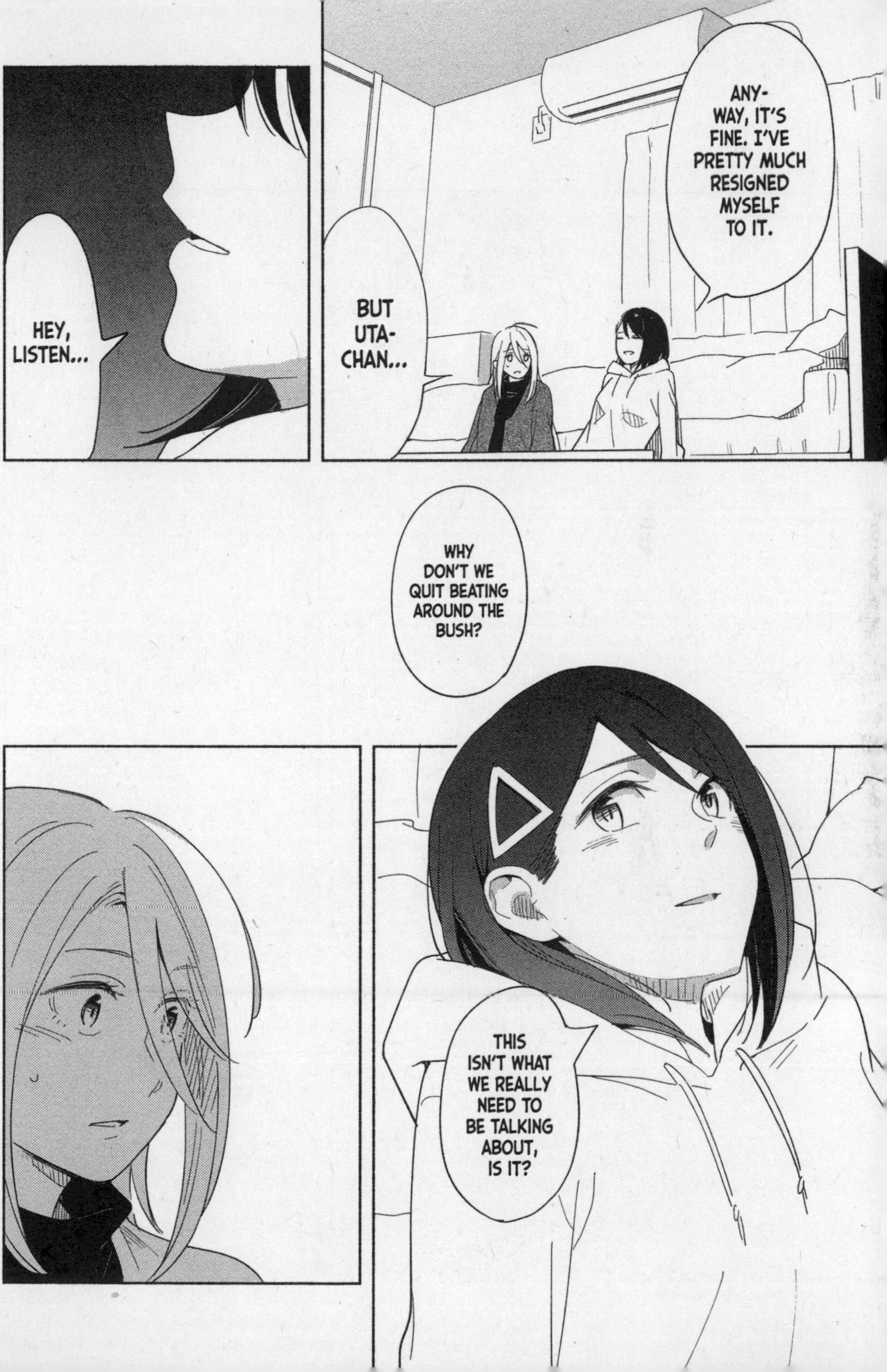
ANY-WAY, IT'S FINE. I'VE PRETTY MUCH RESIGNED MYSELF TO IT.
BUT UTA-CHAN...
HEY, LISTEN...
WHY DON'T WE QUIT BEATING AROUND THE BUSH?
THIS ISN'T WHAT WE REALLY NEED TO BE TALKING ABOUT, IS IT?

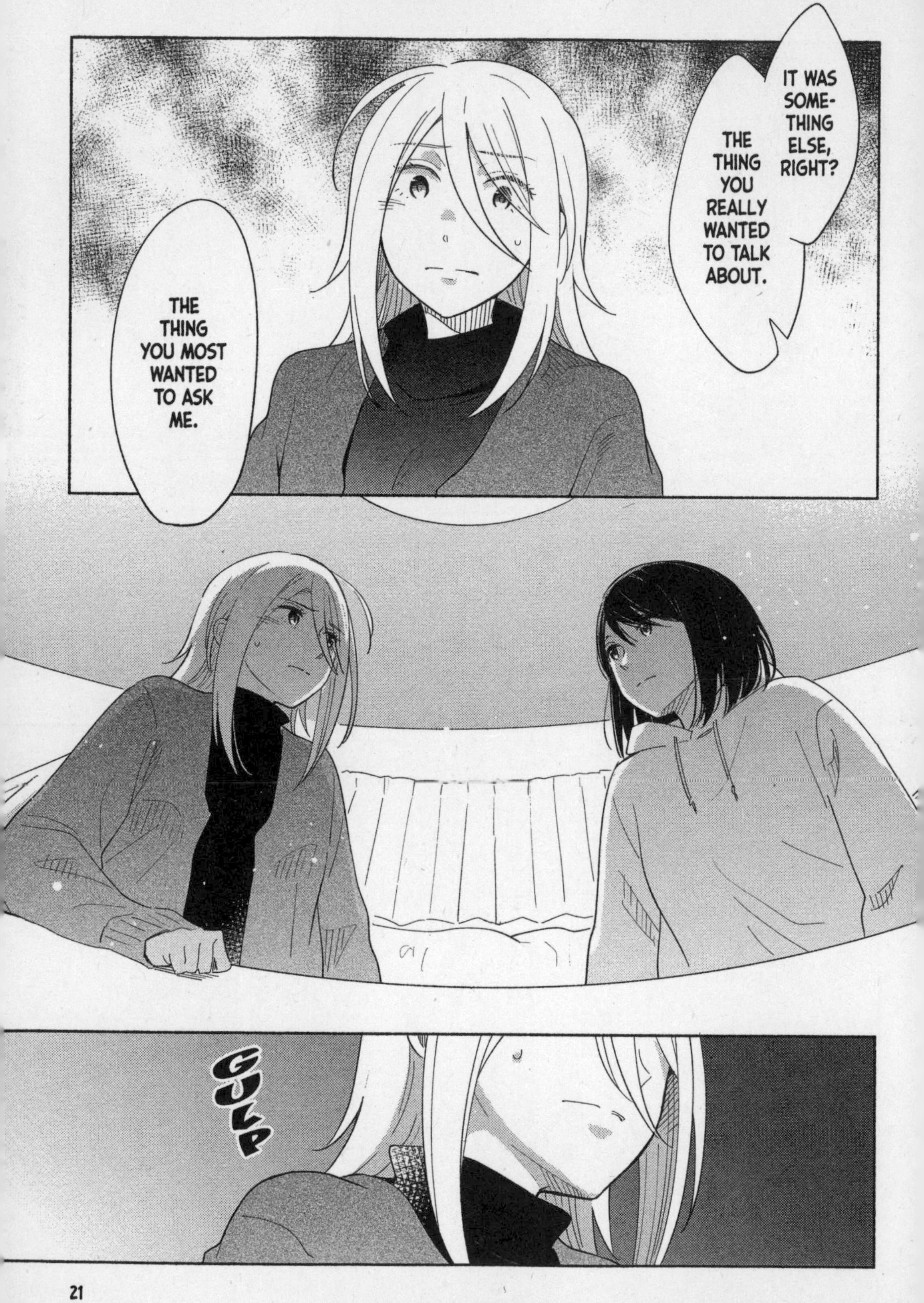
IT WAS SOME-THING ELSE, RIGHT?
THE THING YOU REALLY WANTED TO TALK ABOUT.
THE THING YOU MOST WANTED TO ASK ME.
GULP

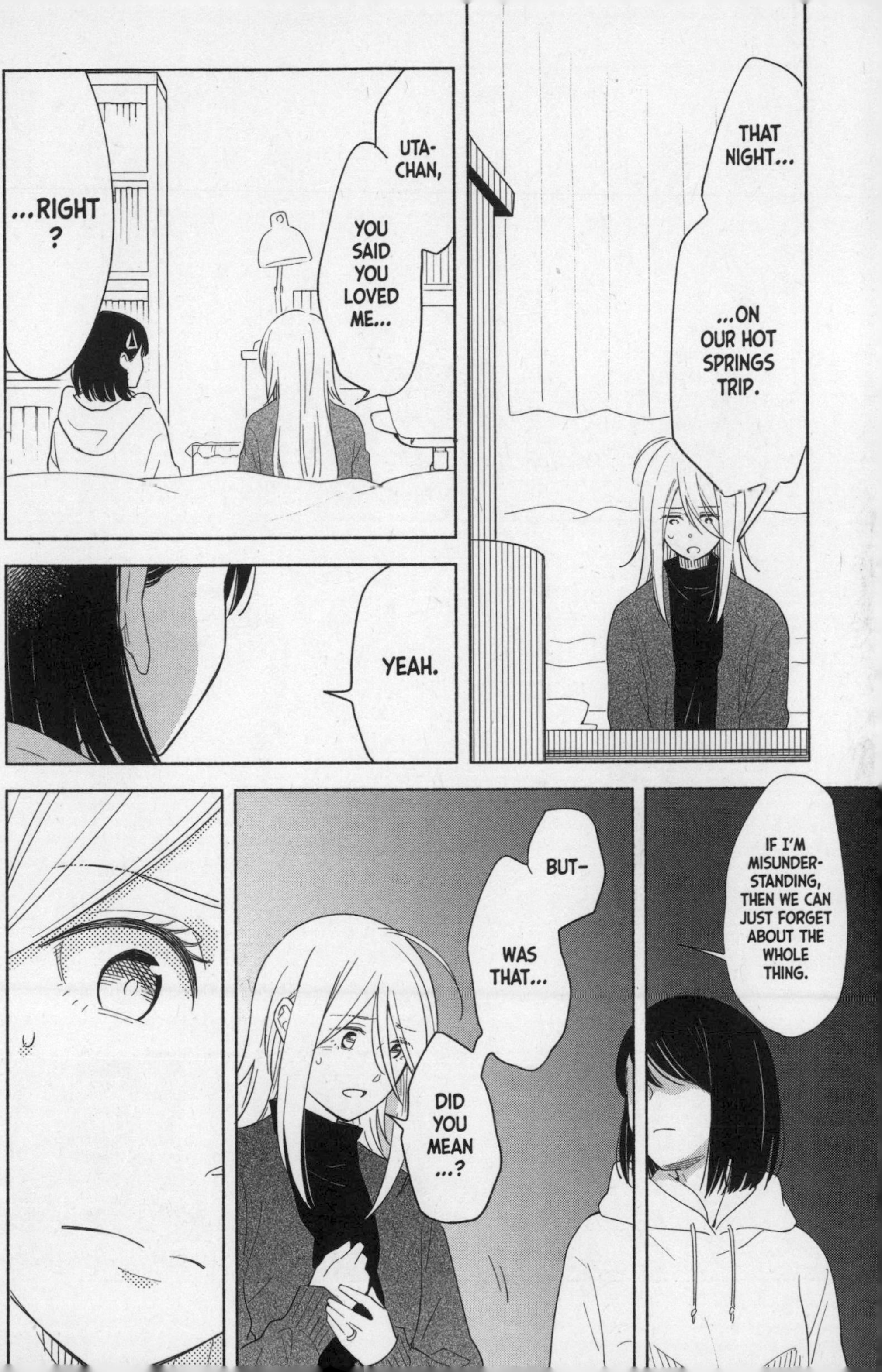
THAT NIGHT...
...ON OUR HOT SPRINGS TRIP.
UTA-CHAN,
YOU SAID YOU LOVED ME...
...RIGHT?
YEAH.
IF I'M MISUNDERSTANDING, THEN WE CAN JUST FORGET ABOUT THE WHOLE THING.
BUT-
WAS THAT...
DID YOU MEAN ...?

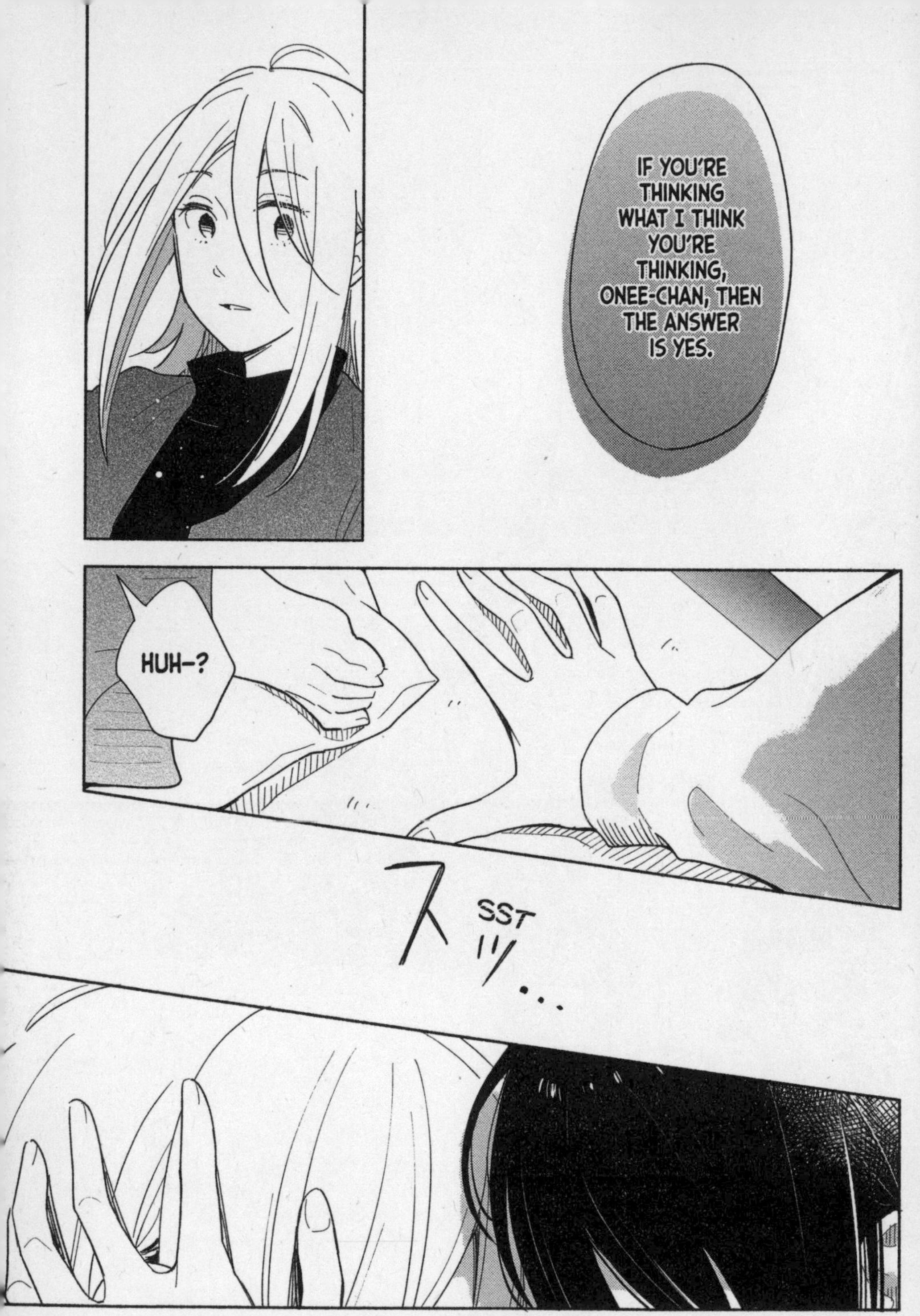
IF YOU'RE THINKING WHAT I THINK YOU'RE THINKING, ONEE-CHAN, THEN THE ANSWER IS YES.
HUH-?
スッ
SST
...

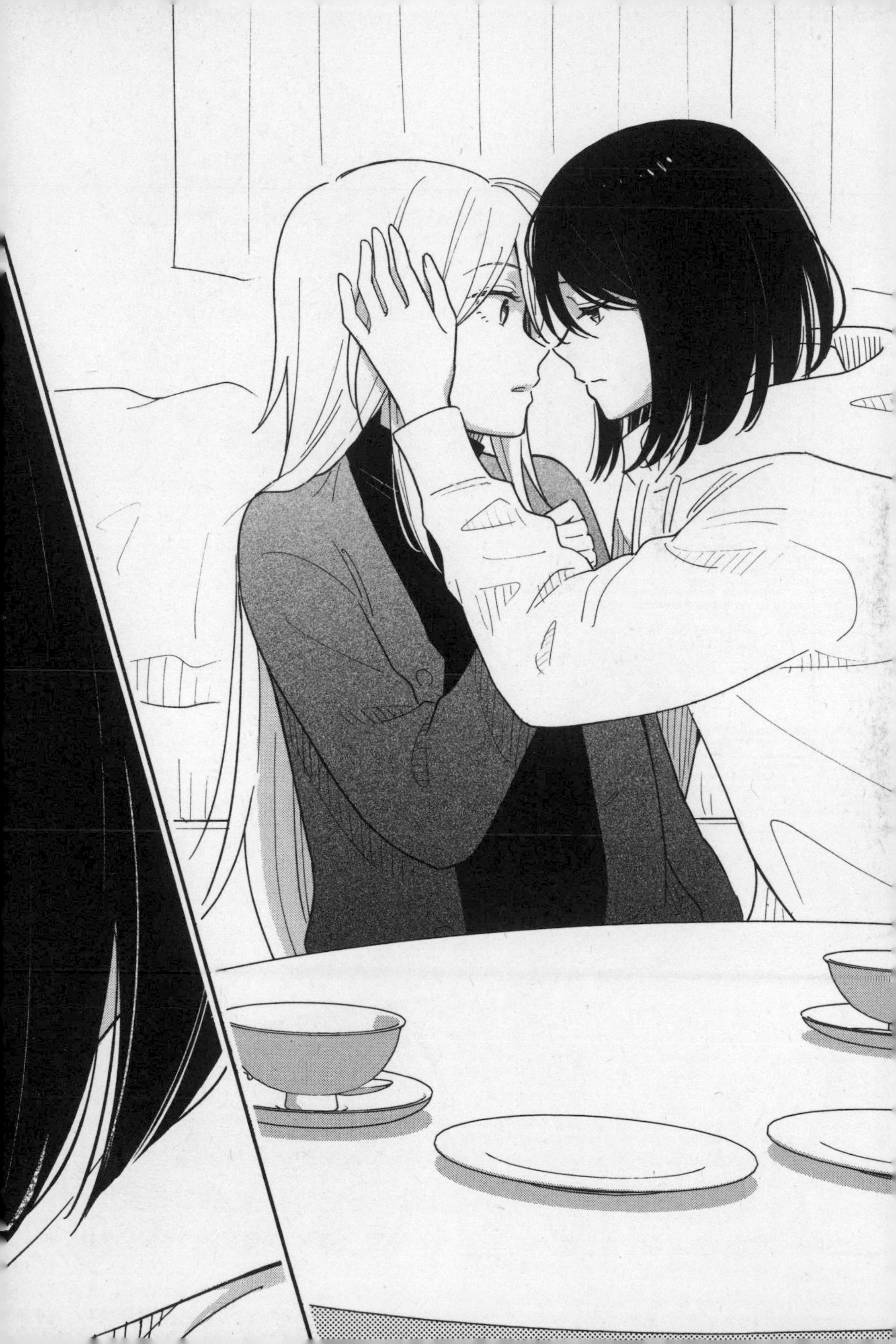

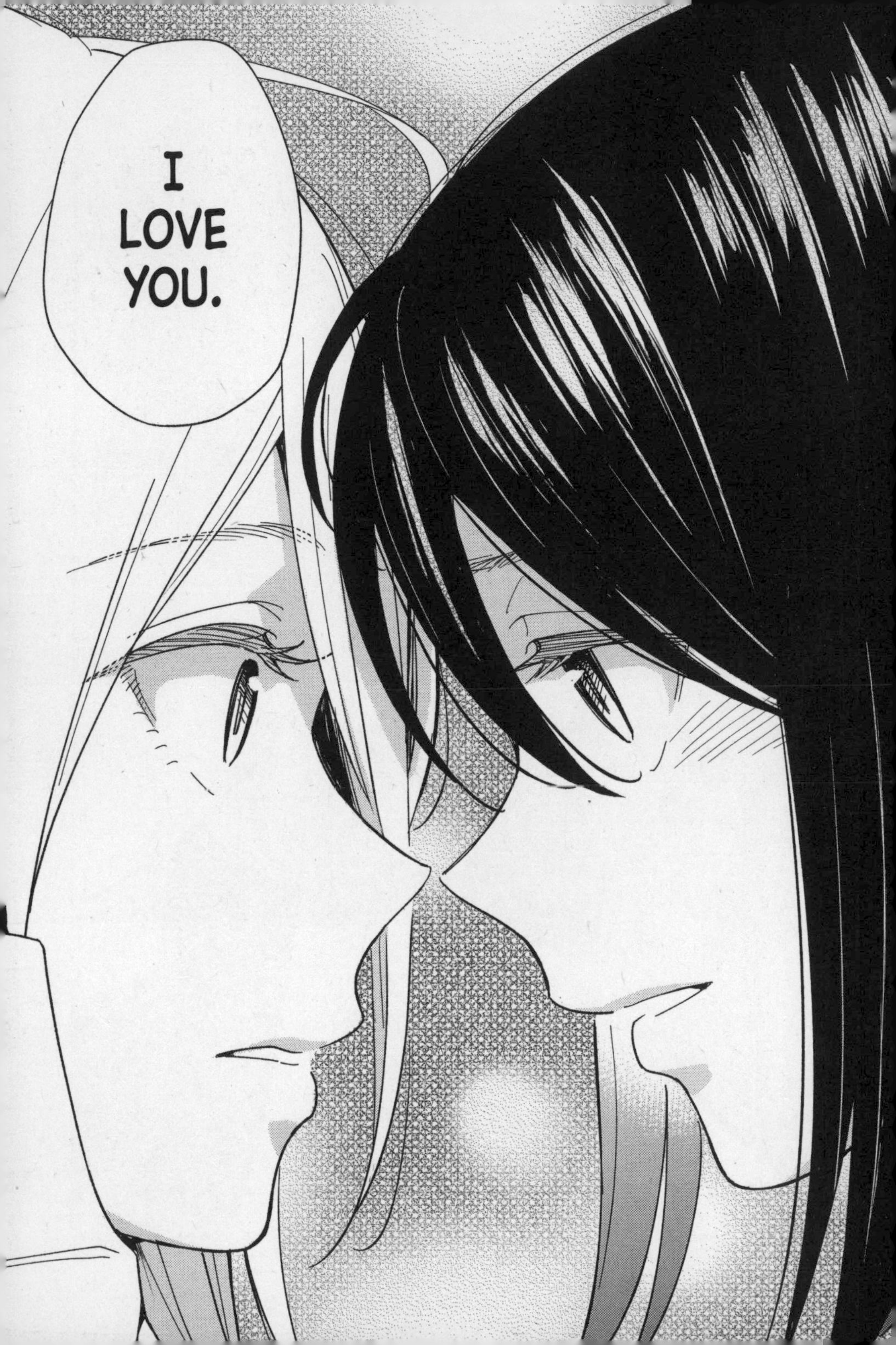
I LOVE YOU.

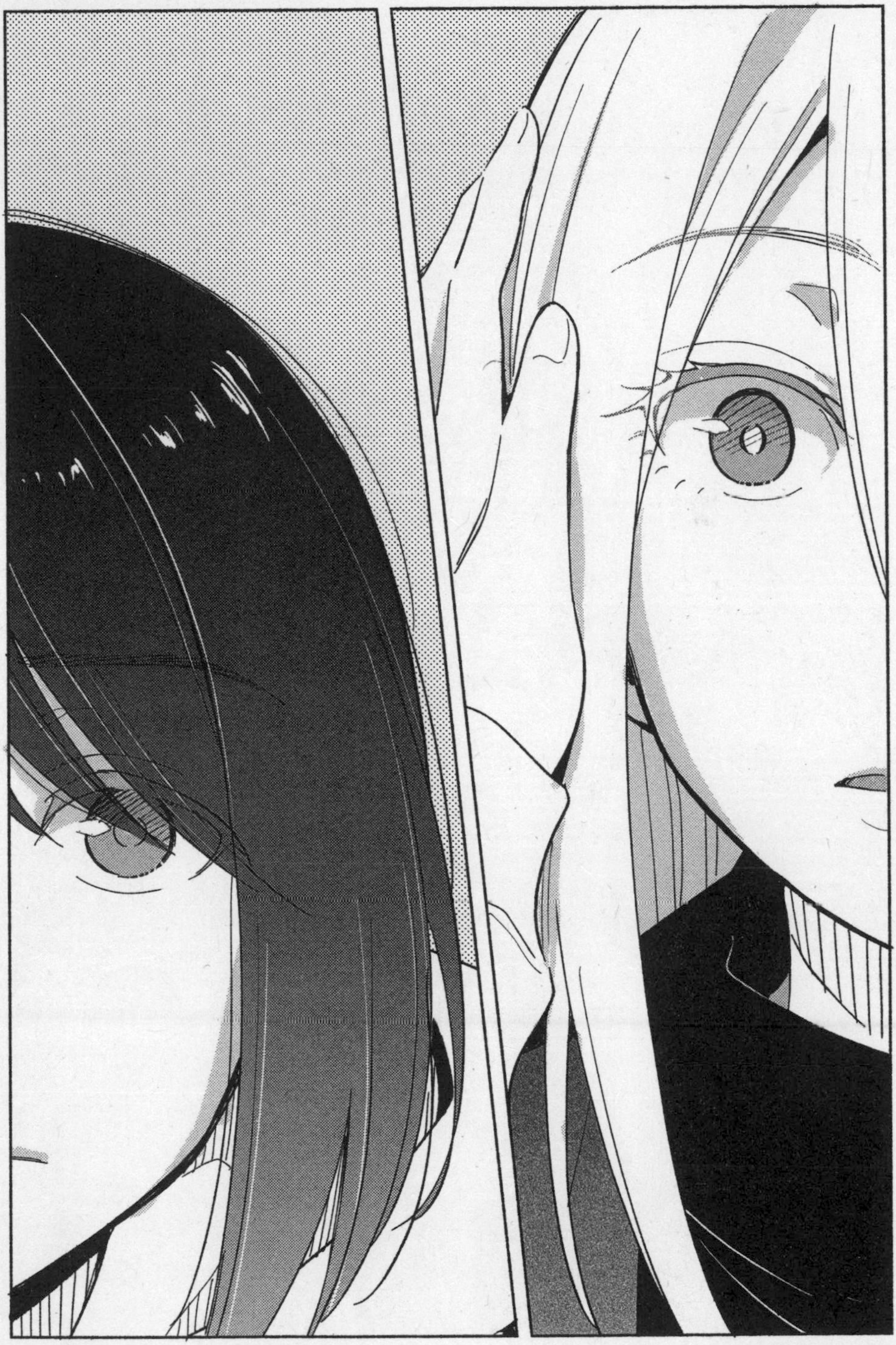

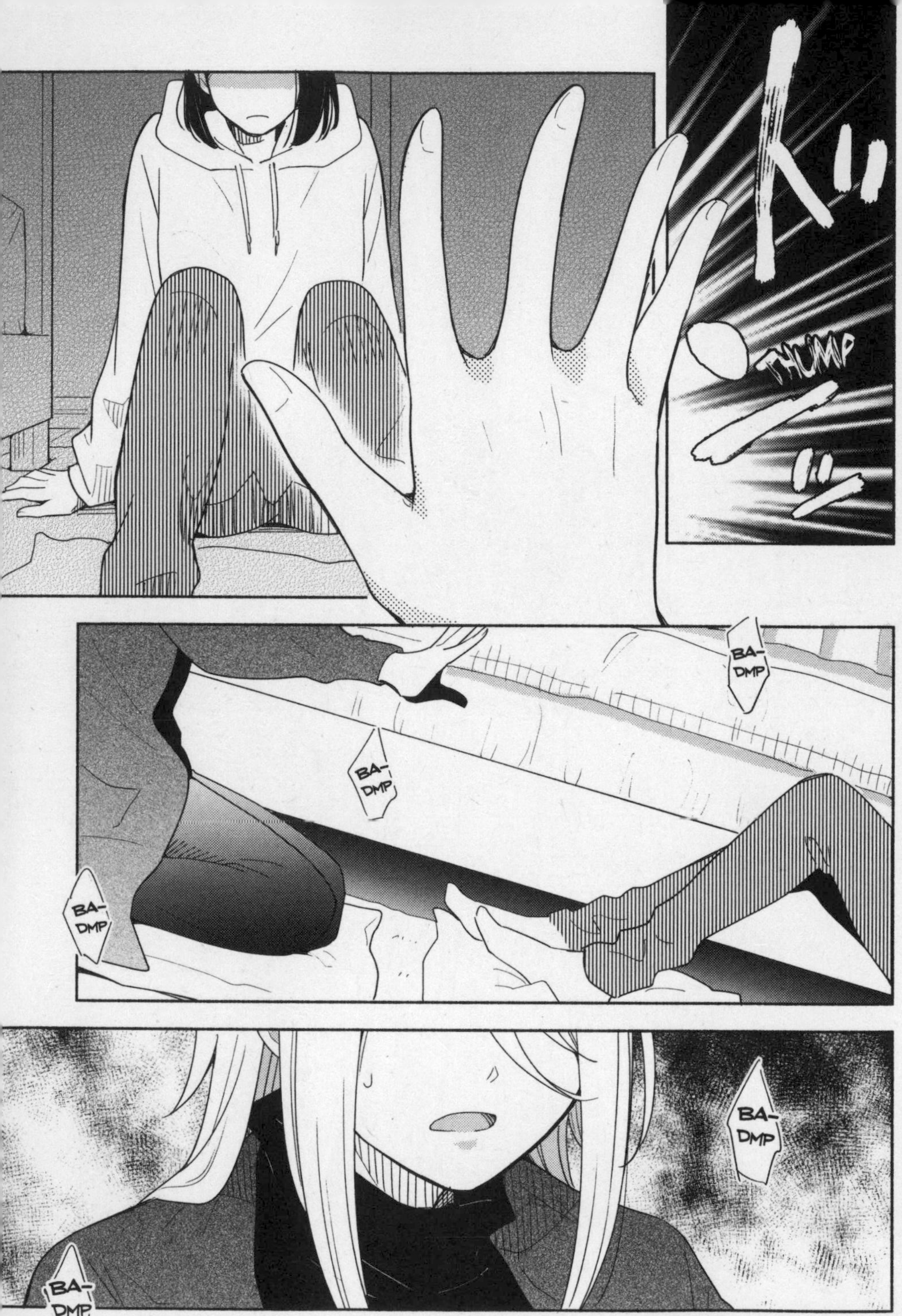
ドッ
THUMP
BA-DMP
BA-DMP
BA-DMP
BA-DMP
BA-DMP

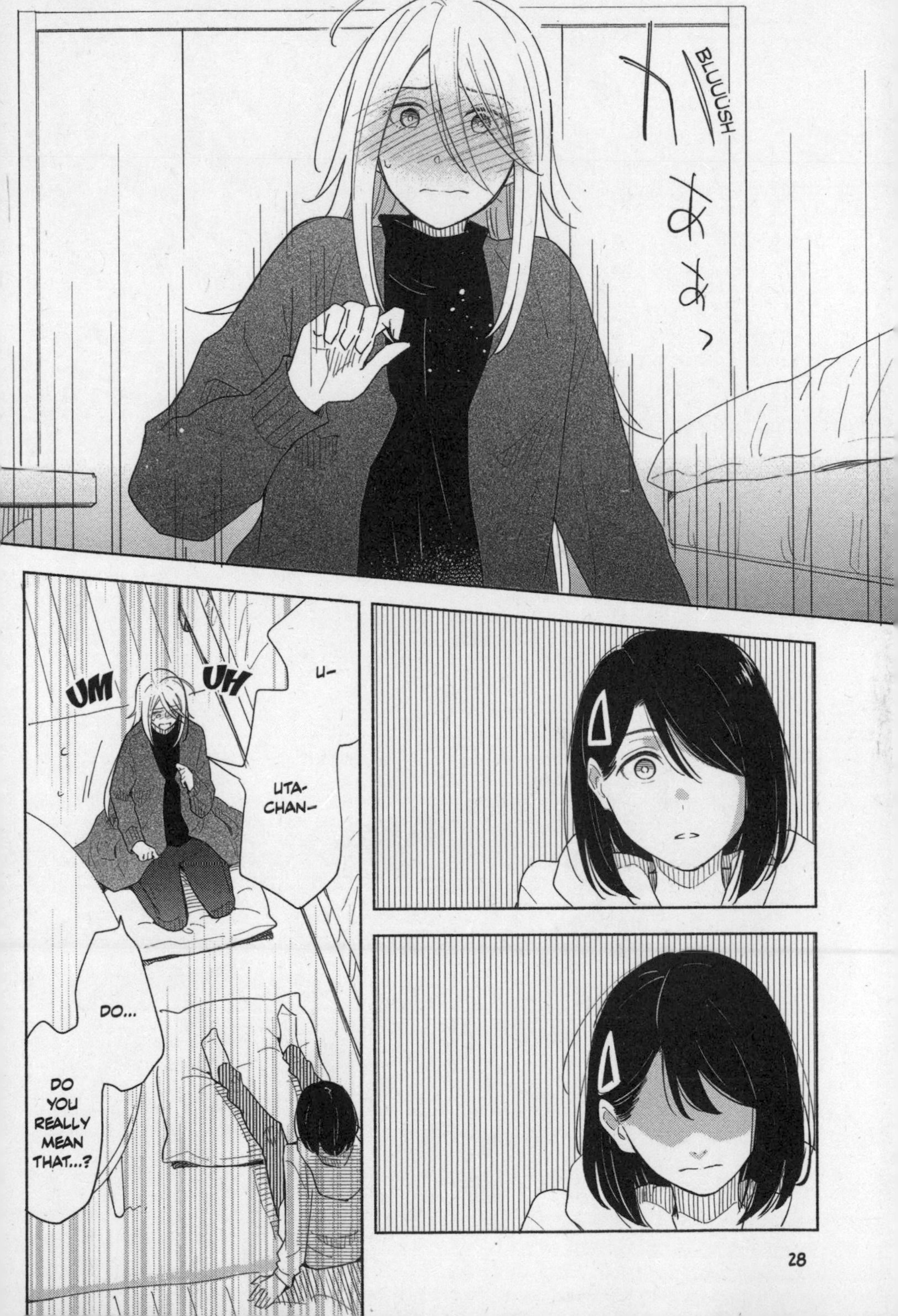
BLUUUSH
ああっ
U-
UH
UM
UTA-CHAN-
DO...
DO YOU REALLY MEAN THAT...?

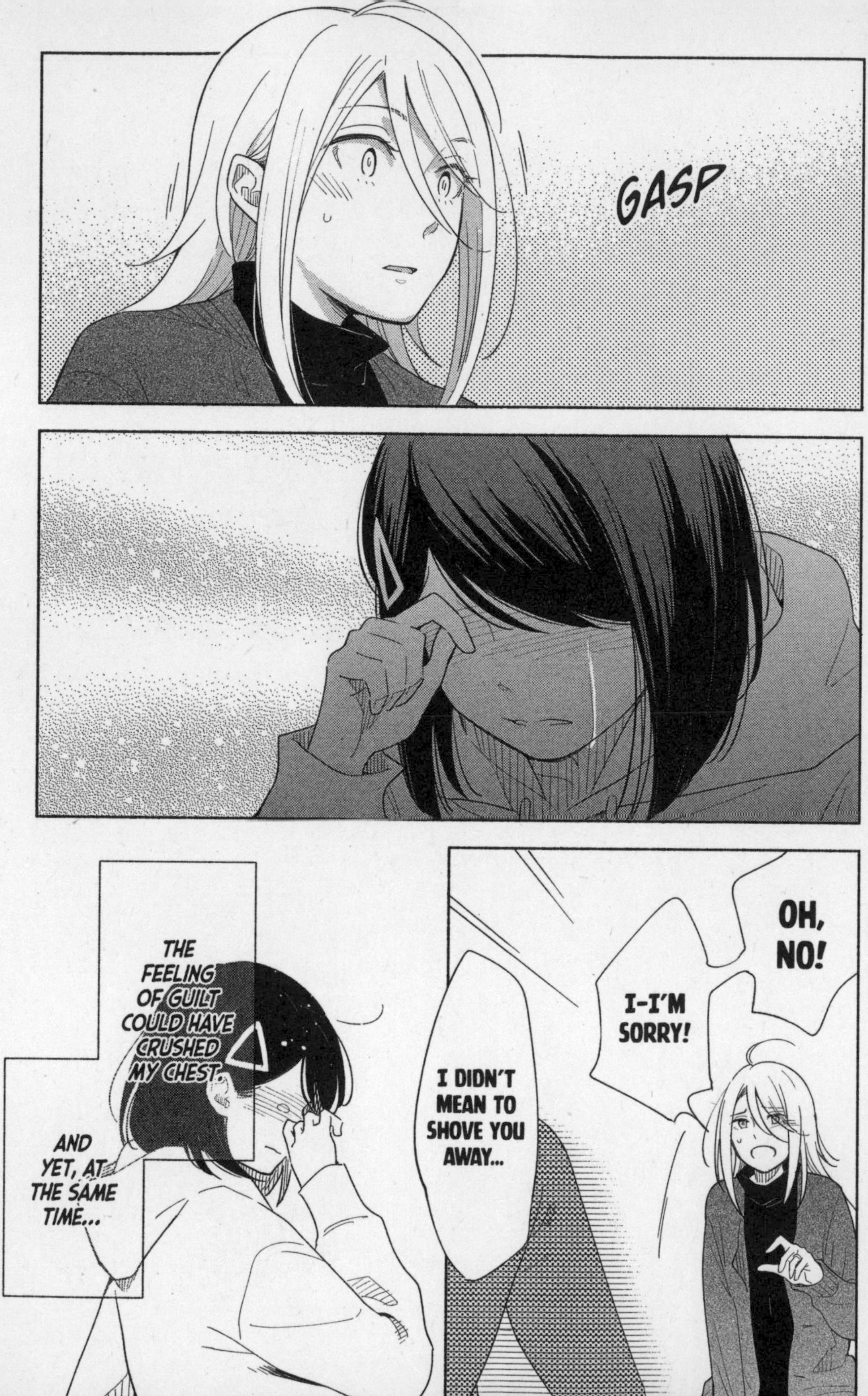
GASP
OH, NO!
I-I'M SORRY!
I DIDN'T MEAN TO SHOVE YOU AWAY...
THE FEELING OF GUILT COULD HAVE CRUSHED MY CHEST.
AND YET, AT THE SAME TIME...

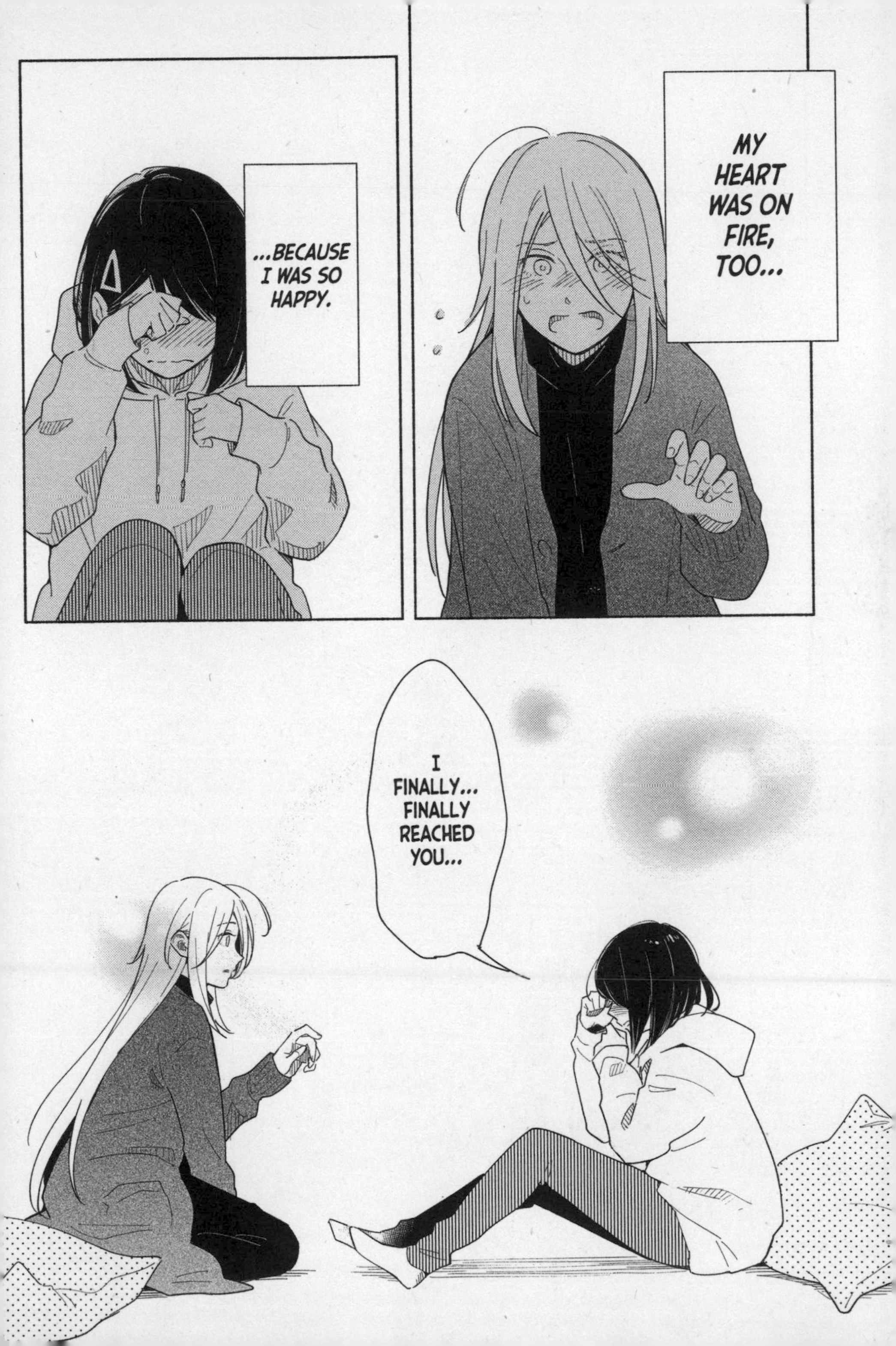
MY HEART WAS ON FIRE, TOO...
...BECAUSE I WAS SO HAPPY.
I FINALLY... FINALLY REACHED YOU...

If I Could
Reach You

If I Could
Reach You

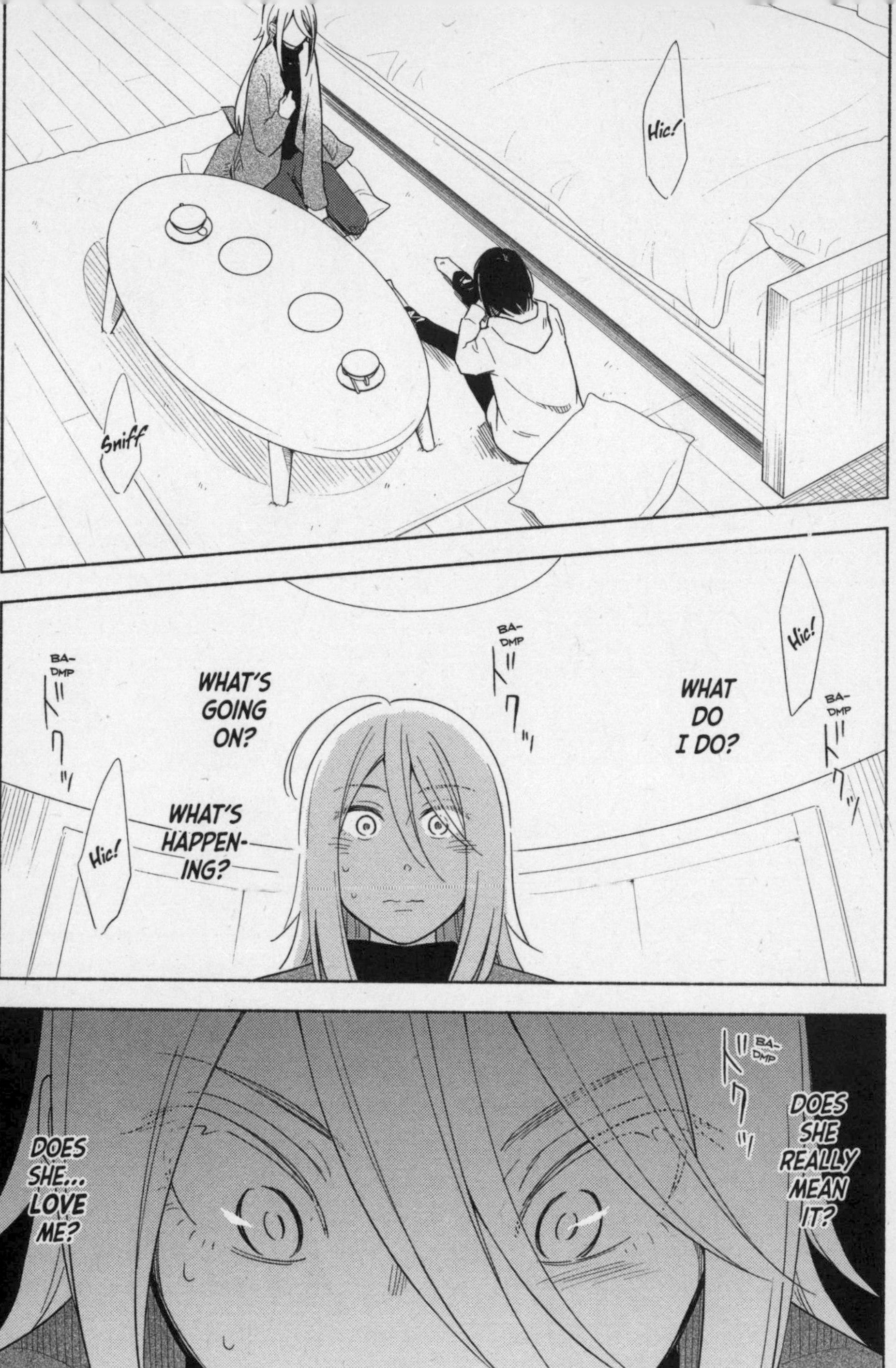
Hic!
Sniff
Hic!
BA-DMP
WHAT DO I DO?
BA-DMP
WHAT'S GOING ON?
WHAT'S HAPPENING?
BA-DMP
Hic!
BA-DMP
DOES SHE REALLY MEAN IT?
DOES SHE... LOVE ME?
BA-DMP

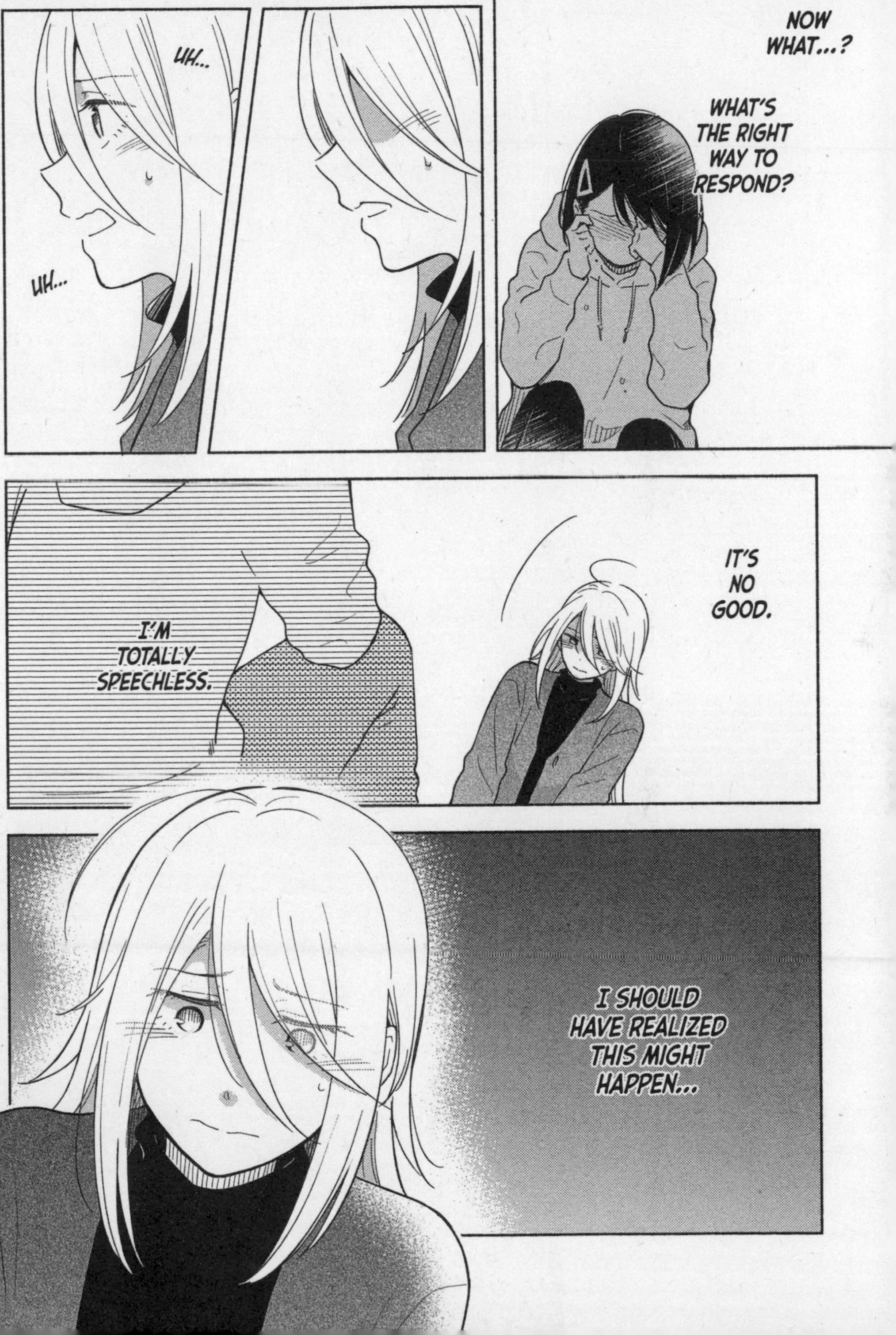
NOW WHAT...?
WHAT'S THE RIGHT WAY TO RESPOND?
UH...
UH...
IT'S NO GOOD.
I'M TOTALLY SPEECHLESS.
I SHOULD HAVE REALIZED THIS MIGHT HAPPEN...

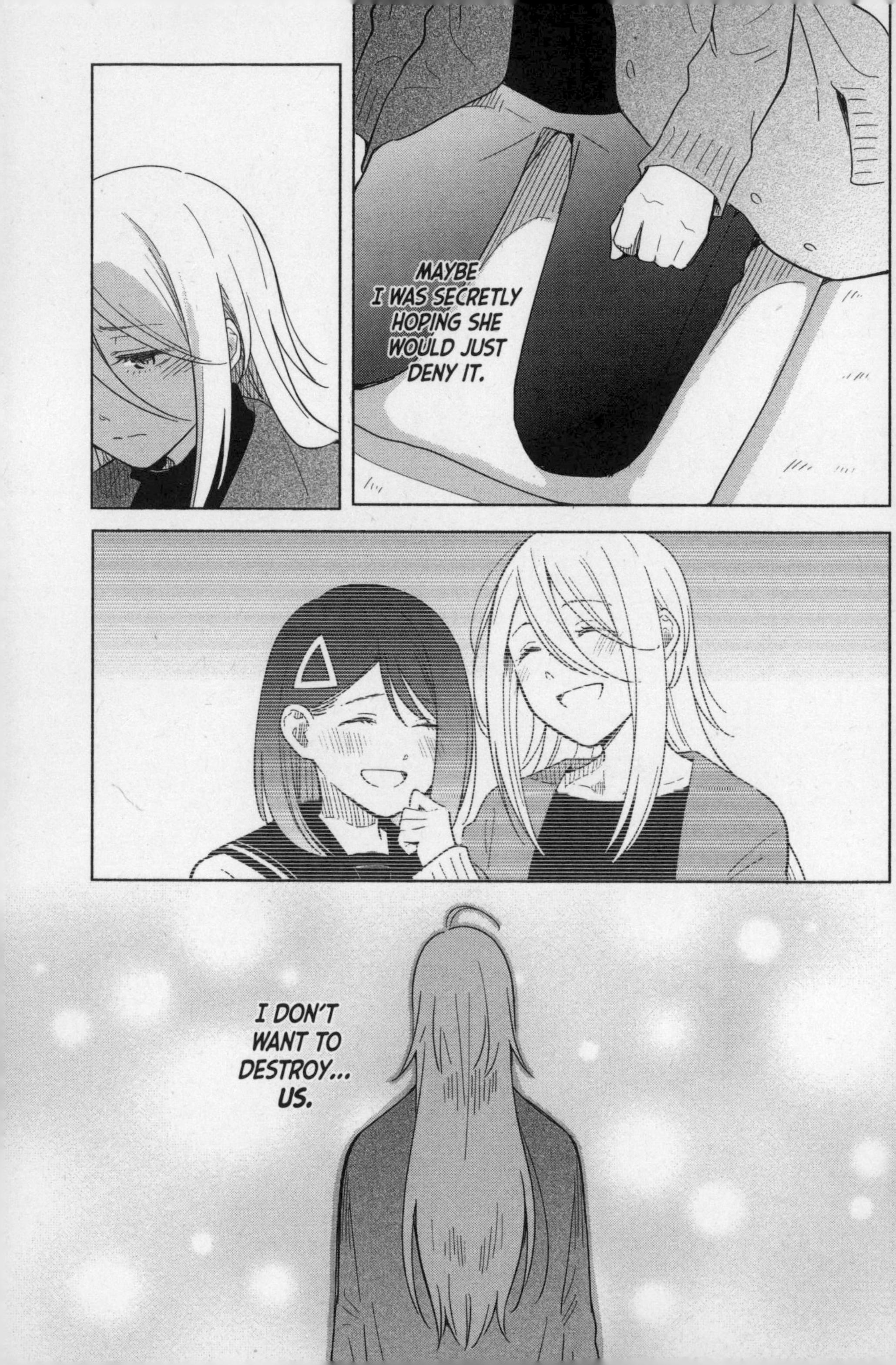
MAYBE I WAS SECRETLY HOPING SHE WOULD JUST DENY IT.
I DON'T WANT TO DESTROY... US.

Chapter 22

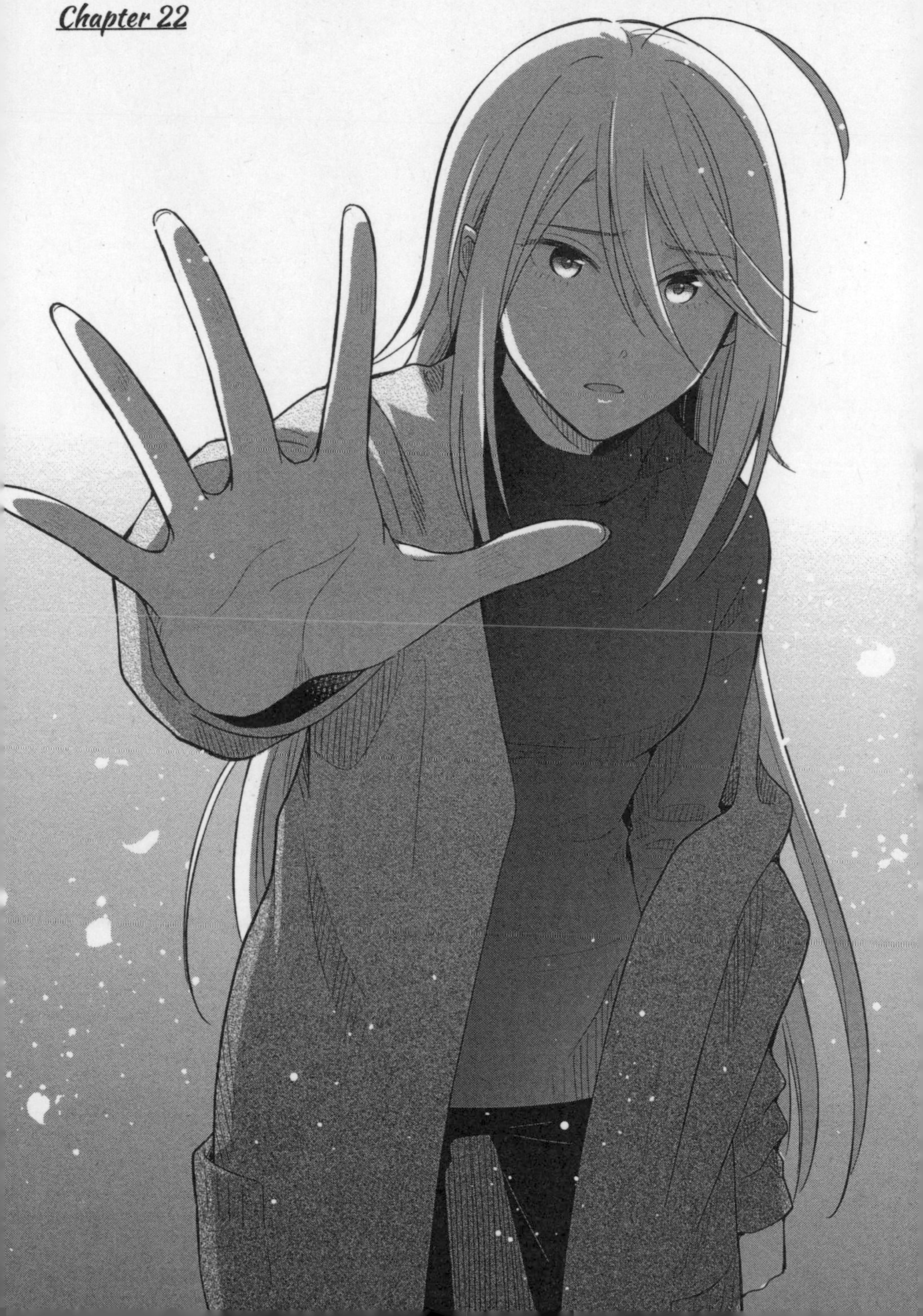

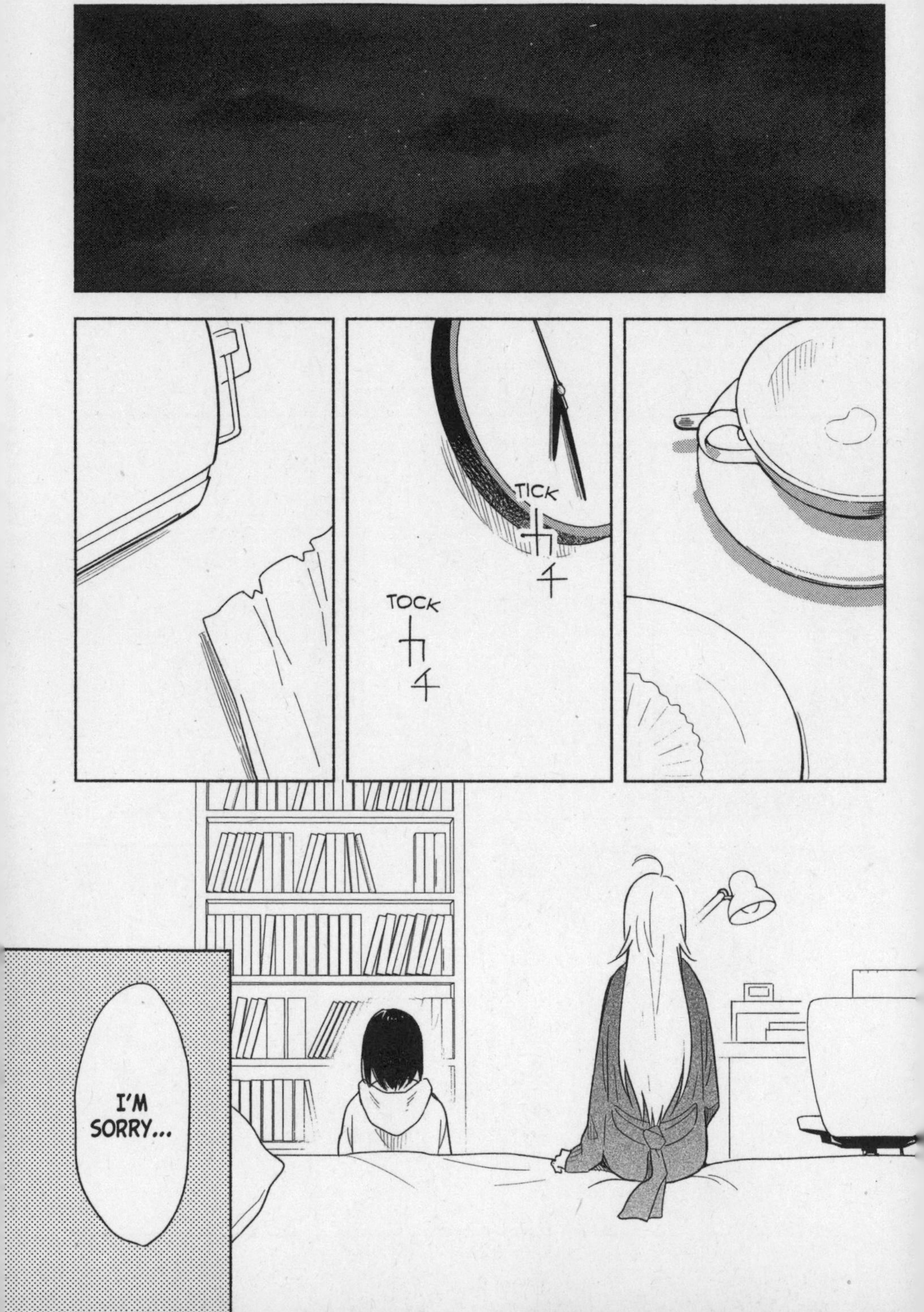
TICK
カチ
TOCK
カチ
I'M SORRY...

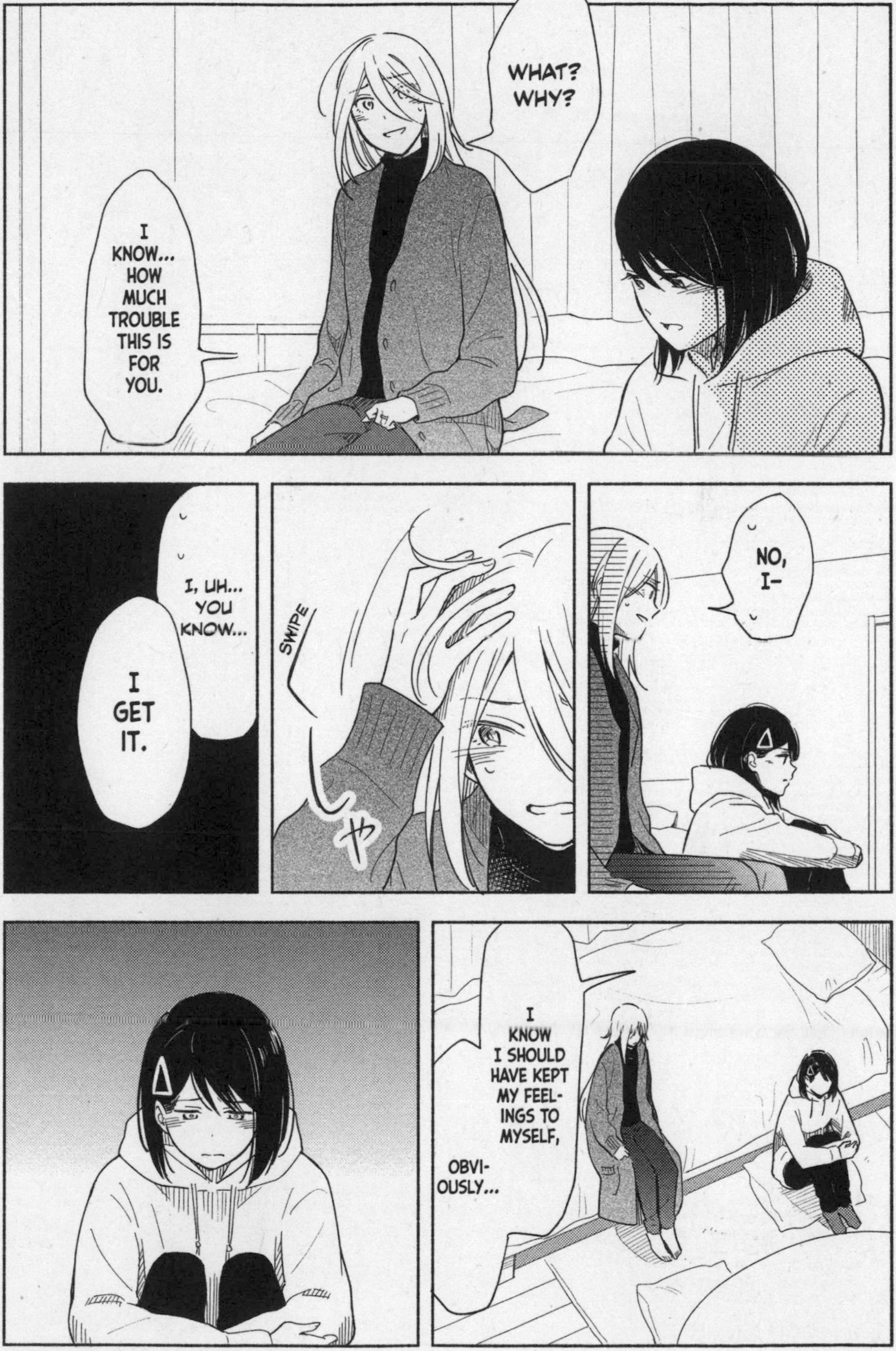
WHAT? WHY?
I KNOW... HOW MUCH TROUBLE THIS IS FOR YOU.
NO, I–
SWIPE
I, UH... YOU KNOW...
I GET IT.
I KNOW I SHOULD HAVE KEPT MY FEEL-INGS TO MYSELF,
OBVI-OUSLY...

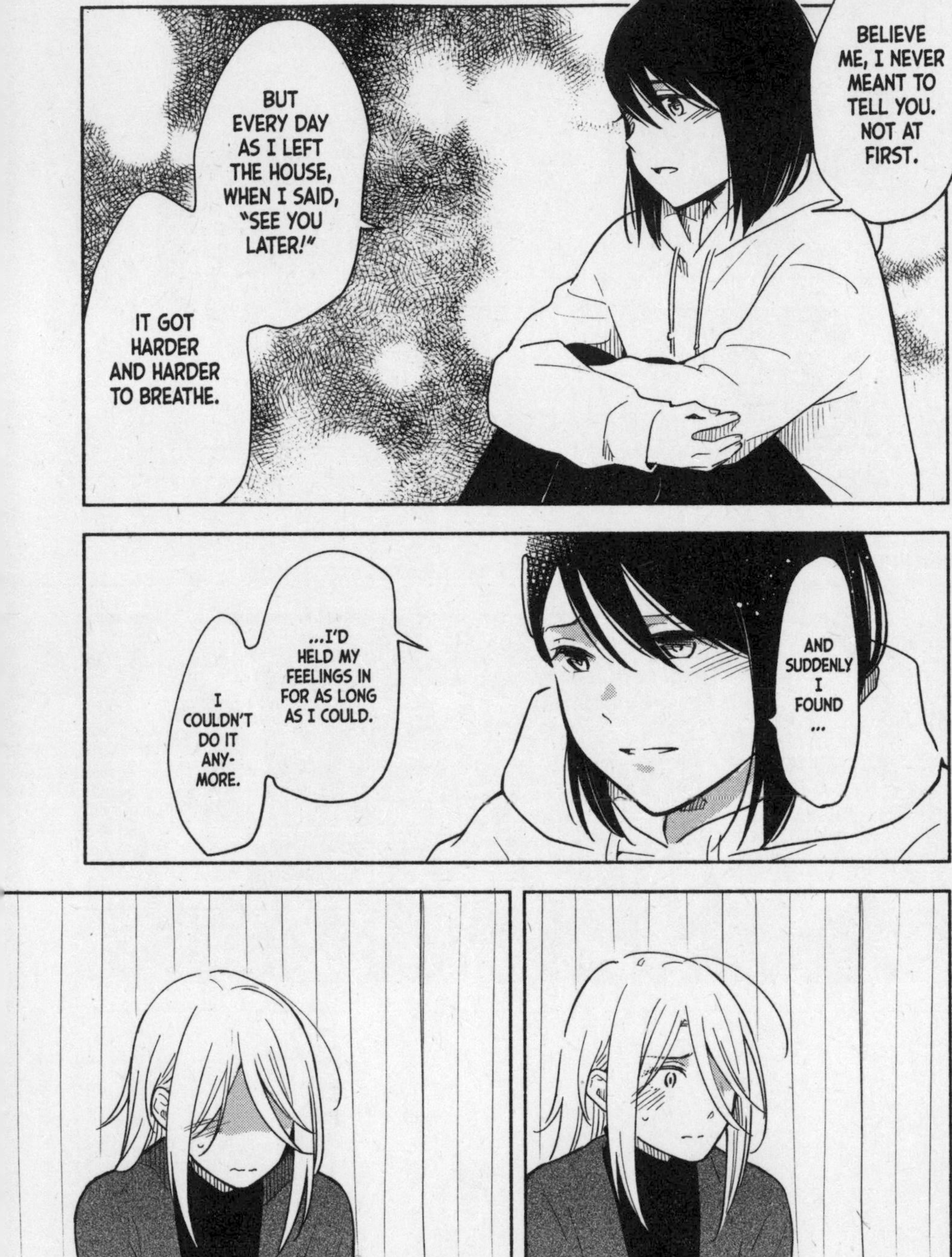
BELIEVE ME, I NEVER MEANT TO TELL YOU. NOT AT FIRST.
BUT EVERY DAY AS I LEFT THE HOUSE, WHEN I SAID, "SEE YOU LATER!"
IT GOT HARDER AND HARDER TO BREATHE.
AND SUDDENLY I FOUND ...
...I'D HELD MY FEELINGS IN FOR AS LONG AS I COULD.
I COULDN'T DO IT ANY-MORE.

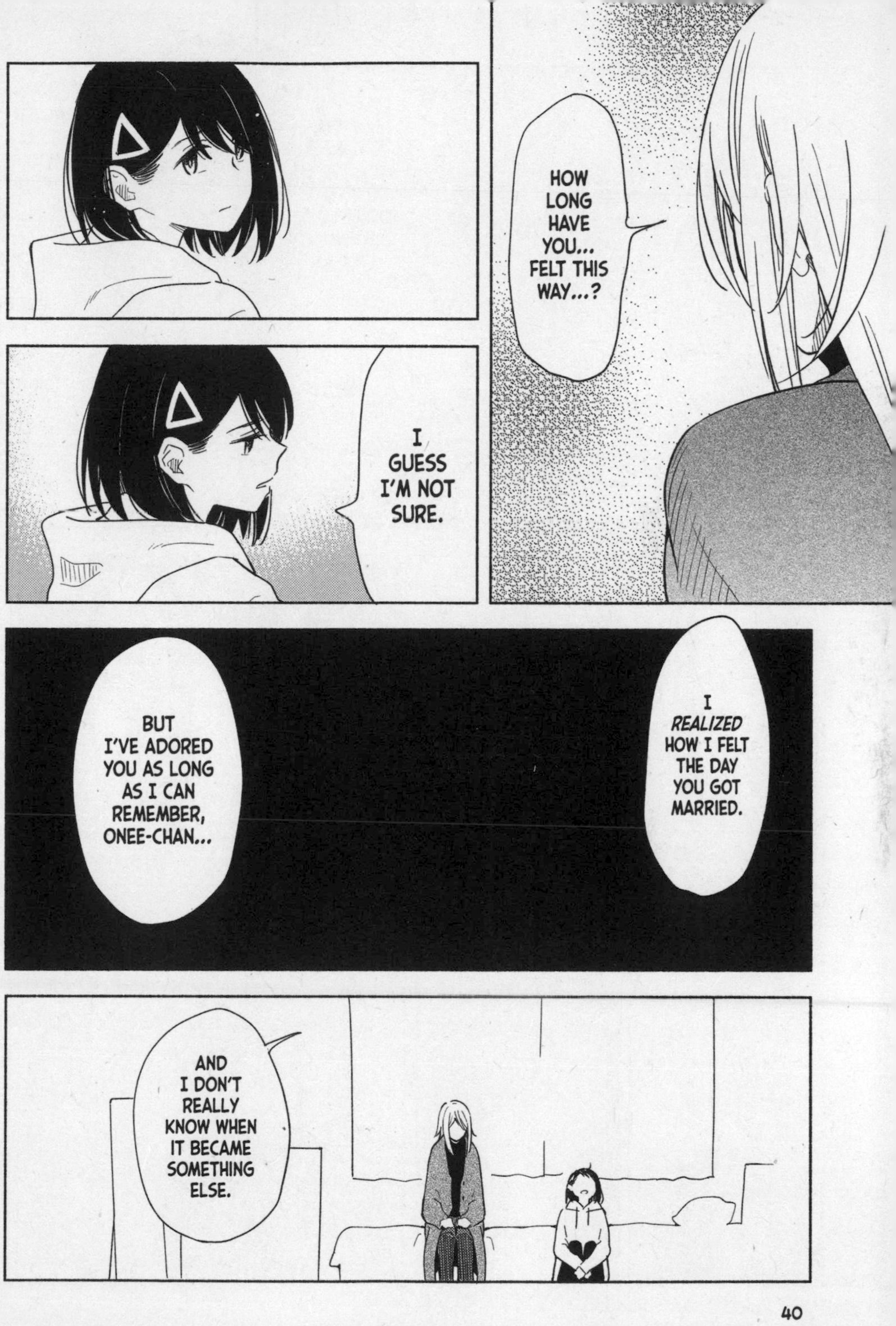
HOW LONG HAVE YOU... FELT THIS WAY...?
I GUESS I'M NOT SURE.
I *REALIZED* HOW I FELT THE DAY YOU GOT MARRIED.
BUT I'VE ADORED YOU AS LONG AS I CAN REMEMBER, ONEE-CHAN...
AND I DON'T REALLY KNOW WHEN IT BECAME SOMETHING ELSE.

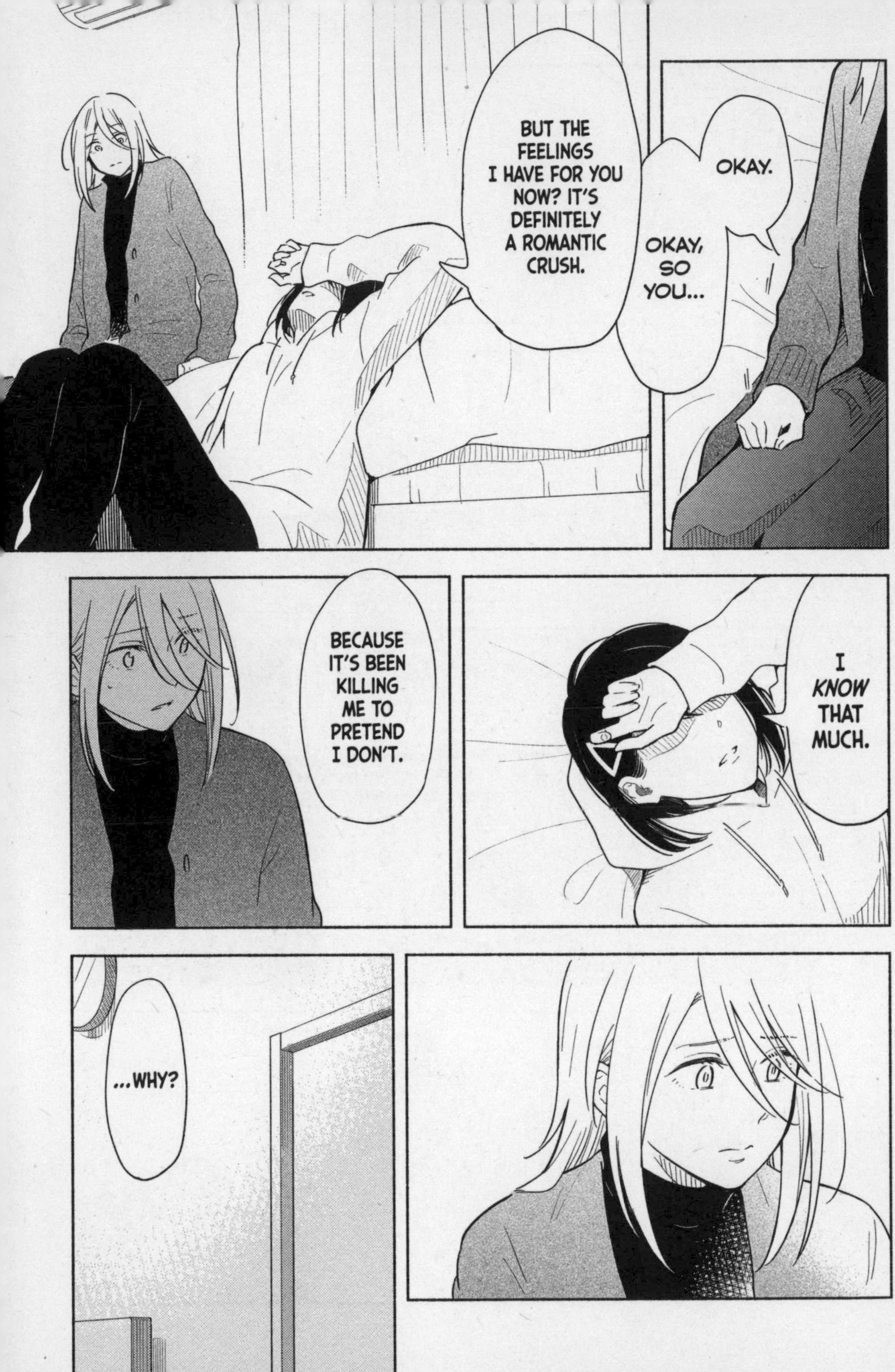
OKAY.
OKAY, SO YOU...
BUT THE FEELINGS I HAVE FOR YOU NOW? IT'S DEFINITELY A ROMANTIC CRUSH.
I *KNOW* THAT MUCH.
BECAUSE IT'S BEEN KILLING ME TO PRETEND I DON'T.
...WHY?

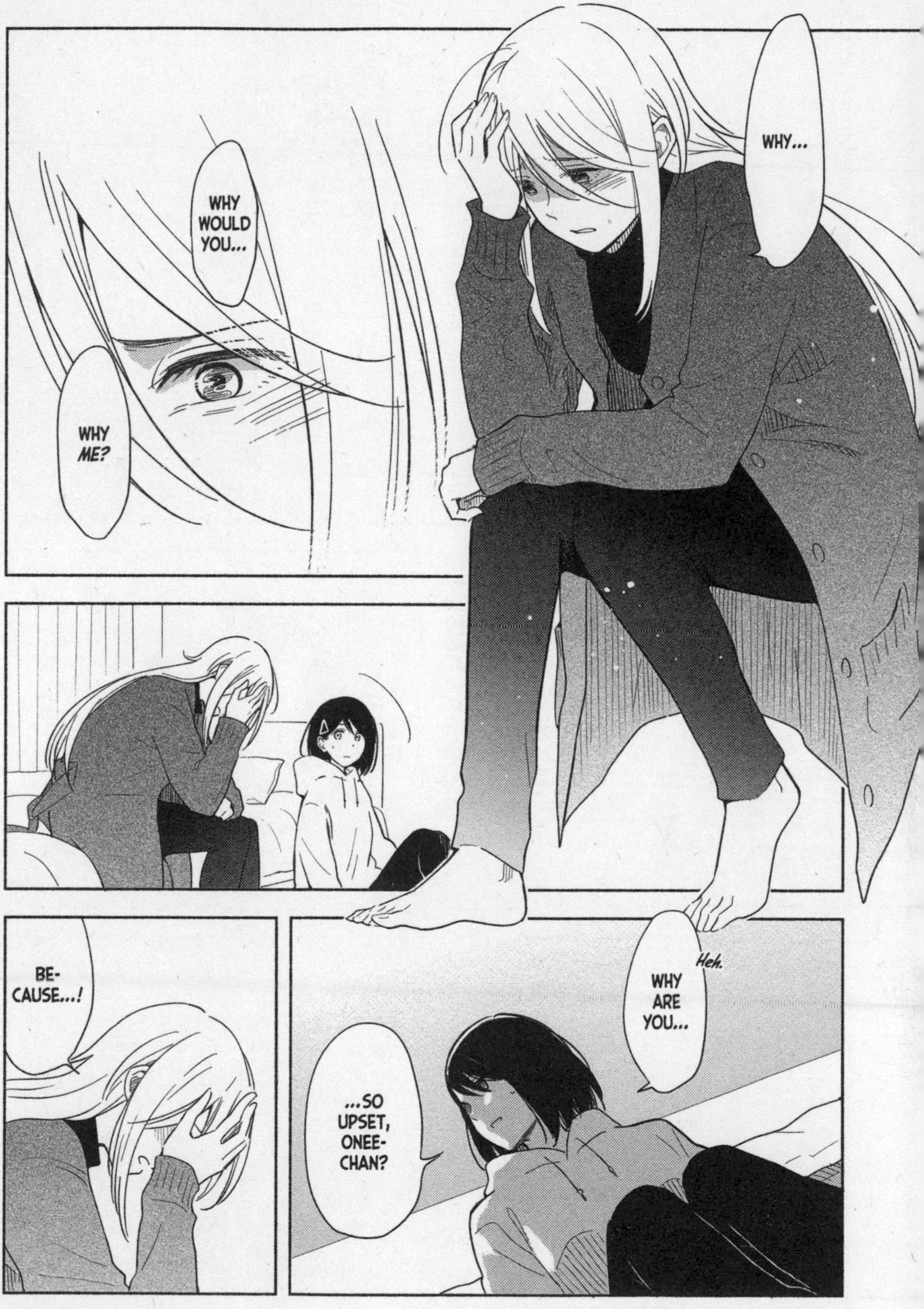
WHY...
WHY WOULD YOU...
WHY ME?
Heh.
WHY ARE YOU...
...SO UPSET, ONEE-CHAN?
BE-CAUSE...!

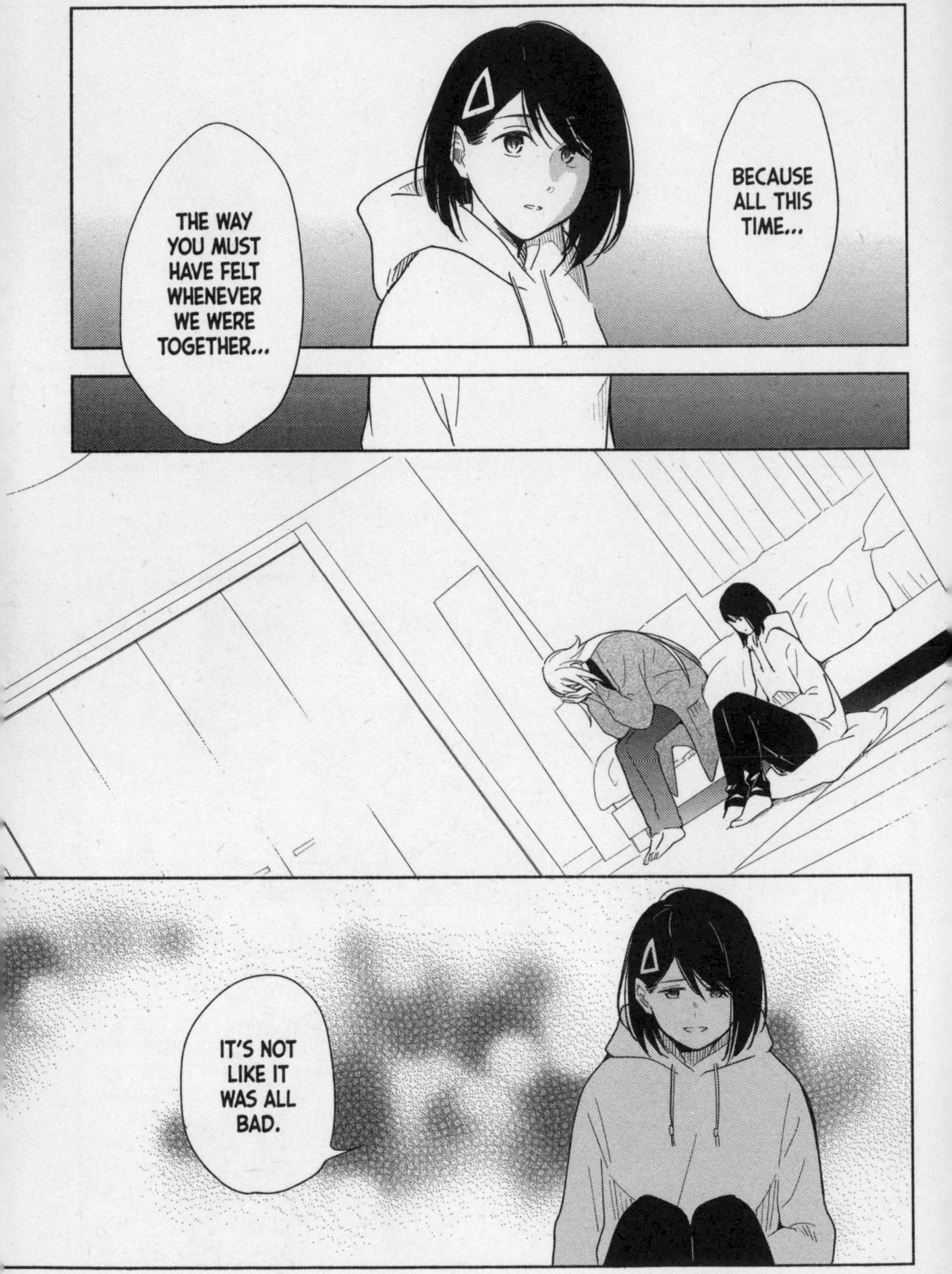
BECAUSE ALL THIS TIME...
THE WAY YOU MUST HAVE FELT WHENEVER WE WERE TOGETHER...
IT'S NOT LIKE IT WAS ALL BAD.

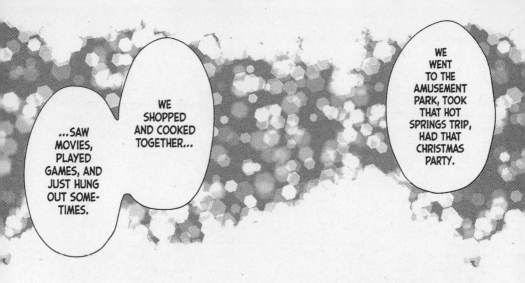

WE WENT TO THE AMUSEMENT PARK, TOOK THAT HOT SPRINGS TRIP, HAD THAT CHRISTMAS PARTY.

WE SHOPPED AND COOKED TOGETHER...

...SAW MOVIES, PLAYED GAMES, AND JUST HUNG OUT SOMETIMES.

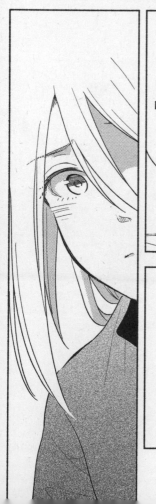

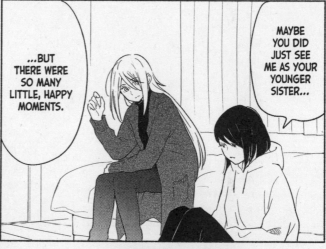

MAYBE YOU DID JUST SEE ME AS YOUR YOUNGER SISTER...

...BUT THERE WERE SO MANY LITTLE, HAPPY MOMENTS.

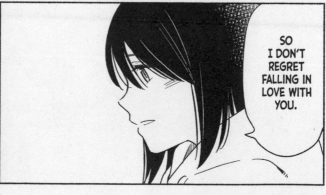

SO I DON'T REGRET FALLING IN LOVE WITH YOU.

44

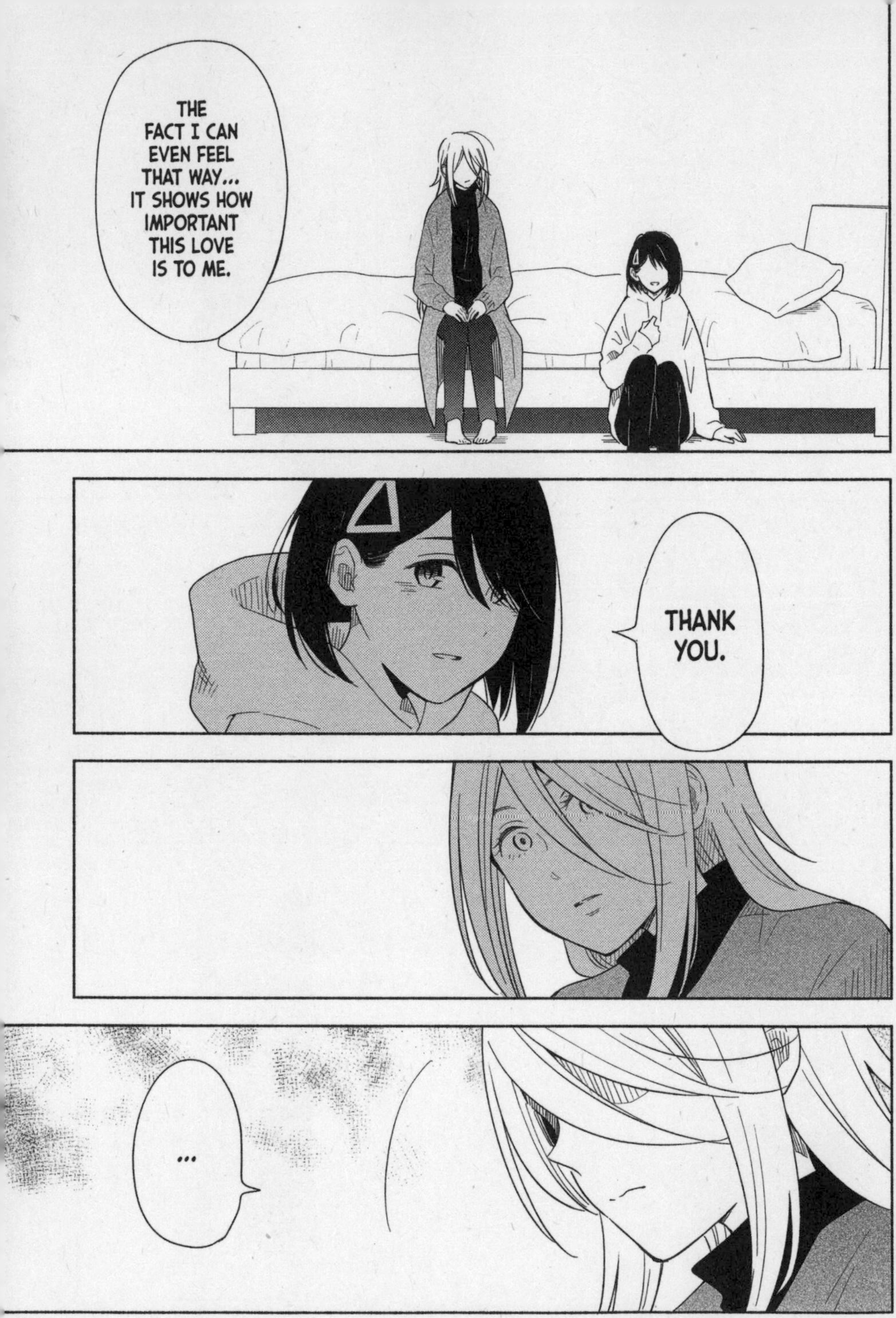
THE FACT I CAN EVEN FEEL THAT WAY... IT SHOWS HOW IMPORTANT THIS LOVE IS TO ME.
THANK YOU.
...

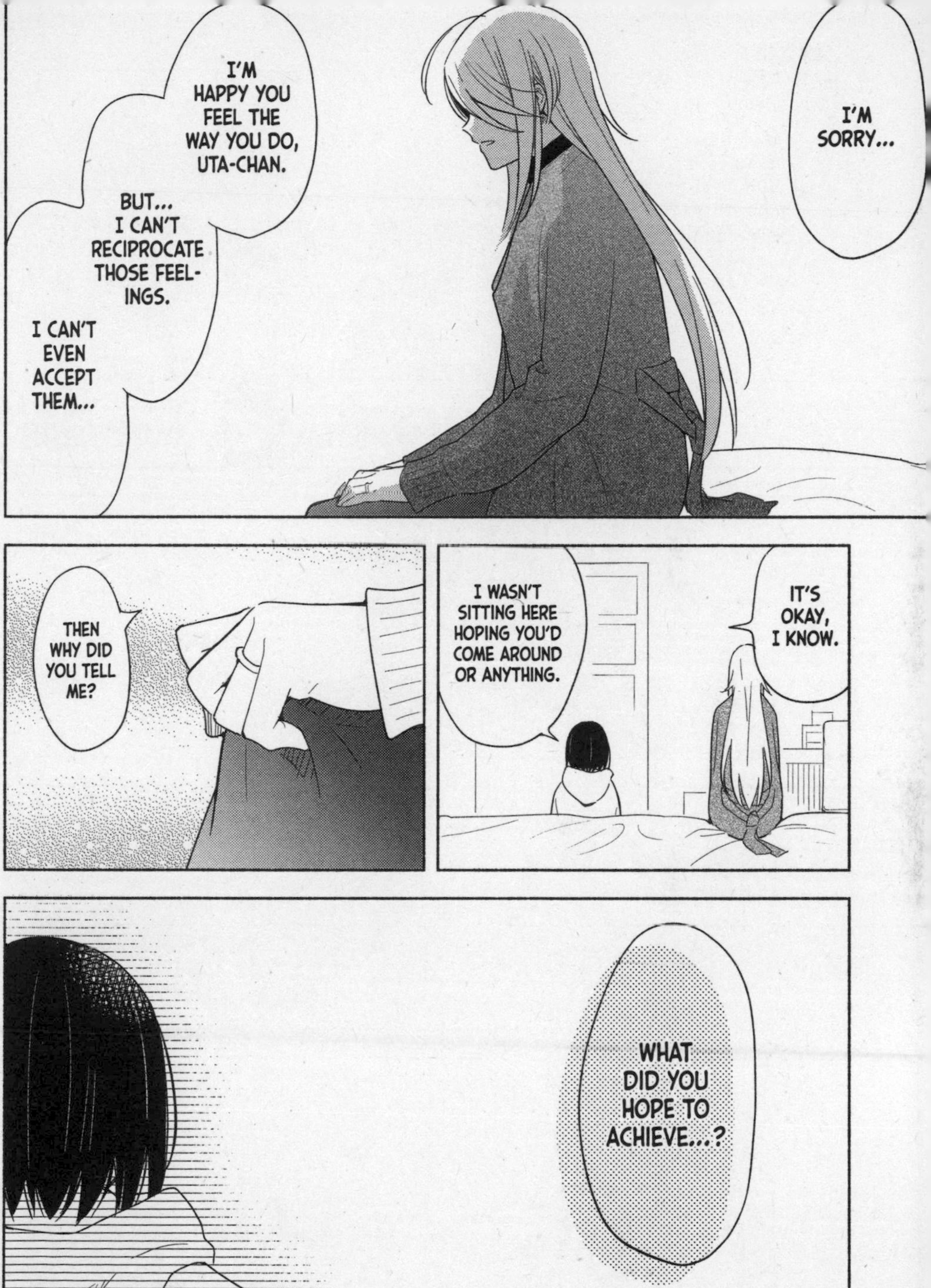
I'M SORRY...
I'M HAPPY YOU FEEL THE WAY YOU DO, UTA-CHAN.
BUT... I CAN'T RECIPROCATE THOSE FEEL-INGS.
I CAN'T EVEN ACCEPT THEM...
IT'S OKAY, I KNOW.
I WASN'T SITTING HERE HOPING YOU'D COME AROUND OR ANYTHING.
THEN WHY DID YOU TELL ME?
WHAT DID YOU HOPE TO ACHIEVE...?

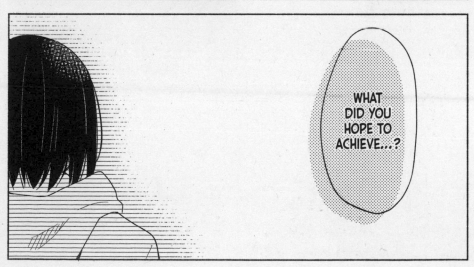

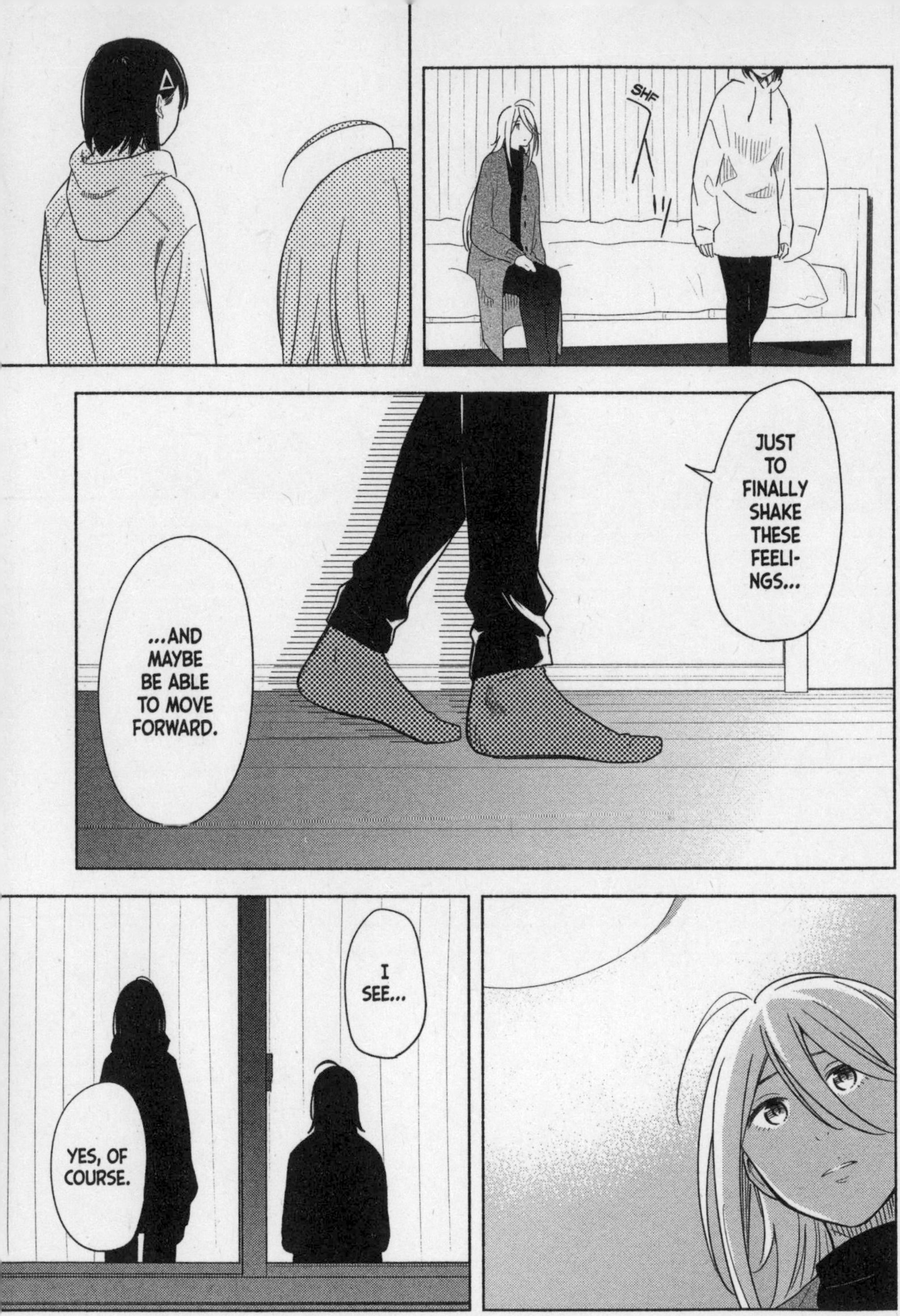
SHF
JUST TO FINALLY SHAKE THESE FEELI-NGS...
...AND MAYBE BE ABLE TO MOVE FORWARD.
I SEE...
YES, OF COURSE.

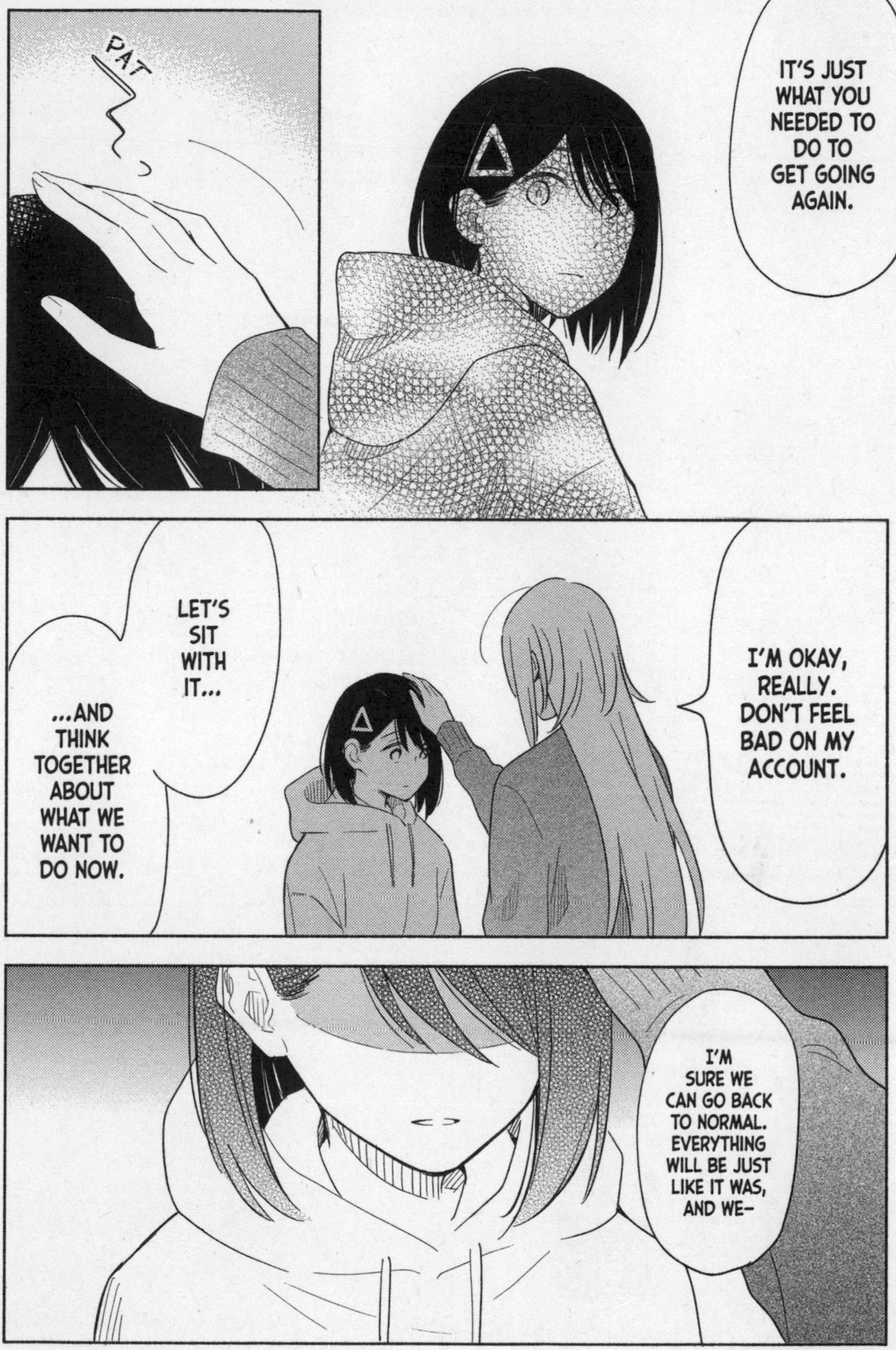
IT'S JUST WHAT YOU NEEDED TO DO TO GET GOING AGAIN.
PAT
I'M OKAY, REALLY. DON'T FEEL BAD ON MY ACCOUNT.
LET'S SIT WITH IT...
...AND THINK TOGETHER ABOUT WHAT WE WANT TO DO NOW.
I'M SURE WE CAN GO BACK TO NORMAL. EVERYTHING WILL BE JUST LIKE IT WAS, AND WE–

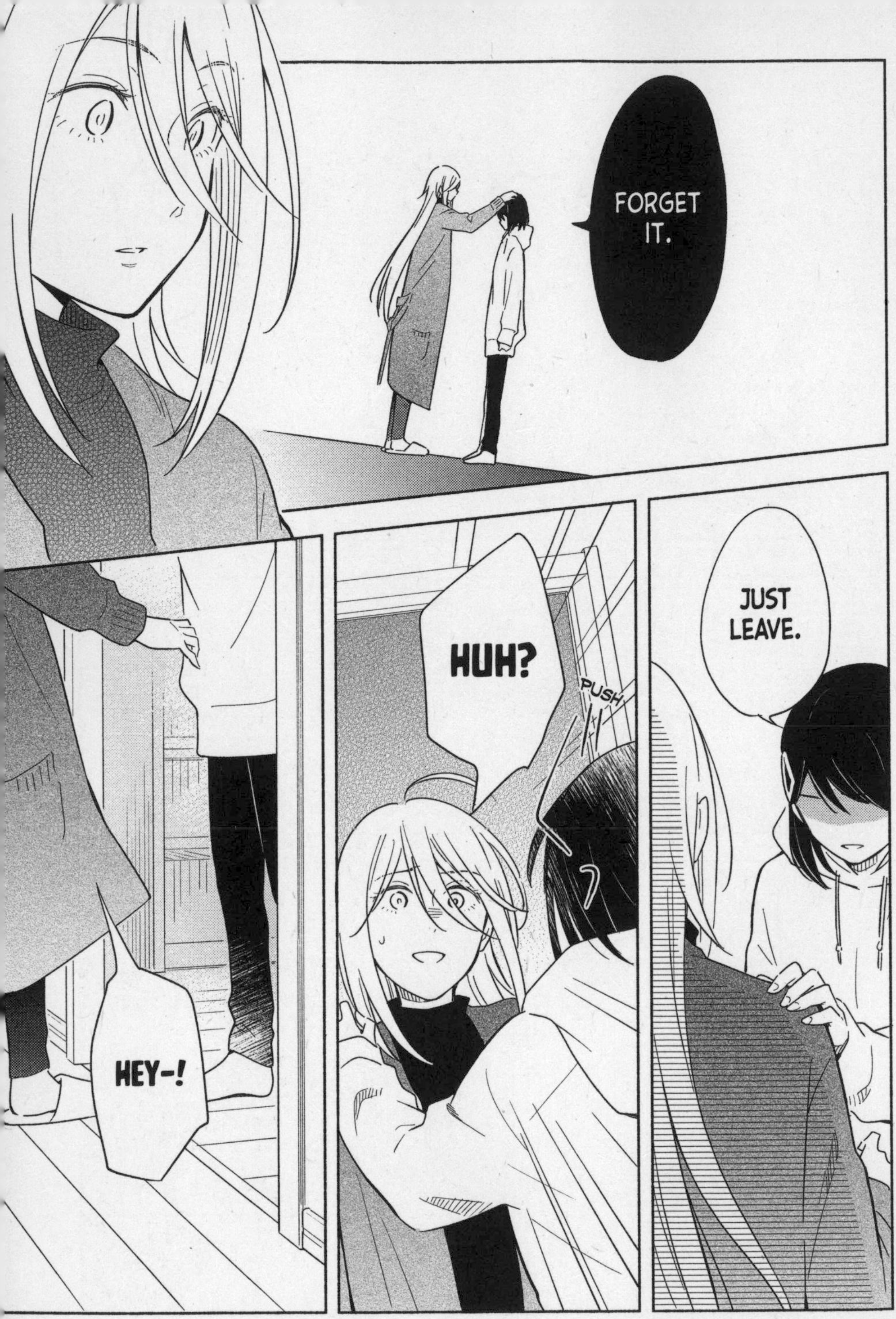
FORGET IT.
JUST LEAVE.
HUH?
PUSH
HEY-!

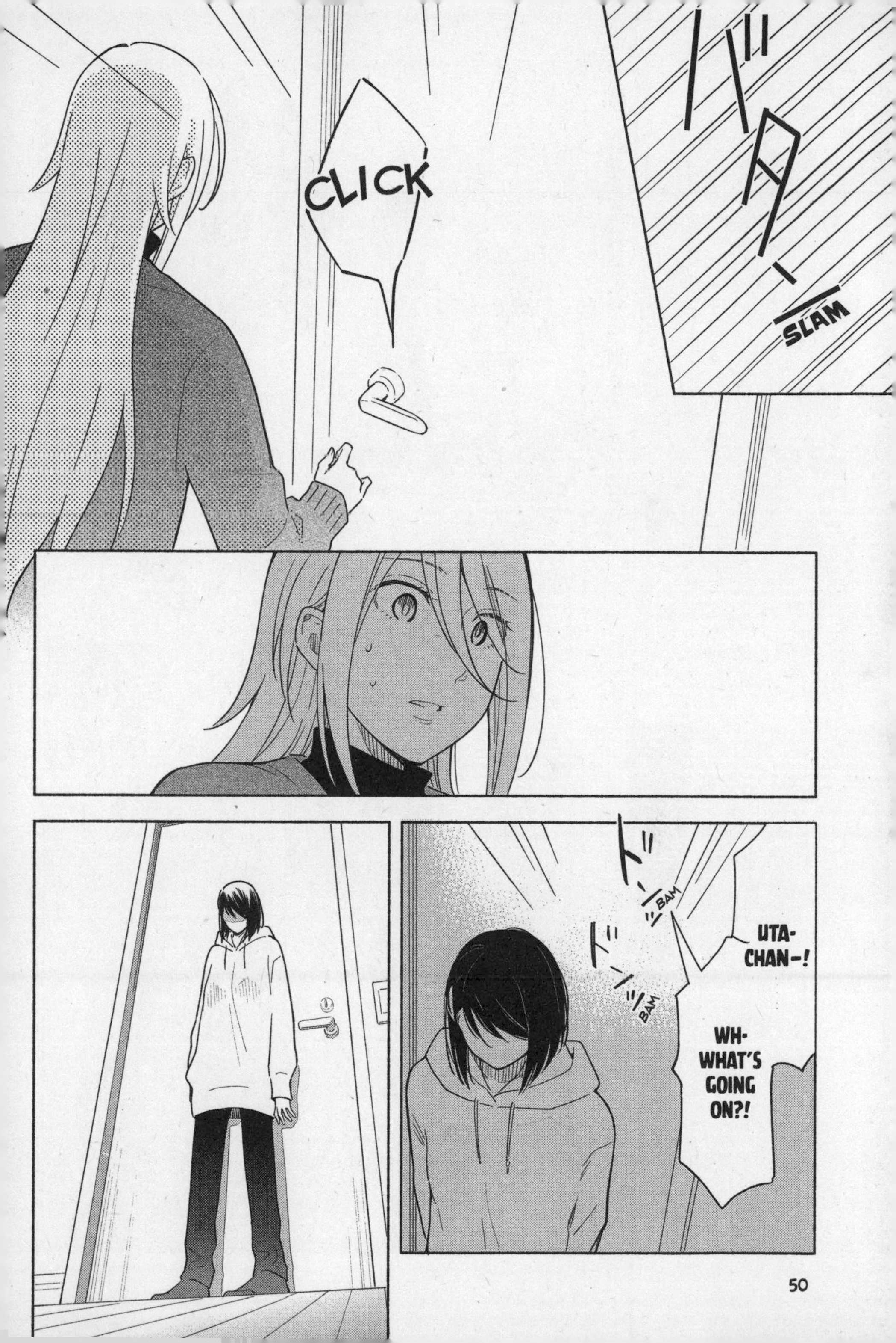
バタ
SLAM
CLICK
BAM
BAM
UTA-CHAN-!
WH-WHAT'S GOING ON?!

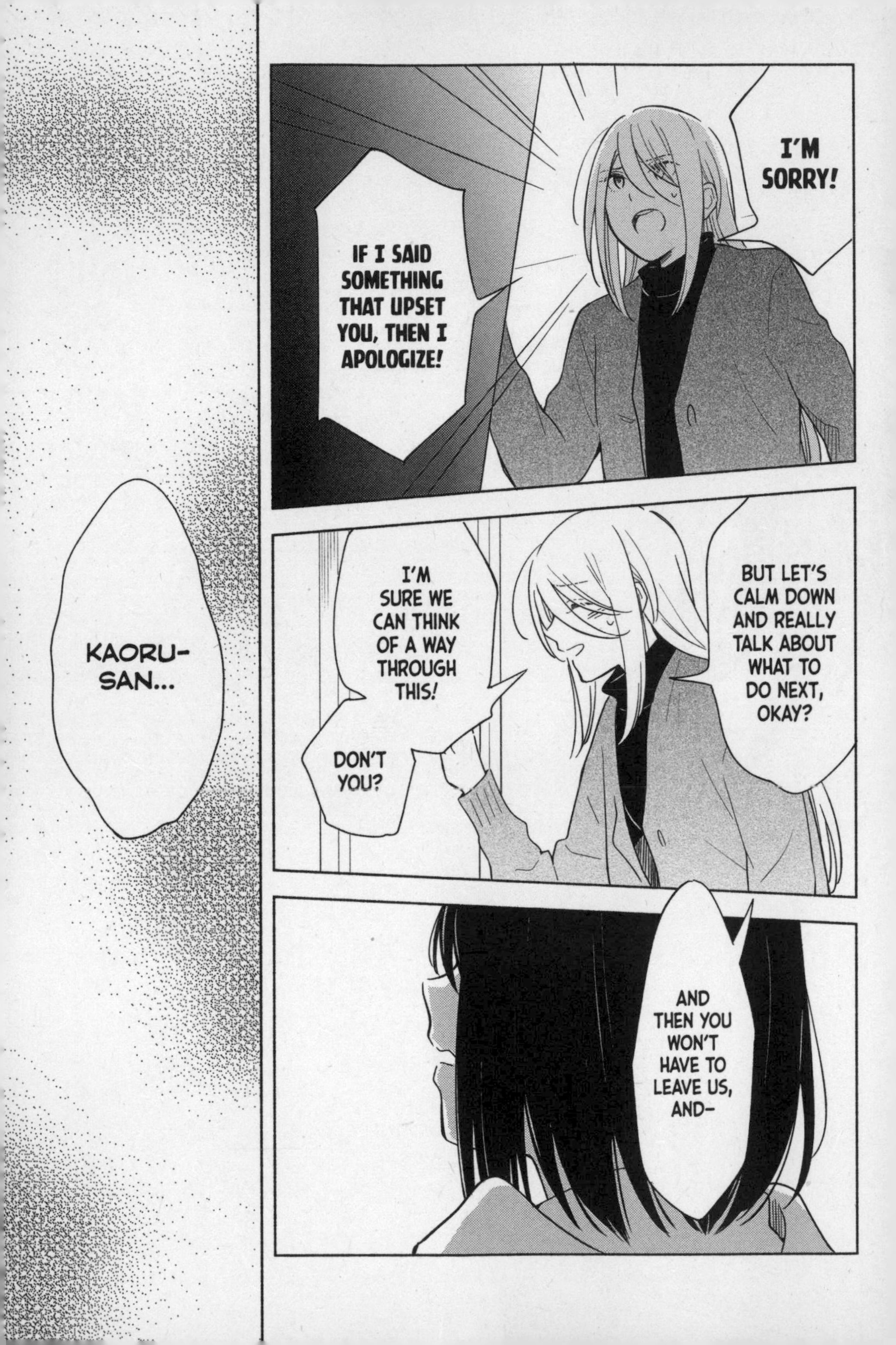
I'M SORRY!
IF I SAID SOMETHING THAT UPSET YOU, THEN I APOLOGIZE!
BUT LET'S CALM DOWN AND REALLY TALK ABOUT WHAT TO DO NEXT, OKAY?
I'M SURE WE CAN THINK OF A WAY THROUGH THIS!
DON'T YOU?
AND THEN YOU WON'T HAVE TO LEAVE US, AND–
KAORU-SAN...

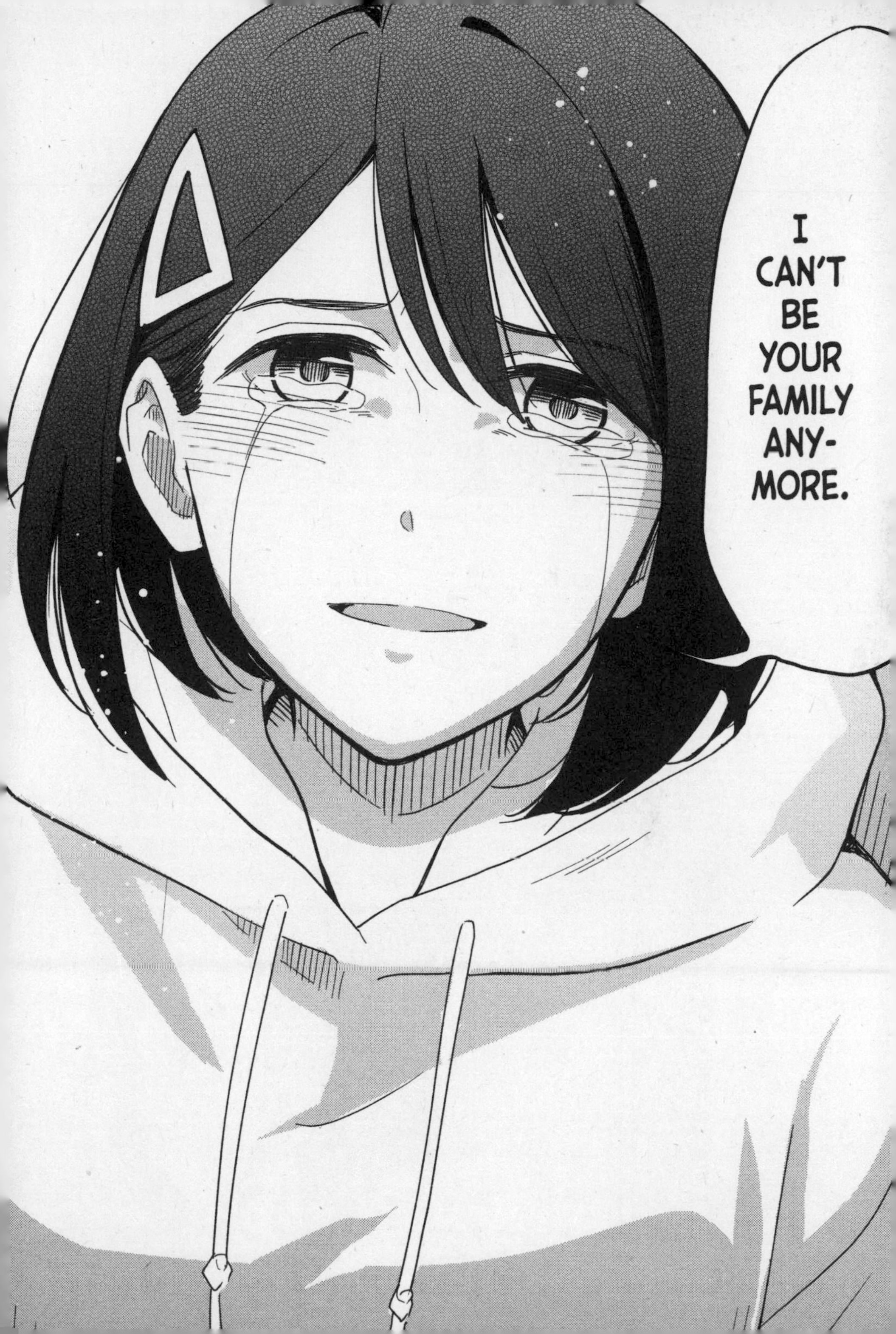
I CAN'T BE YOUR FAMILY ANY- MORE.

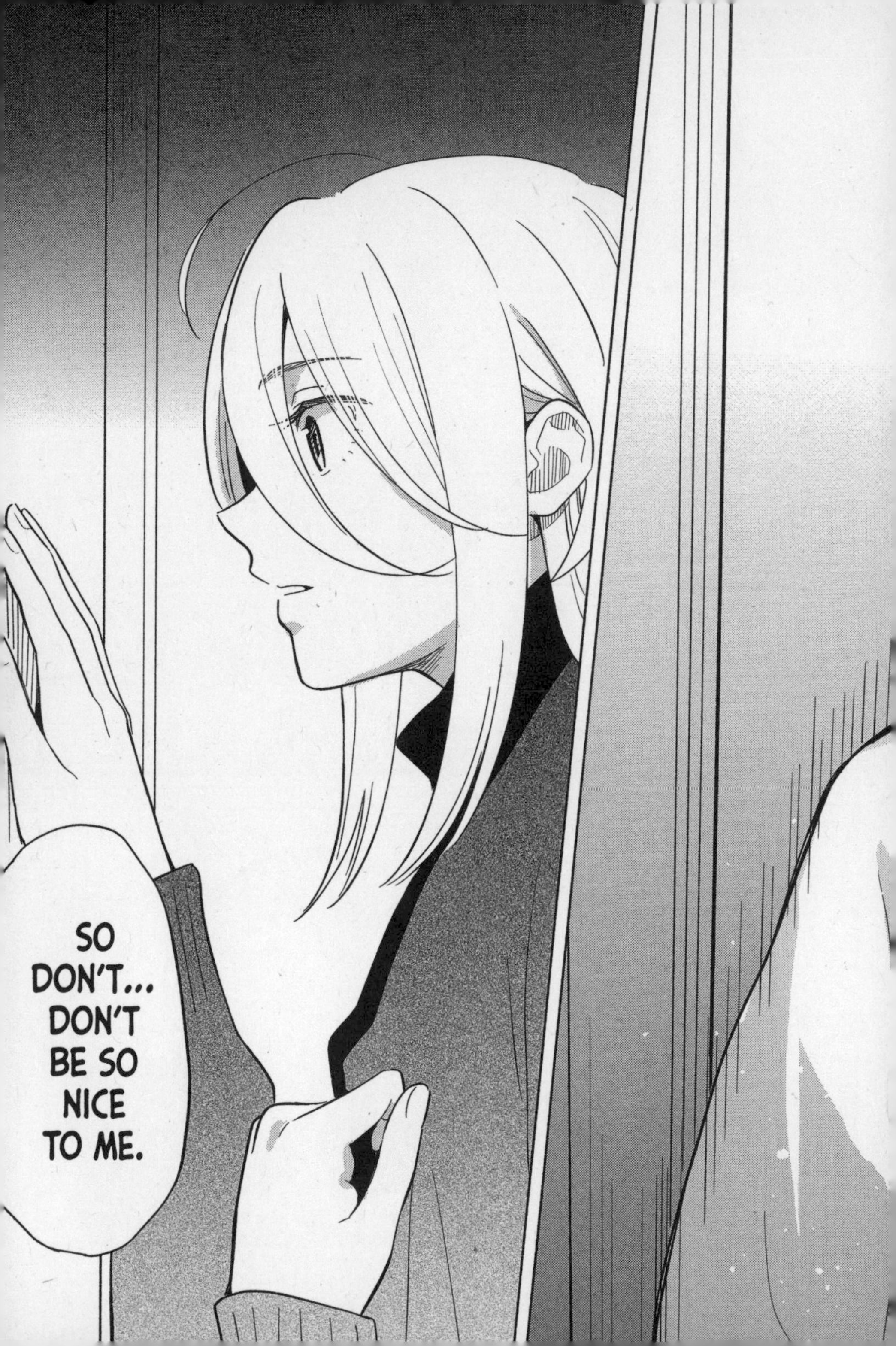
SO DON'T... DON'T BE SO NICE TO ME.

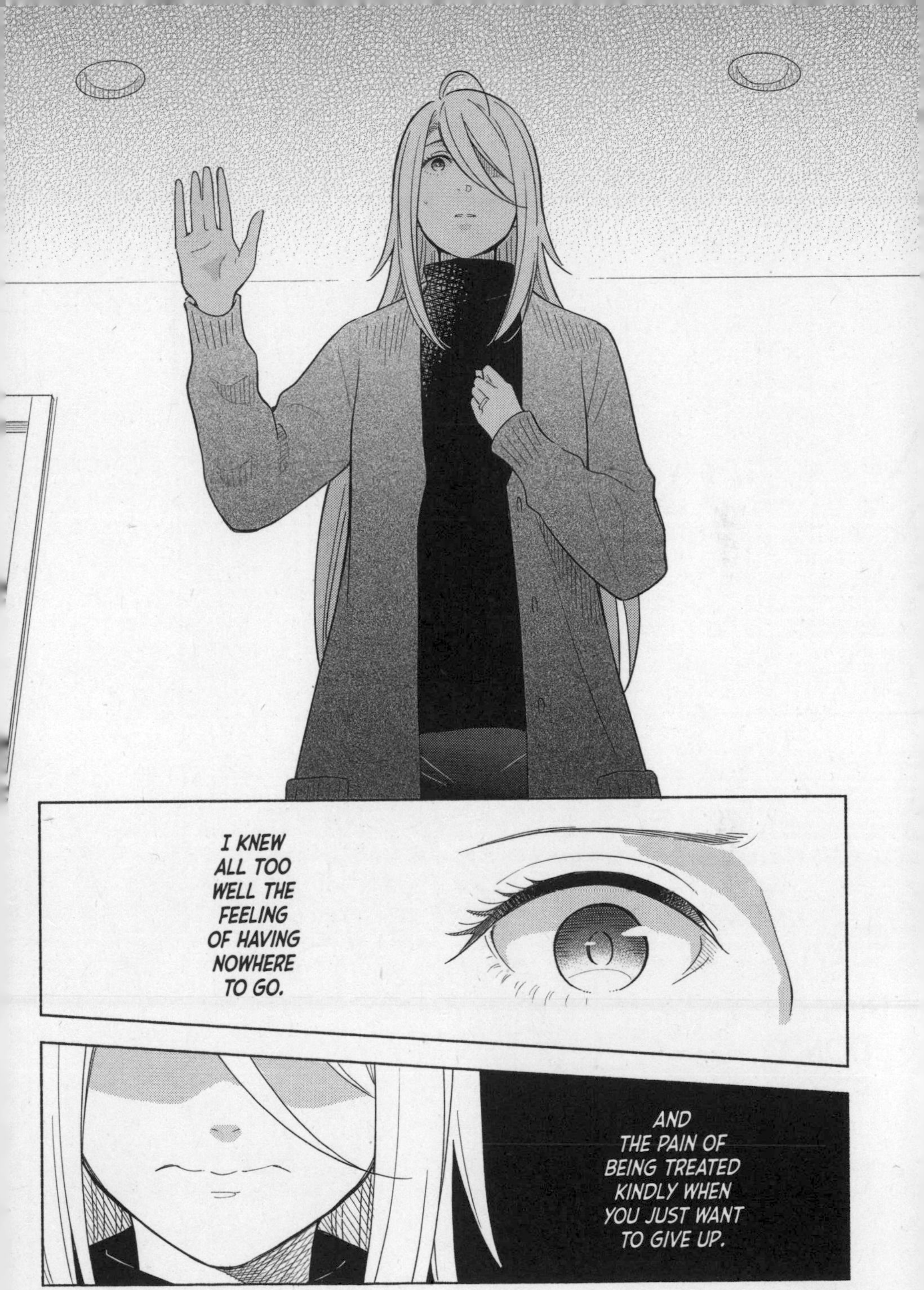
I KNEW ALL TOO WELL THE FEELING OF HAVING NOWHERE TO GO.
AND THE PAIN OF BEING TREATED KINDLY WHEN YOU JUST WANT TO GIVE UP.

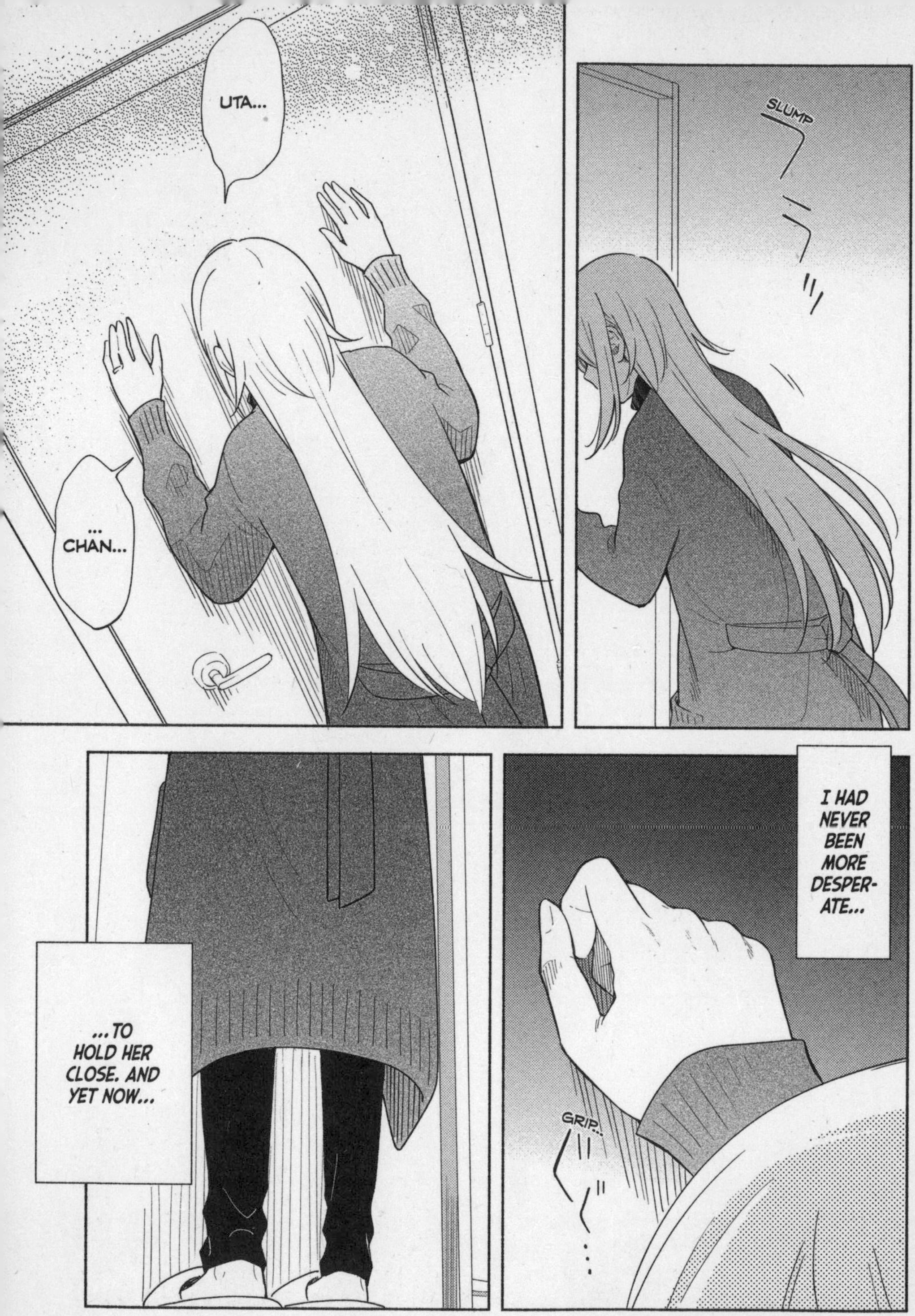
SLUMP
UTA...
...CHAN...
I HAD NEVER BEEN MORE DESPERATE...
GRIP...
...TO HOLD HER CLOSE. AND YET NOW...

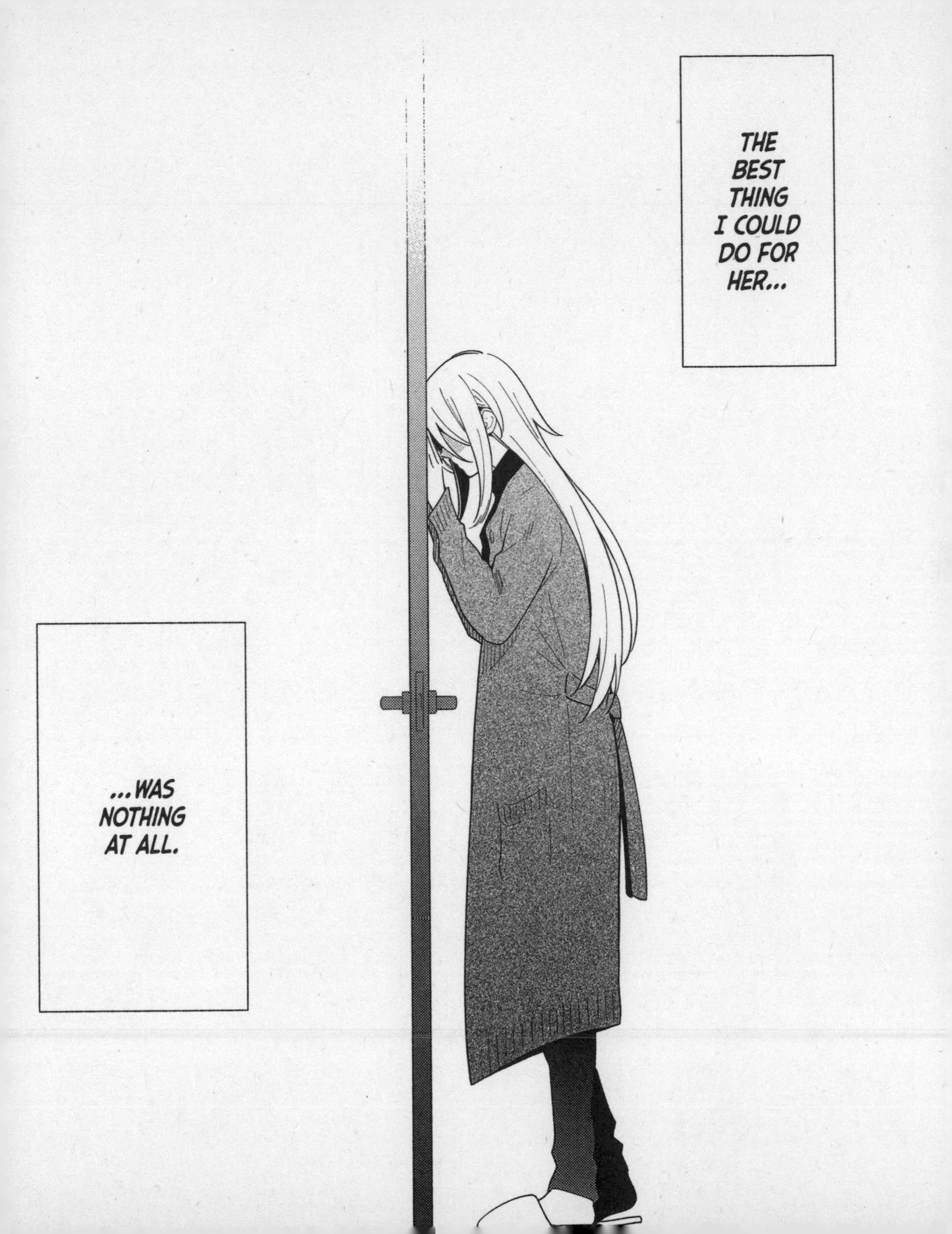
THE BEST THING I COULD DO FOR HER...
...WAS NOTHING AT ALL.

If I Could
Reach You

If I Could
Reach You

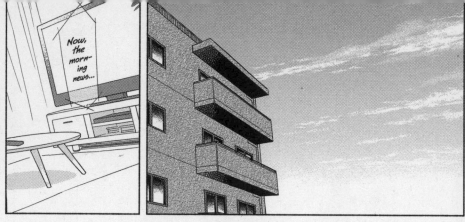

Now, the morning news...

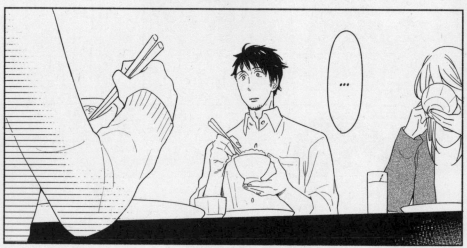

...

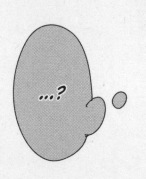

...?

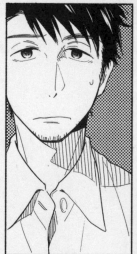

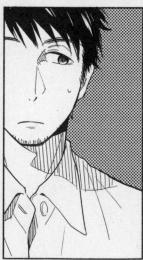

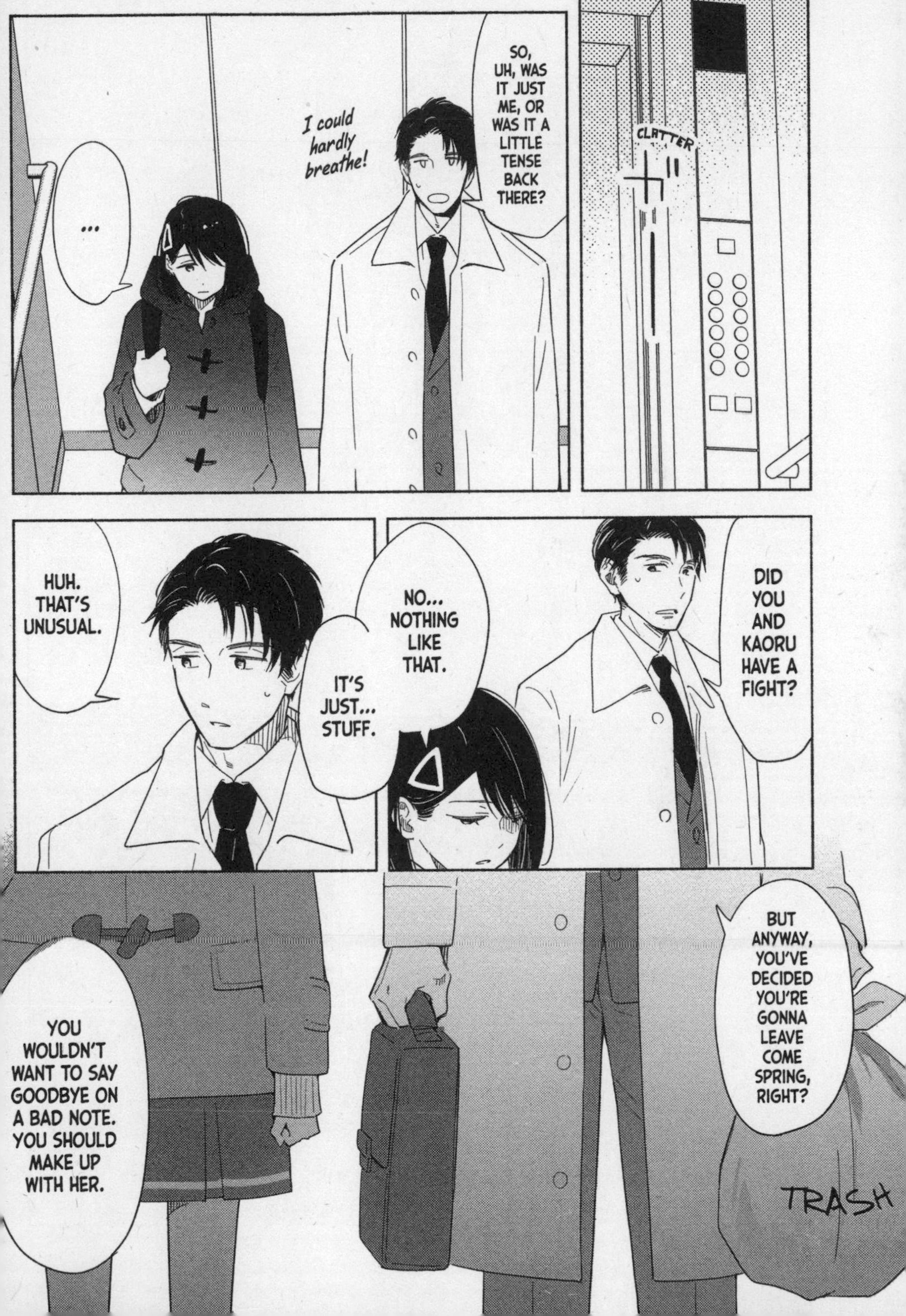
CLATTER
SO, UH, WAS IT JUST ME, OR WAS IT A LITTLE TENSE BACK THERE?
I could hardly breathe!
...
DID YOU AND KAORU HAVE A FIGHT?
NO... NOTHING LIKE THAT.
IT'S JUST... STUFF.
HUH. THAT'S UNUSUAL.
BUT ANYWAY, YOU'VE DECIDED YOU'RE GONNA LEAVE COME SPRING, RIGHT?
TRASH
YOU WOULDN'T WANT TO SAY GOODBYE ON A BAD NOTE. YOU SHOULD MAKE UP WITH HER.

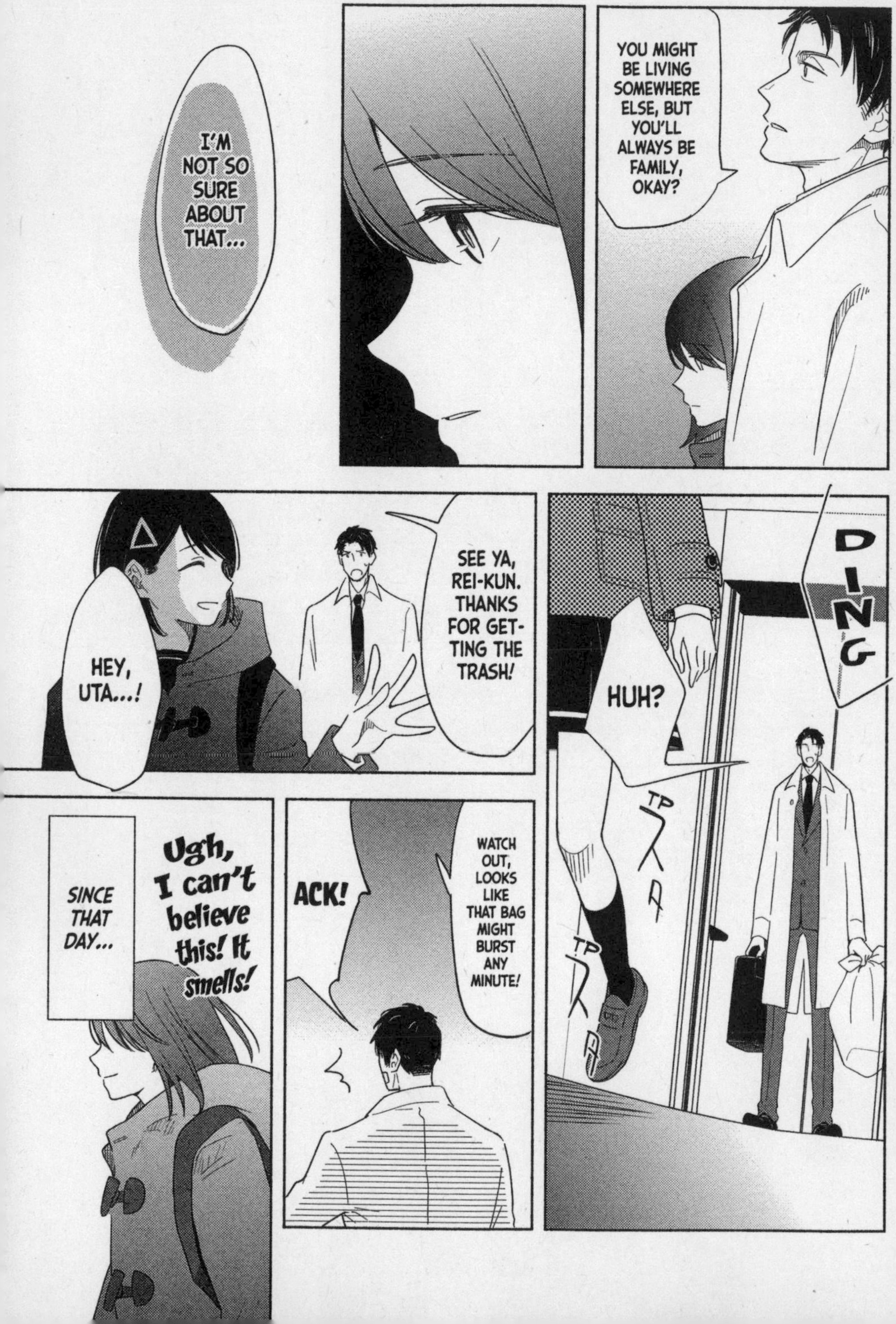
YOU MIGHT BE LIVING SOMEWHERE ELSE, BUT YOU'LL ALWAYS BE FAMILY, OKAY?
I'M NOT SO SURE ABOUT THAT...
DING
HUH?
TP
TP
SEE YA, REI-KUN. THANKS FOR GET-TING THE TRASH!
HEY, UTA...!
WATCH OUT, LOOKS LIKE THAT BAG MIGHT BURST ANY MINUTE!
ACK!
Ugh, I can't believe this! It smells!
SINCE THAT DAY...

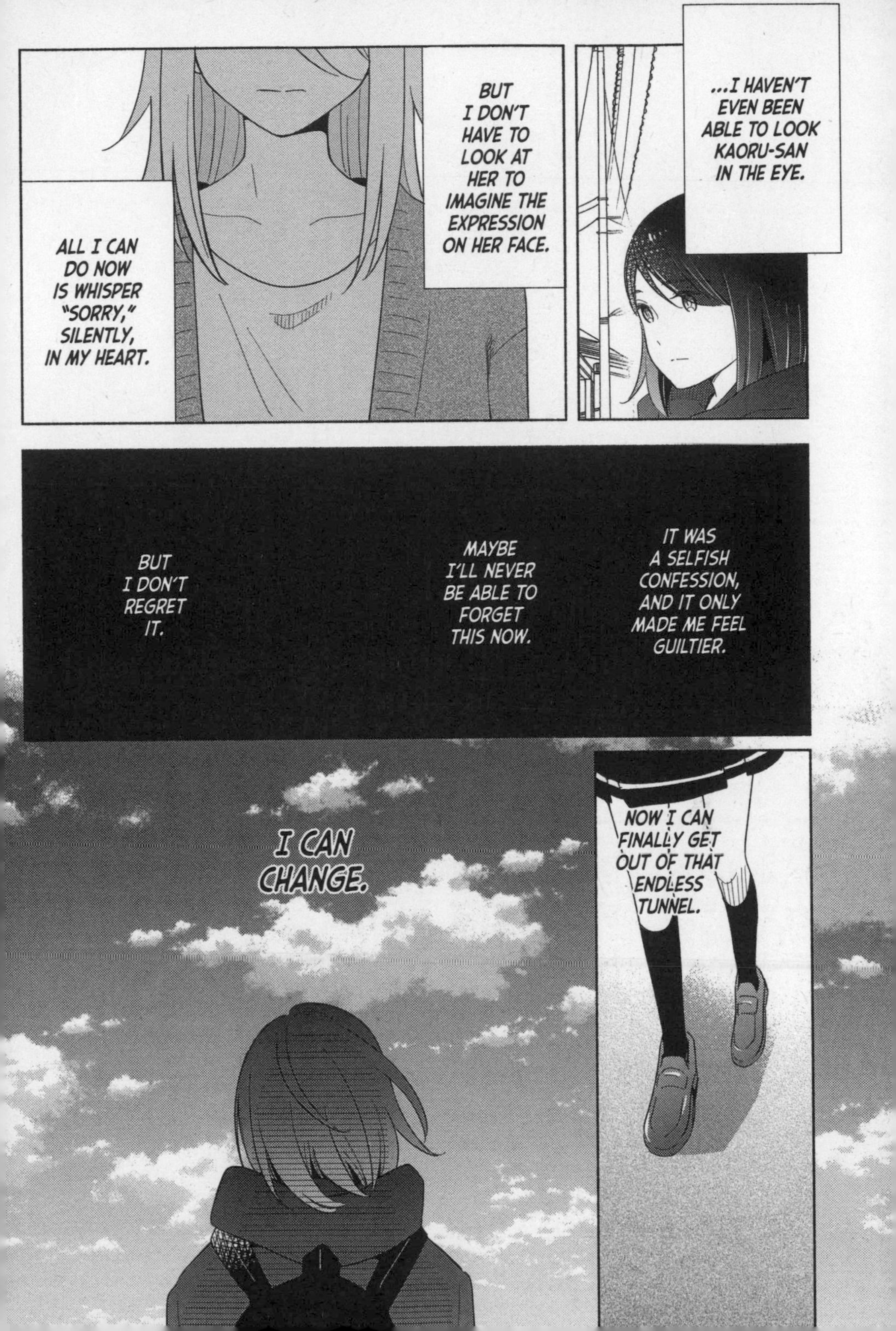
...I HAVEN'T EVEN BEEN ABLE TO LOOK KAORU-SAN IN THE EYE.
BUT I DON'T HAVE TO LOOK AT HER TO IMAGINE THE EXPRESSION ON HER FACE.
ALL I CAN DO NOW IS WHISPER "SORRY," SILENTLY, IN MY HEART.
IT WAS A SELFISH CONFESSION, AND IT ONLY MADE ME FEEL GUILTIER.
MAYBE I'LL NEVER BE ABLE TO FORGET THIS NOW.
BUT I DON'T REGRET IT.
NOW I CAN FINALLY GET OUT OF THAT ENDLESS TUNNEL.
I CAN CHANGE.

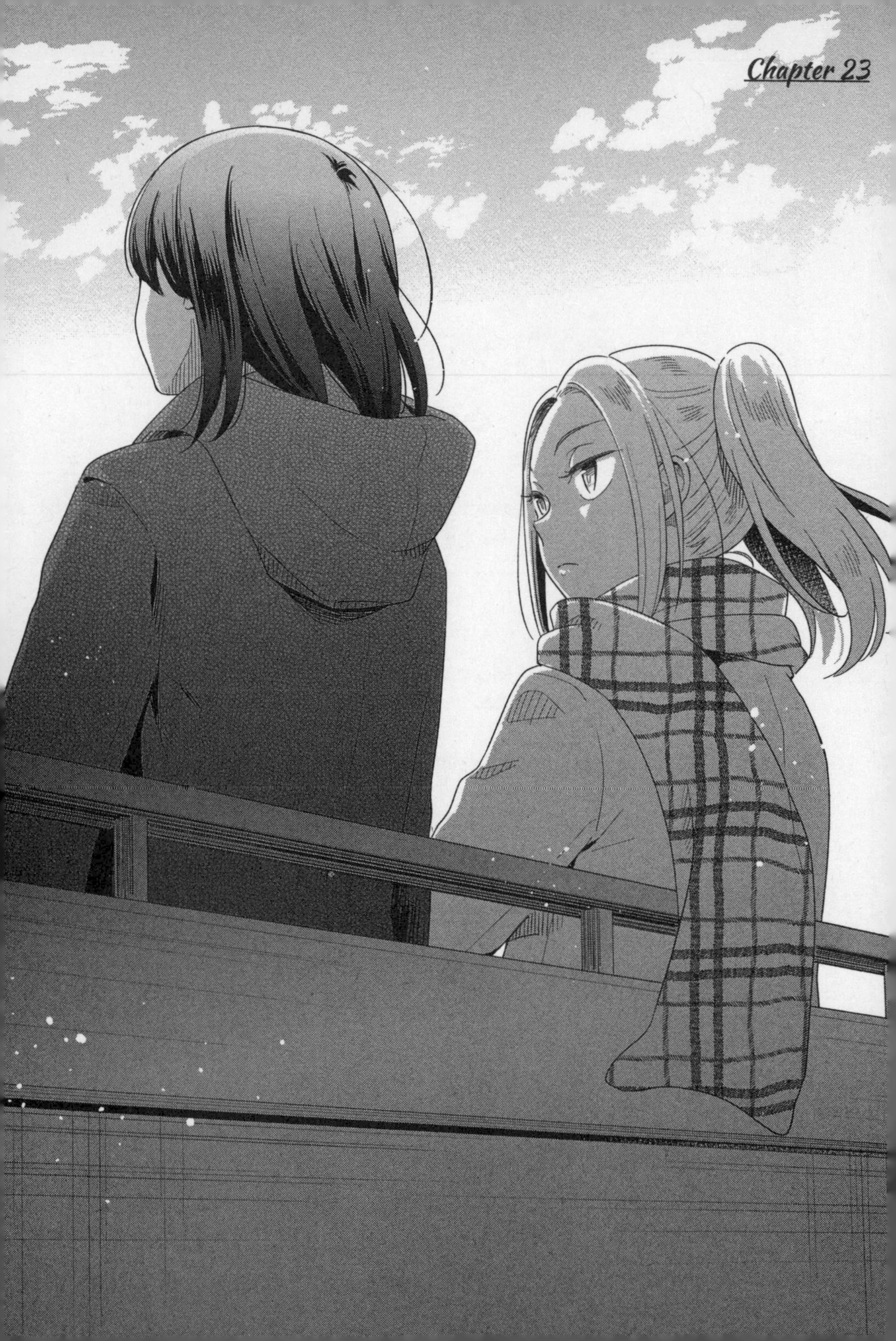
Chapter 23

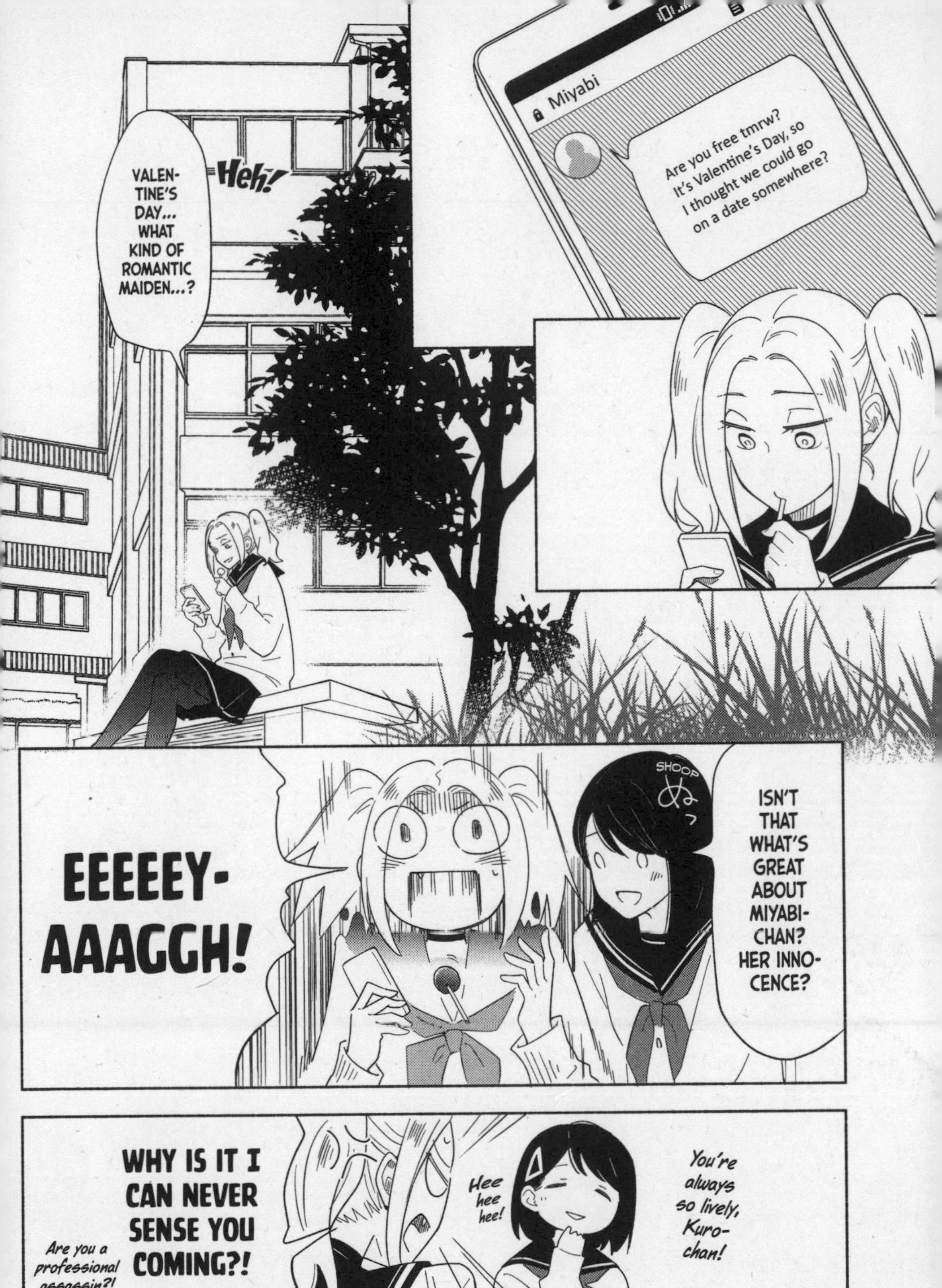
Miyabi
Are you free tmrw? It's Valentine's Day, so I thought we could go on a date somewhere?
Heh!
VALENTINE'S DAY... WHAT KIND OF ROMANTIC MAIDEN...?
ISN'T THAT WHAT'S GREAT ABOUT MIYABI-CHAN? HER INNOCENCE?
SHOOP
EEEEEY-AAAGGH!
You're always so lively, Kuro-chan!
Hee hee hee!
WHY IS IT I CAN NEVER SENSE YOU COMING?!
Are you a professional assassin?!

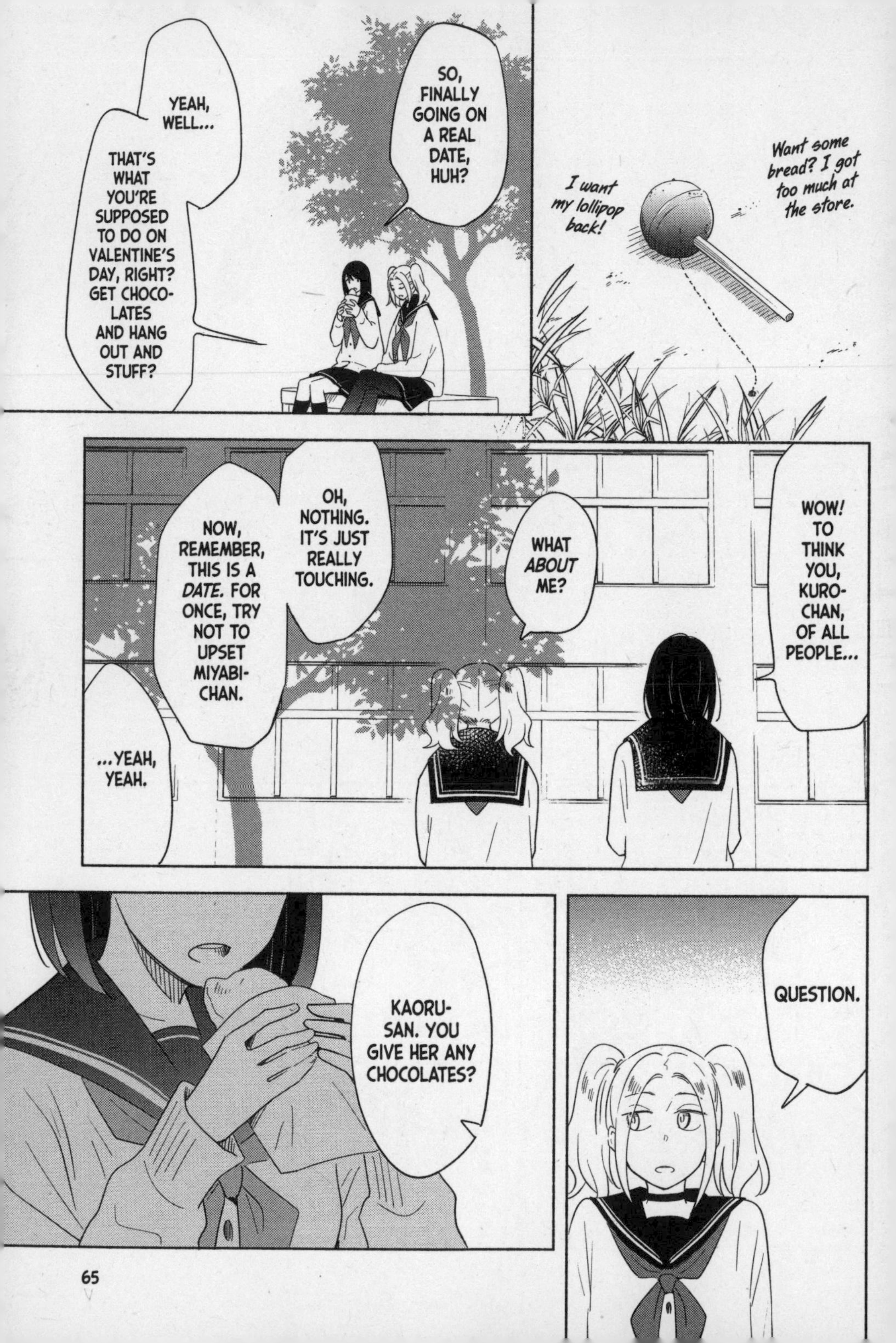

Want some bread? I got too much at the store.
I want my lollipop back!
SO, FINALLY GOING ON A REAL DATE, HUH?
YEAH, WELL...
THAT'S WHAT YOU'RE SUPPOSED TO DO ON VALENTINE'S DAY, RIGHT? GET CHOCO-LATES AND HANG OUT AND STUFF?
WOW! TO THINK YOU, KURO-CHAN, OF ALL PEOPLE...
WHAT ABOUT ME?
OH, NOTHING. IT'S JUST REALLY TOUCHING.
NOW, REMEMBER, THIS IS A DATE. FOR ONCE, TRY NOT TO UPSET MIYABI-CHAN.
...YEAH, YEAH.
QUESTION.
KAORU-SAN. YOU GIVE HER ANY CHOCOLATES?

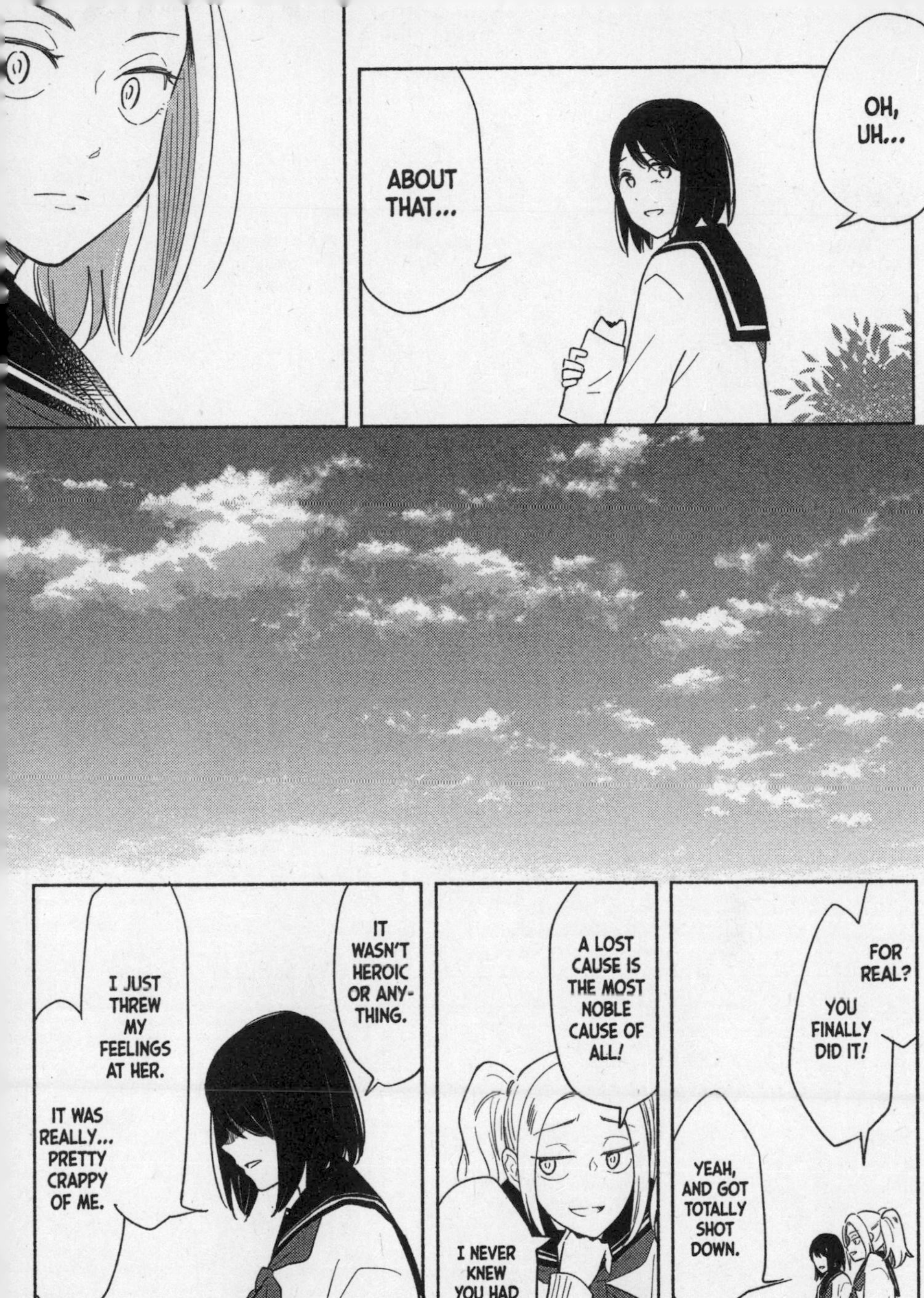
OH, UH...
ABOUT THAT...
FOR REAL?
YOU FINALLY DID IT!
YEAH, AND GOT TOTALLY SHOT DOWN.
A LOST CAUSE IS THE MOST NOBLE CAUSE OF ALL!
I NEVER KNEW YOU HAD THE GUTS, UTA-CHAN.
IT WASN'T HEROIC OR ANY-THING.
I JUST THREW MY FEELINGS AT HER.
IT WAS REALLY... PRETTY CRAPPY OF ME.

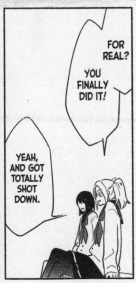

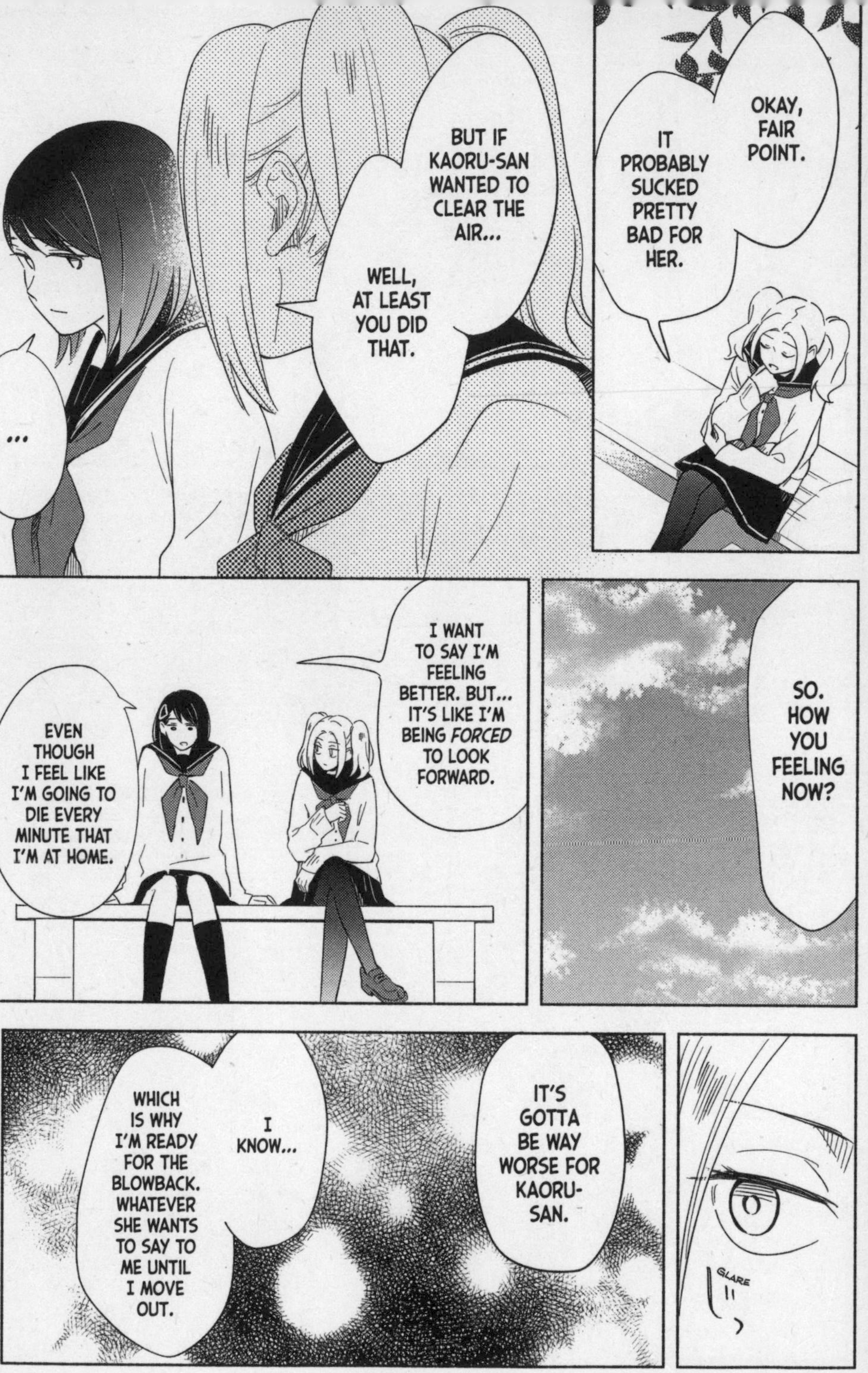
OKAY, FAIR POINT.
IT PROBABLY SUCKED PRETTY BAD FOR HER.
BUT IF KAORU-SAN WANTED TO CLEAR THE AIR...
WELL, AT LEAST YOU DID THAT.
...
SO. HOW YOU FEELING NOW?
I WANT TO SAY I'M FEELING BETTER. BUT... IT'S LIKE I'M BEING *FORCED* TO LOOK FORWARD.
EVEN THOUGH I FEEL LIKE I'M GOING TO DIE EVERY MINUTE THAT I'M AT HOME.
GLARE
IT'S GOTTA BE WAY WORSE FOR KAORU-SAN.
I KNOW...
WHICH IS WHY I'M READY FOR THE BLOWBACK. WHATEVER SHE WANTS TO SAY TO ME UNTIL I MOVE OUT.

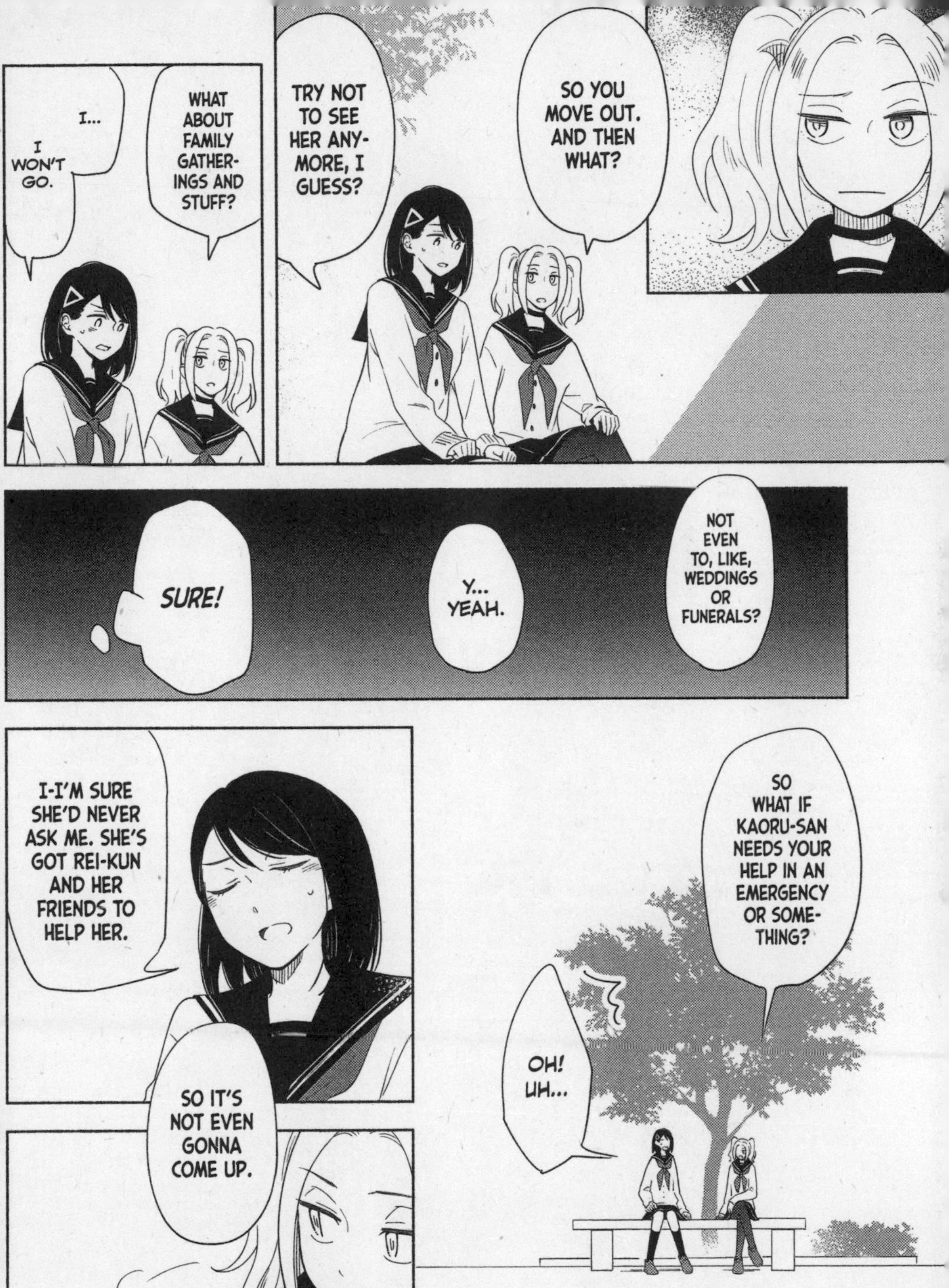
SO YOU MOVE OUT. AND THEN WHAT?
TRY NOT TO SEE HER ANYMORE, I GUESS?
WHAT ABOUT FAMILY GATHERINGS AND STUFF?
I... I WON'T GO.
NOT EVEN TO, LIKE, WEDDINGS OR FUNERALS?
Y... YEAH.
SURE!
SO WHAT IF KAORU-SAN NEEDS YOUR HELP IN AN EMERGENCY OR SOMETHING?
OH! UH...
I-I'M SURE SHE'D NEVER ASK ME. SHE'S GOT REI-KUN AND HER FRIENDS TO HELP HER.
SO IT'S NOT EVEN GONNA COME UP.

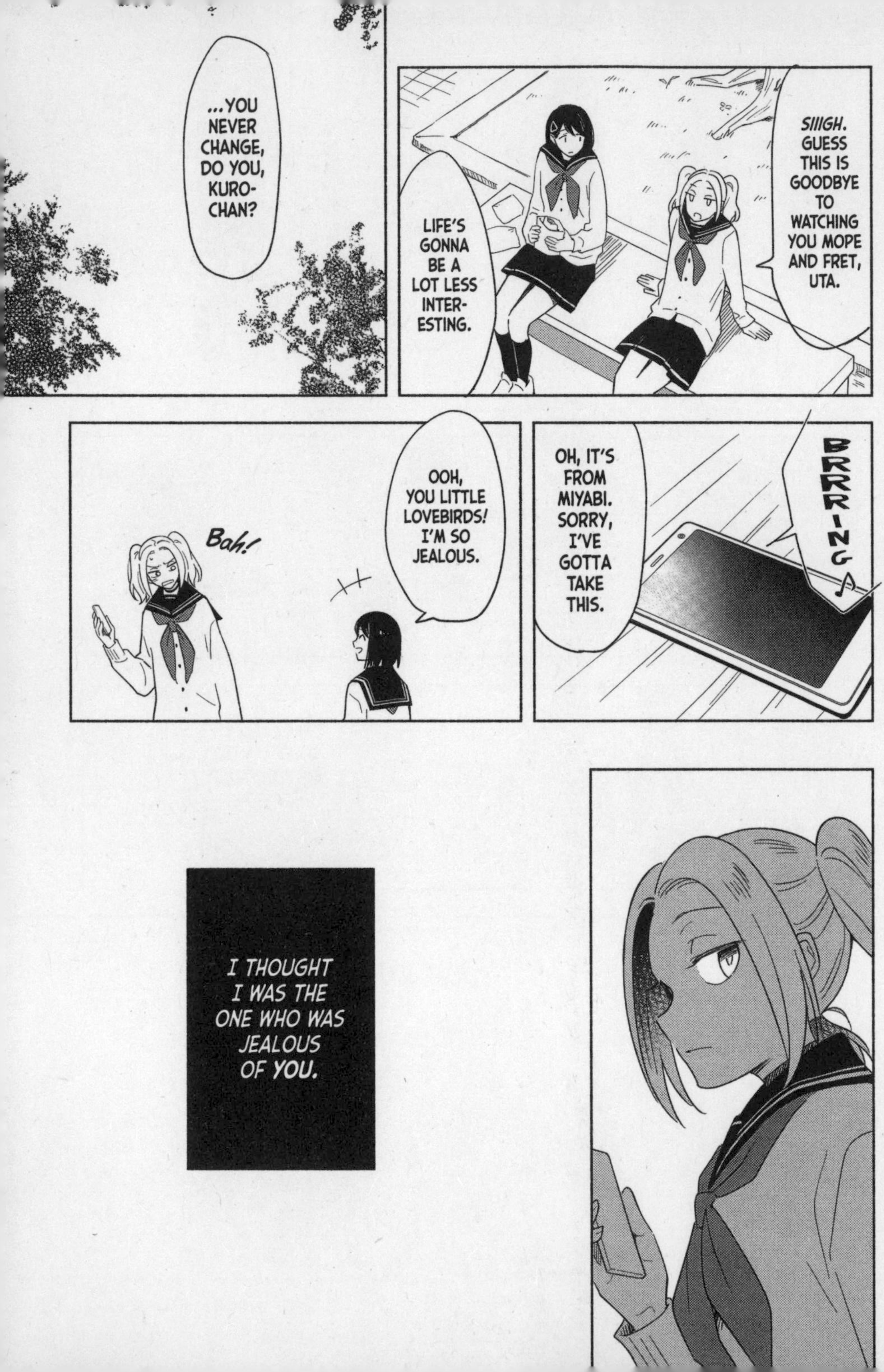

SIIGH. GUESS THIS IS GOODBYE TO WATCHING YOU MOPE AND FRET, UTA.
LIFE'S GONNA BE A LOT LESS INTER-ESTING.
...YOU NEVER CHANGE, DO YOU, KURO-CHAN?
BRRRING
OH, IT'S FROM MIYABI. SORRY, I'VE GOTTA TAKE THIS.
OOH, YOU LITTLE LOVEBIRDS! I'M SO JEALOUS.
Bah!
I THOUGHT I WAS THE ONE WHO WAS JEALOUS OF YOU.

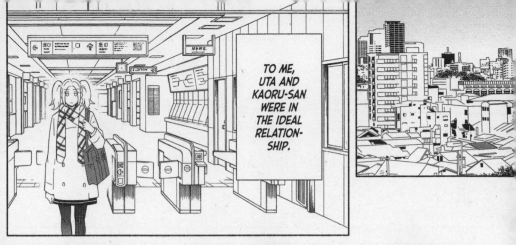

TO ME,
UTA AND
KAORU-SAN
WERE IN
THE IDEAL
RELATION-
SHIP.

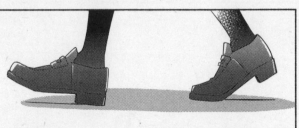

ROMANCE
AND LOVE CAN
SHATTER LIKE
GLASS. BUT THEY
DIDN'T HAVE
TO WORRY
ABOUT THAT.

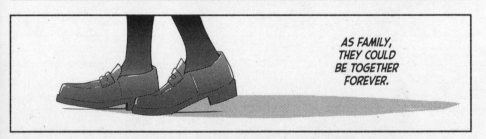

AS FAMILY,
THEY COULD
BE TOGETHER
FOREVER.

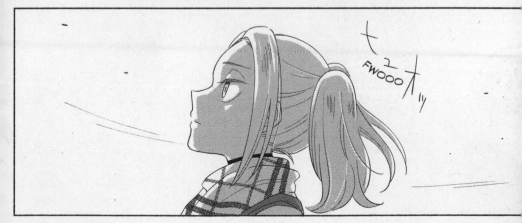

FWOOO

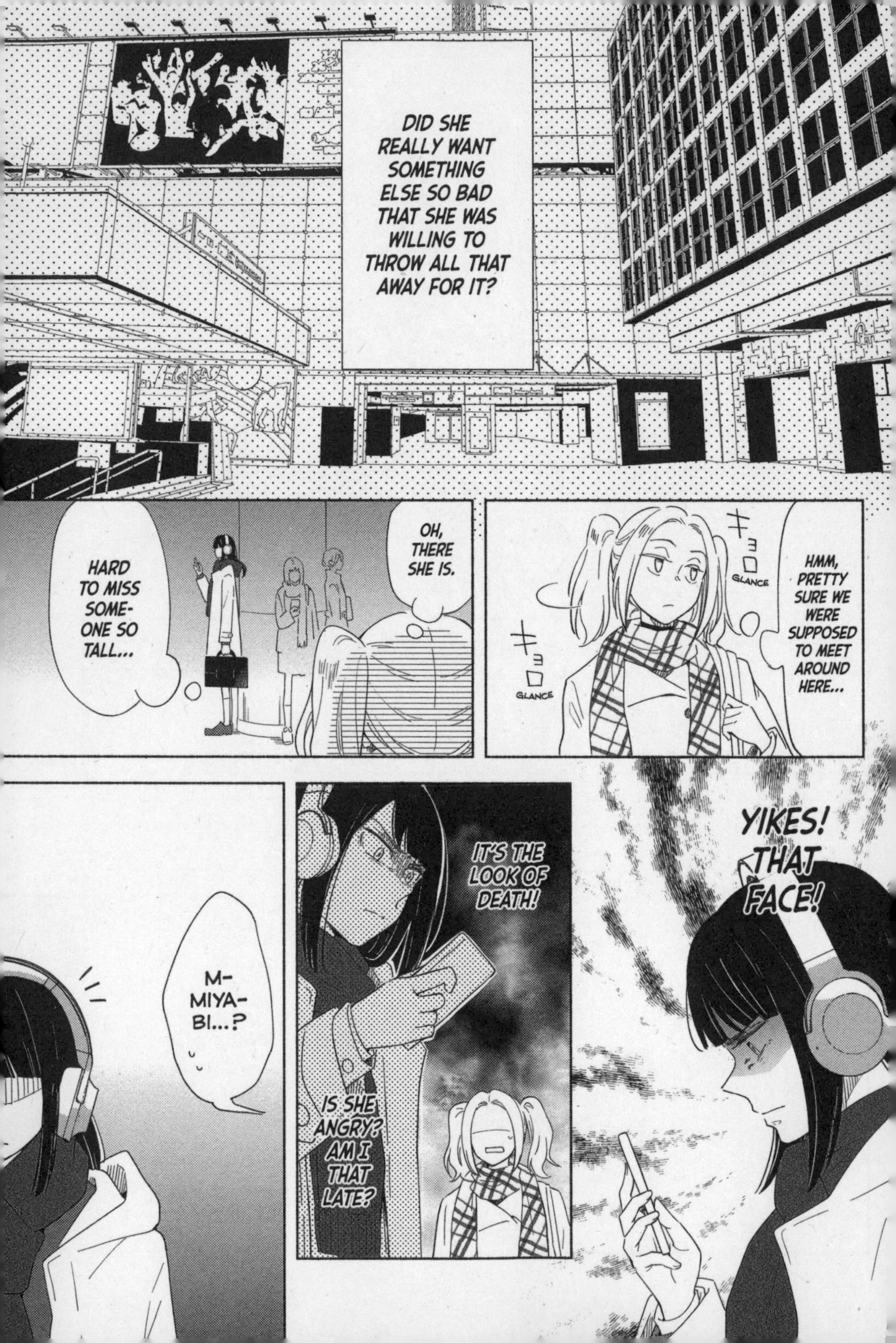
DID SHE REALLY WANT SOMETHING ELSE SO BAD THAT SHE WAS WILLING TO THROW ALL THAT AWAY FOR IT?
キョロ GLANCE
HMM, PRETTY SURE WE WERE SUPPOSED TO MEET AROUND HERE...
キョロ GLANCE
OH, THERE SHE IS.
HARD TO MISS SOME-ONE SO TALL...
YIKES! THAT FACE!
IT'S THE LOOK OF DEATH!
IS SHE ANGRY? AM I THAT LATE?
M-MIYA-BI...?

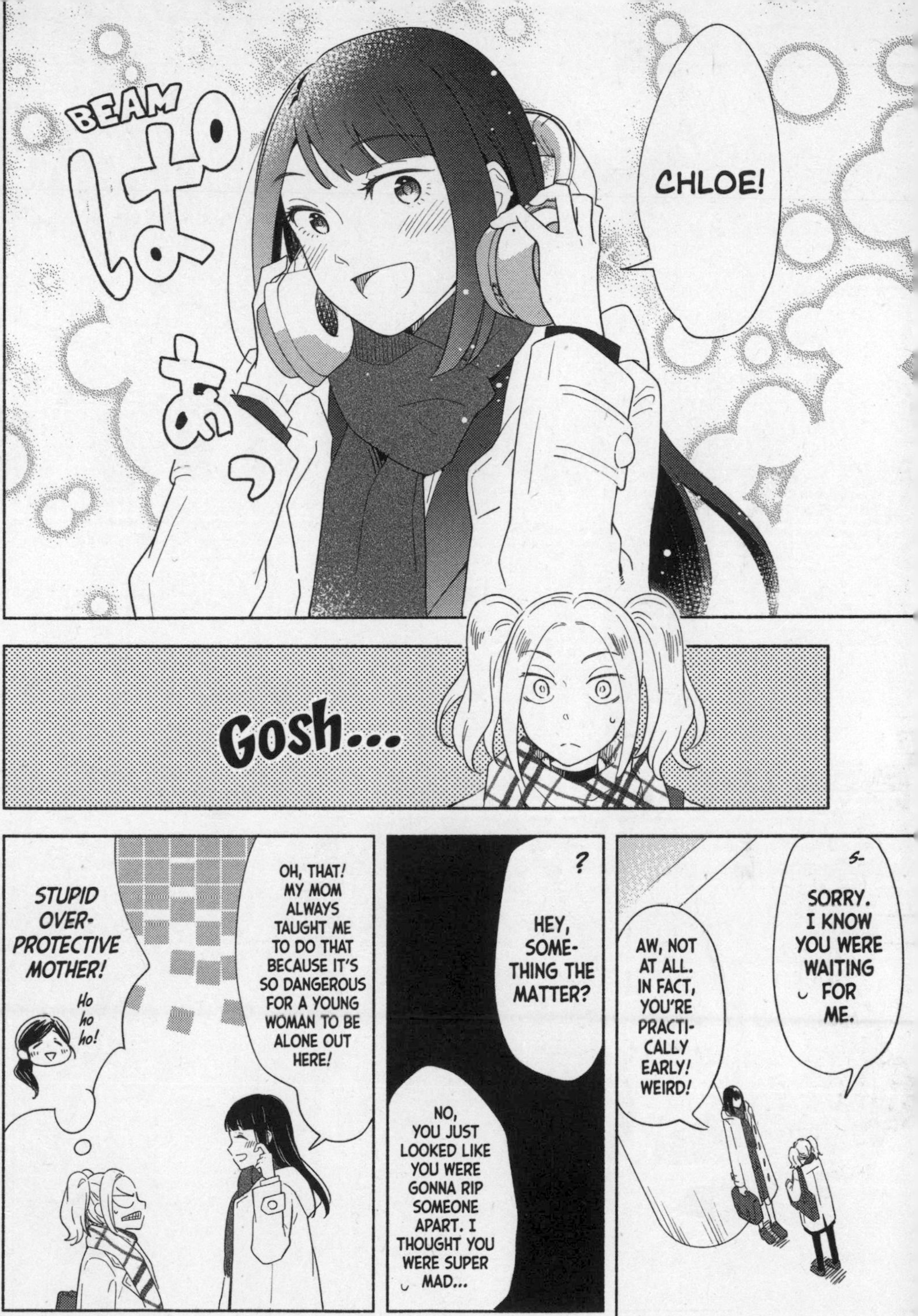
CHLOE!
BEAM
ぱあっ
Gosh...
S-
SORRY. I KNOW YOU WERE WAITING FOR ME.
AW, NOT AT ALL. IN FACT, YOU'RE PRACTICALLY EARLY! WEIRD!
?
HEY, SOMETHING THE MATTER?
NO, YOU JUST LOOKED LIKE YOU WERE GONNA RIP SOMEONE APART. I THOUGHT YOU WERE SUPER MAD...
OH, THAT! MY MOM ALWAYS TAUGHT ME TO DO THAT BECAUSE IT'S SO DANGEROUS FOR A YOUNG WOMAN TO BE ALONE OUT HERE!
STUPID OVERPROTECTIVE MOTHER!
Ho ho ho!

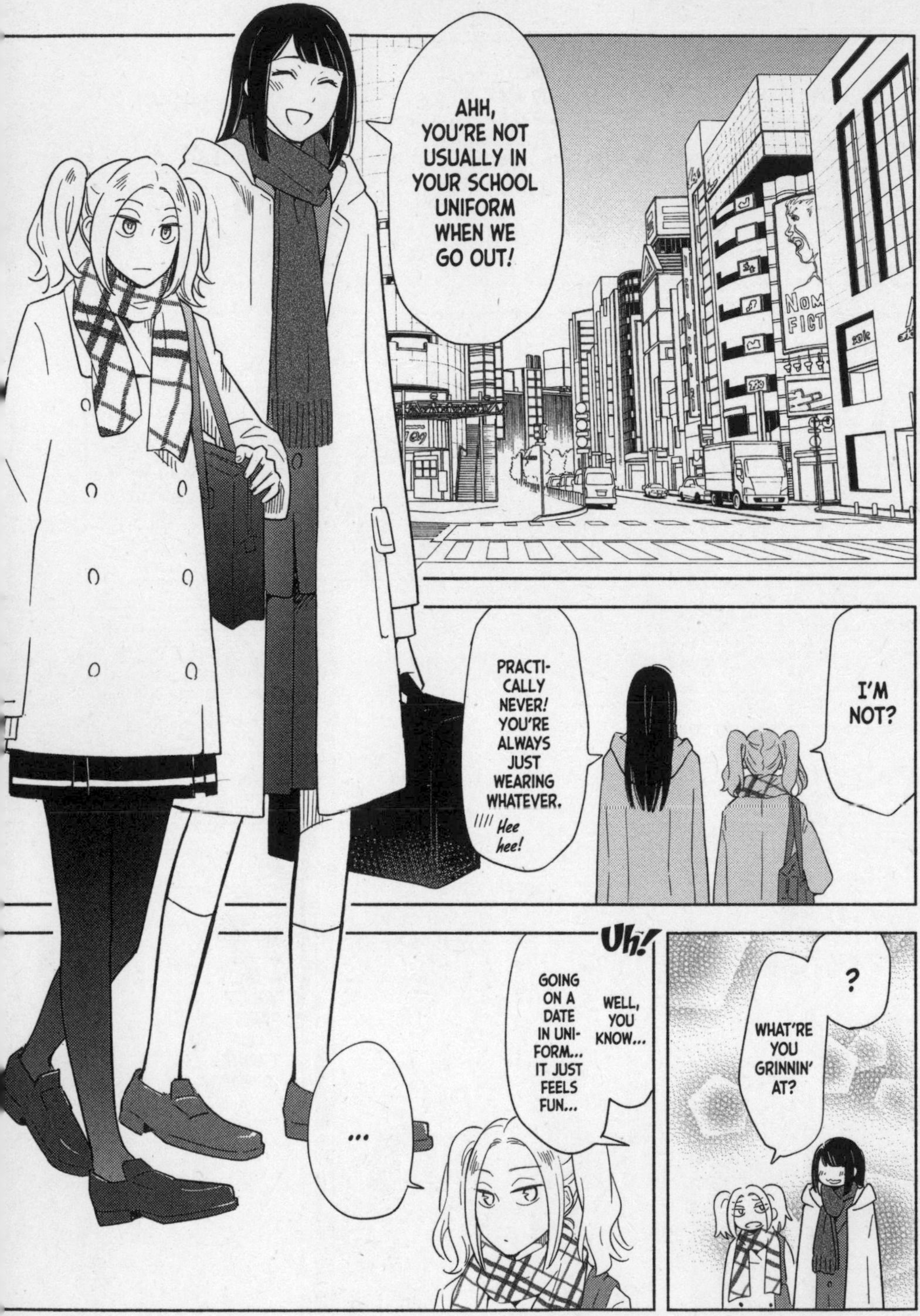
AHH, YOU'RE NOT USUALLY IN YOUR SCHOOL UNIFORM WHEN WE GO OUT!
I'M NOT?
PRACTI-CALLY NEVER! YOU'RE ALWAYS JUST WEARING WHATEVER.
Hee hee!
?
WHAT'RE YOU GRINNIN' AT?
Uh!
WELL, YOU KNOW...
GOING ON A DATE IN UNI-FORM... IT JUST FEELS FUN...
...

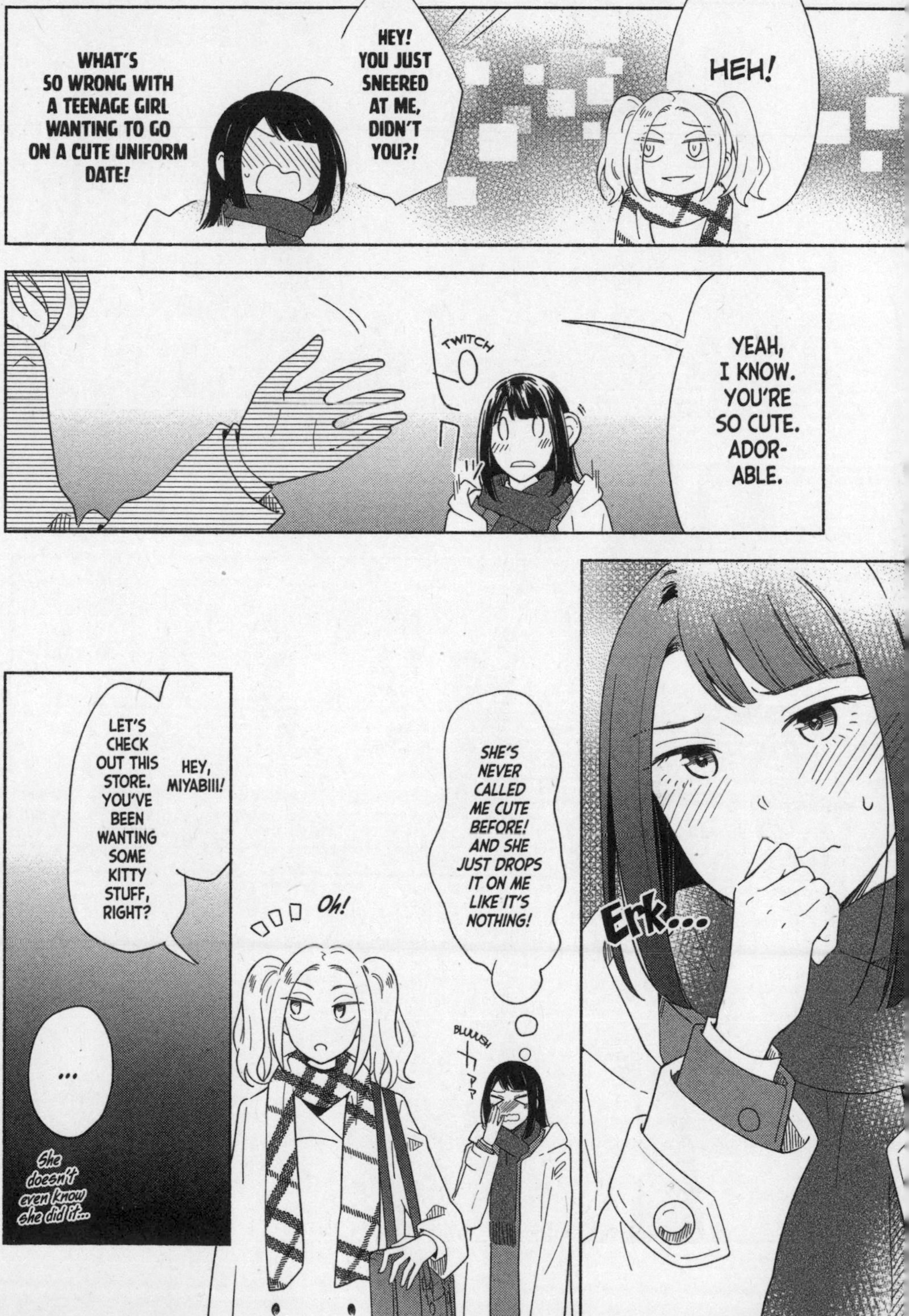
HEH!
HEY! YOU JUST SNEERED AT ME, DIDN'T YOU?!
WHAT'S SO WRONG WITH A TEENAGE GIRL WANTING TO GO ON A CUTE UNIFORM DATE!
YEAH, I KNOW. YOU'RE SO CUTE. ADOR-ABLE.
TWITCH
Erk...
SHE'S NEVER CALLED ME CUTE BEFORE! AND SHE JUST DROPS IT ON ME LIKE IT'S NOTHING!
BLUUUSH
Oh!
HEY, MIYABIII!
LET'S CHECK OUT THIS STORE. YOU'VE BEEN WANTING SOME KITTY STUFF, RIGHT?
...
She doesn't even know she did it...

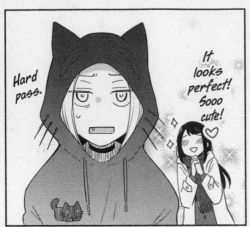

Shopping
Chloe! I found some-thing!
Hm?
It looks perfect! Sooo cute!
Hard pass.
Amusement
I'll show you my demon skills!
Bah!
Stupid machine!
Prizes: zero
I got so many... Would you like one?
Cinema
Screen 4
Bouquet of Love
FWIP
Nooo! I hate horror movies!
ZLRR ズル
ZLRR ズル
4 SCREEN

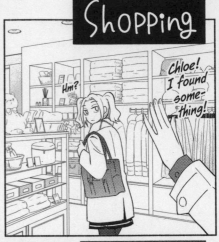

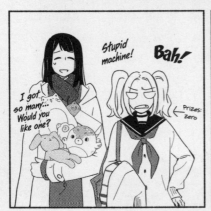

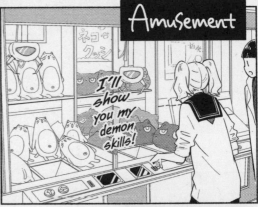

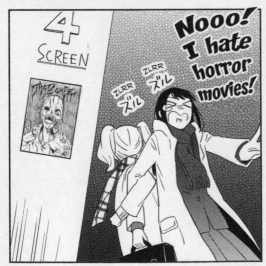

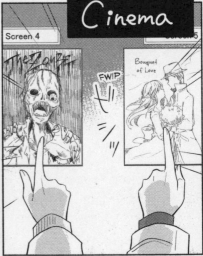

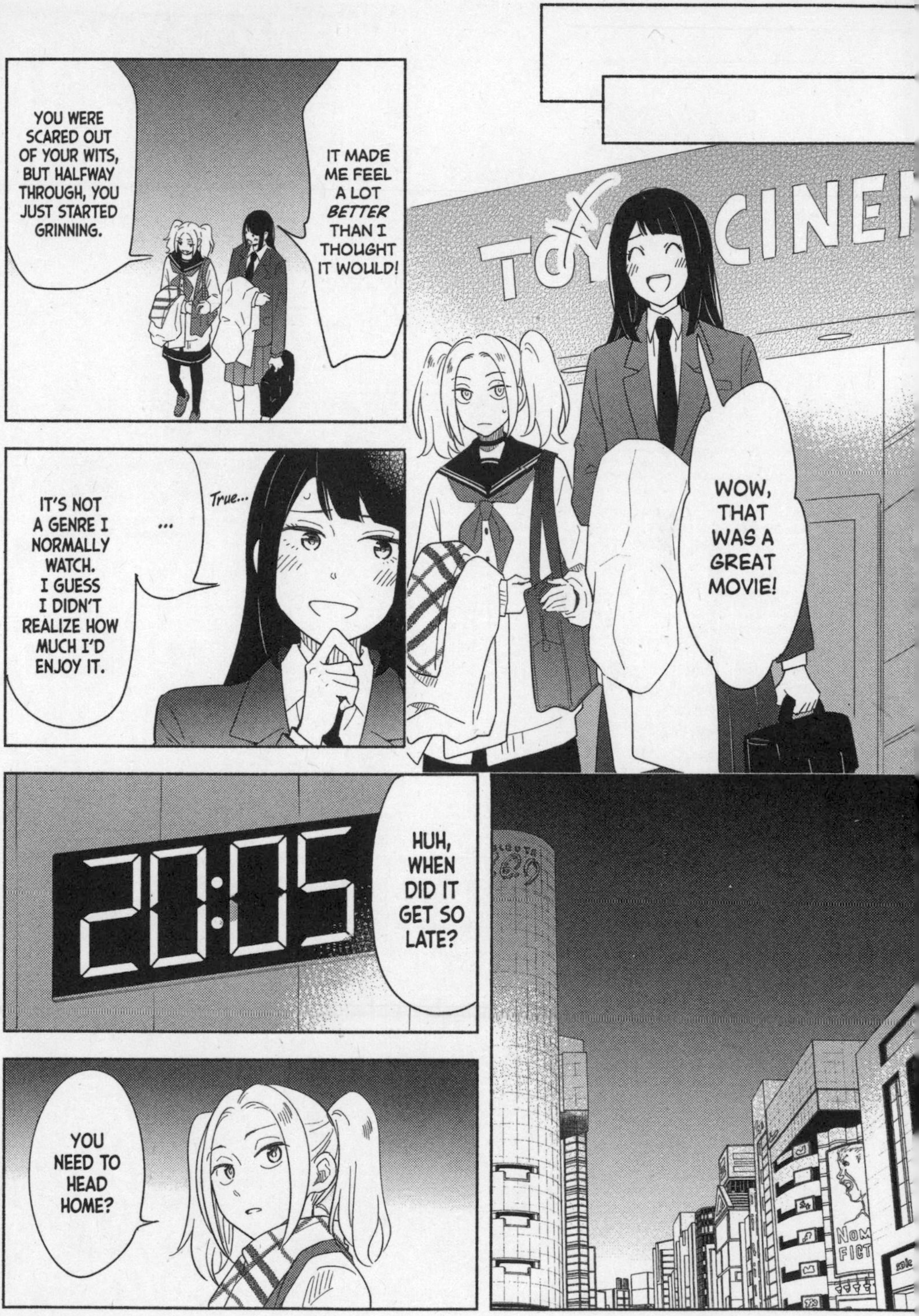
WOW, THAT WAS A GREAT MOVIE!
IT MADE ME FEEL A LOT *BETTER* THAN I THOUGHT IT WOULD!
YOU WERE SCARED OUT OF YOUR WITS, BUT HALFWAY THROUGH, YOU JUST STARTED GRINNING.
True...
...
IT'S NOT A GENRE I NORMALLY WATCH. I GUESS I DIDN'T REALIZE HOW MUCH I'D ENJOY IT.
HUH, WHEN DID IT GET SO LATE?
20:05
YOU NEED TO HEAD HOME?

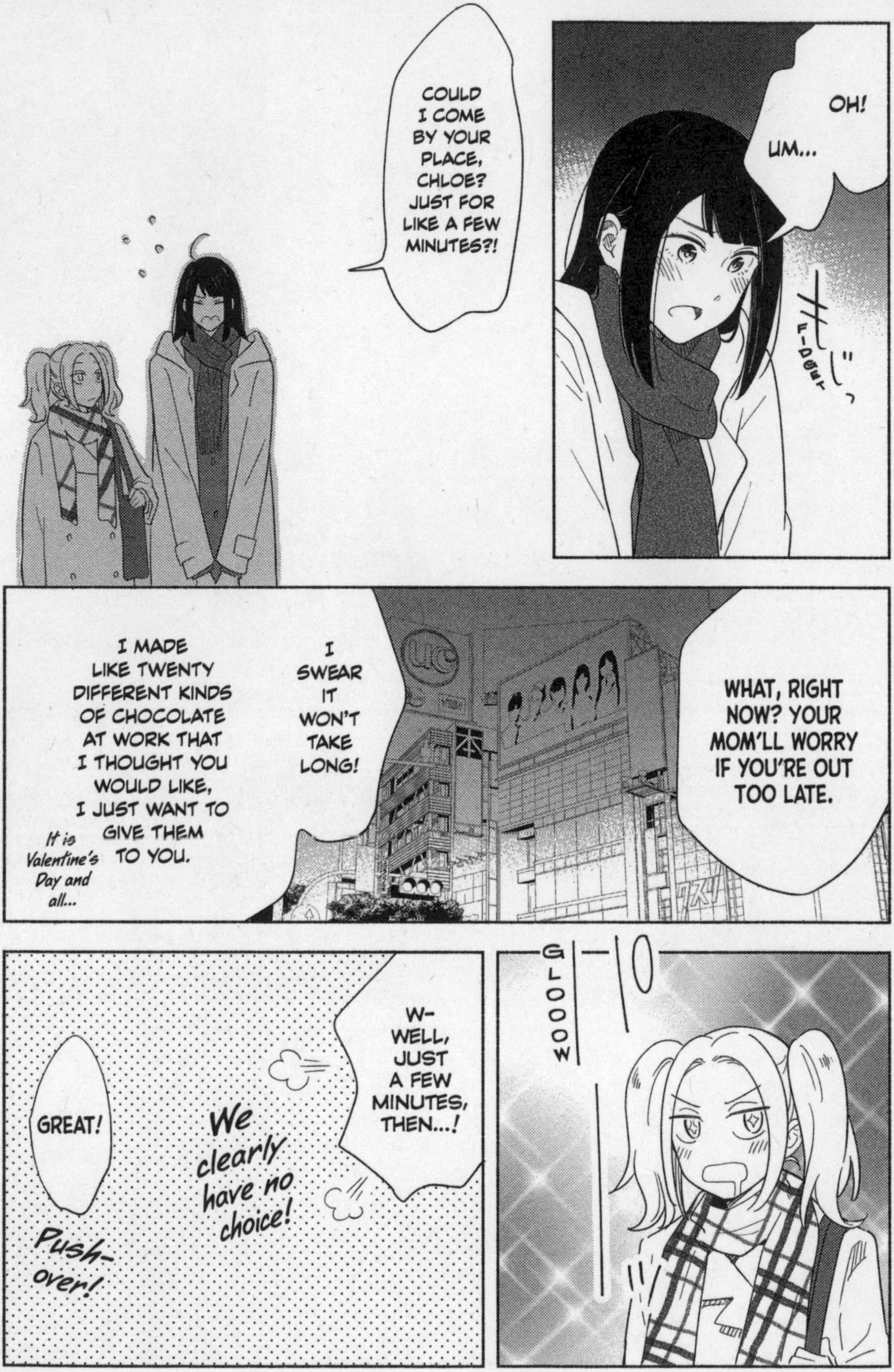

OH!
UM...
FIDGET
COULD I COME BY YOUR PLACE, CHLOE? JUST FOR LIKE A FEW MINUTES?!
WHAT, RIGHT NOW? YOUR MOM'LL WORRY IF YOU'RE OUT TOO LATE.
I SWEAR IT WON'T TAKE LONG!
I MADE LIKE TWENTY DIFFERENT KINDS OF CHOCOLATE AT WORK THAT I THOUGHT YOU WOULD LIKE, I JUST WANT TO GIVE THEM TO YOU.
It is Valentine's Day and all...
GLOOOW
W-WELL, JUST A FEW MINUTES, THEN...!
We clearly have no choice!
GREAT!
Push-over!

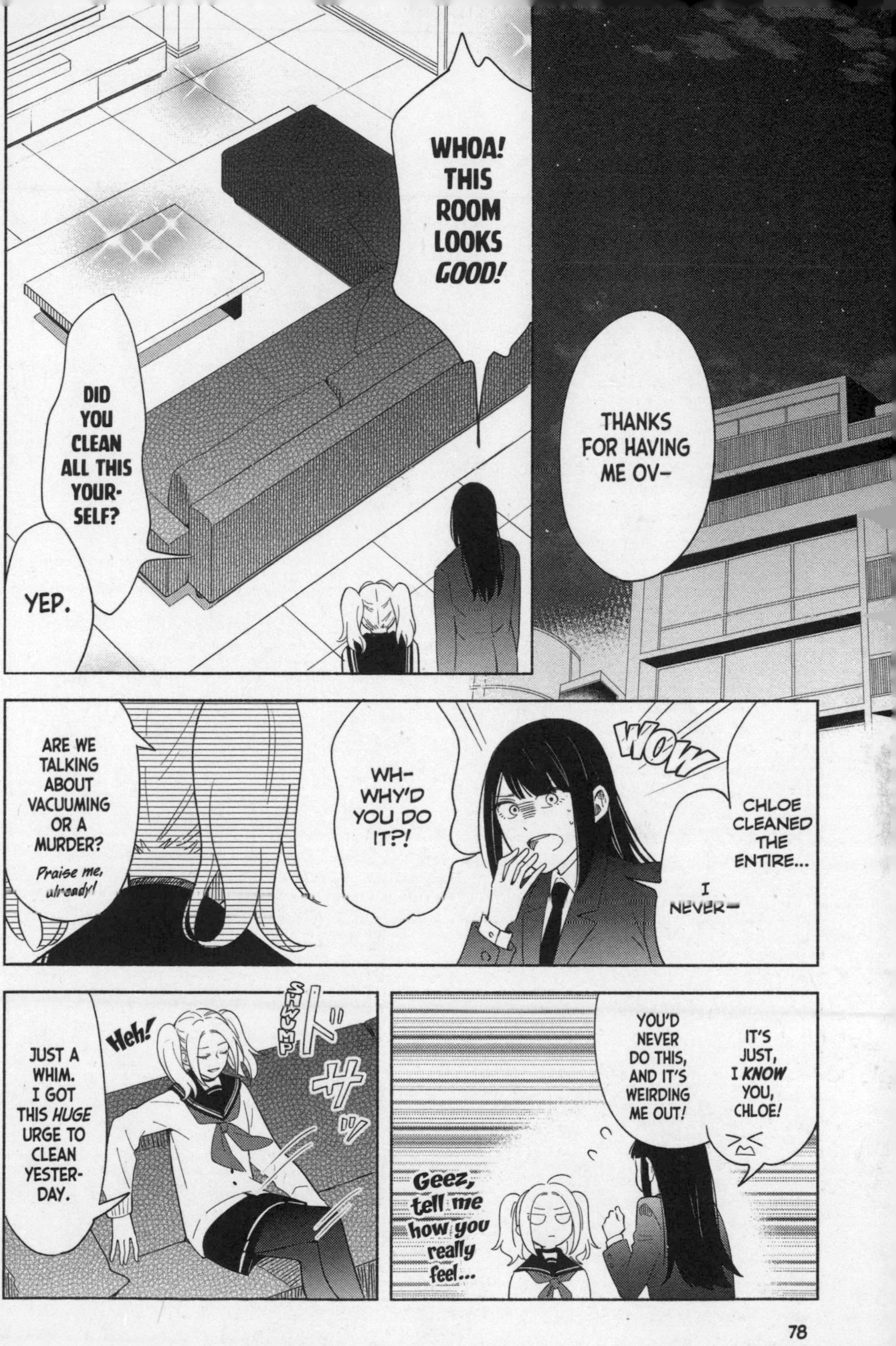
THANKS FOR HAVING ME OV–
WHOA! THIS ROOM LOOKS *GOOD!*
DID YOU CLEAN ALL THIS YOURSELF?
YEP.
WOW
CHLOE CLEANED THE ENTIRE...
I NEVER–
WH- WHY'D YOU DO IT?!
ARE WE TALKING ABOUT VACUUMING OR A MURDER?
Praise me, already!
IT'S JUST, I *KNOW* YOU, CHLOE!
YOU'D NEVER DO THIS, AND IT'S WEIRDING ME OUT!
Geez, tell me how you really feel...
SHWUMP
Heh!
JUST A WHIM. I GOT THIS *HUGE* URGE TO CLEAN YESTERDAY.

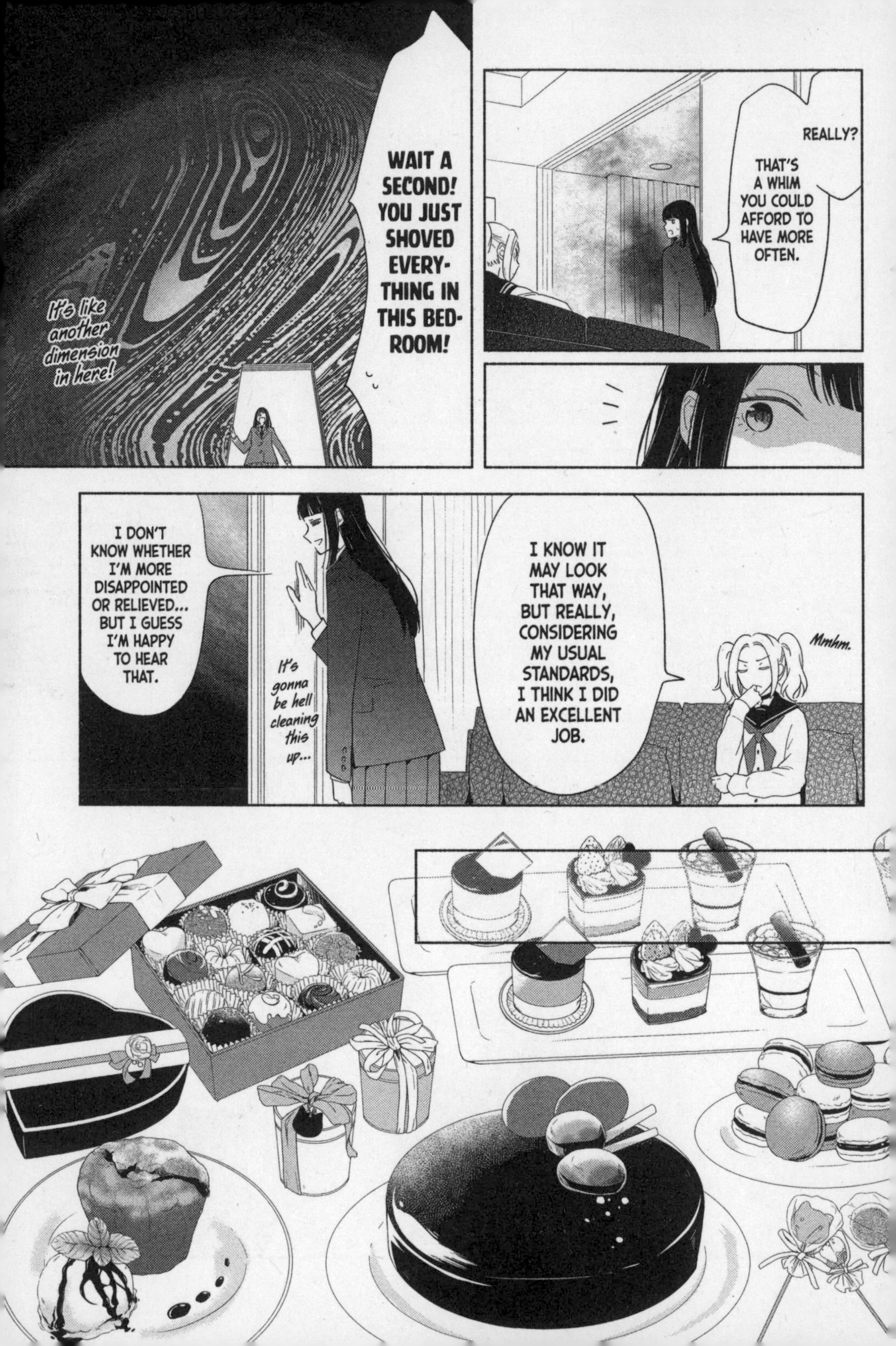
REALLY?
THAT'S A WHIM YOU COULD AFFORD TO HAVE MORE OFTEN.
WAIT A SECOND! YOU JUST SHOVED EVERY-THING IN THIS BED-ROOM!
It's like another dimension in here!
Mmhm.
I KNOW IT MAY LOOK THAT WAY, BUT REALLY, CONSIDERING MY USUAL STANDARDS, I THINK I DID AN EXCELLENT JOB.
I DON'T KNOW WHETHER I'M MORE DISAPPOINTED OR RELIEVED... BUT I GUESS I'M HAPPY TO HEAR THAT.
It's gonna be hell cleaning this up...

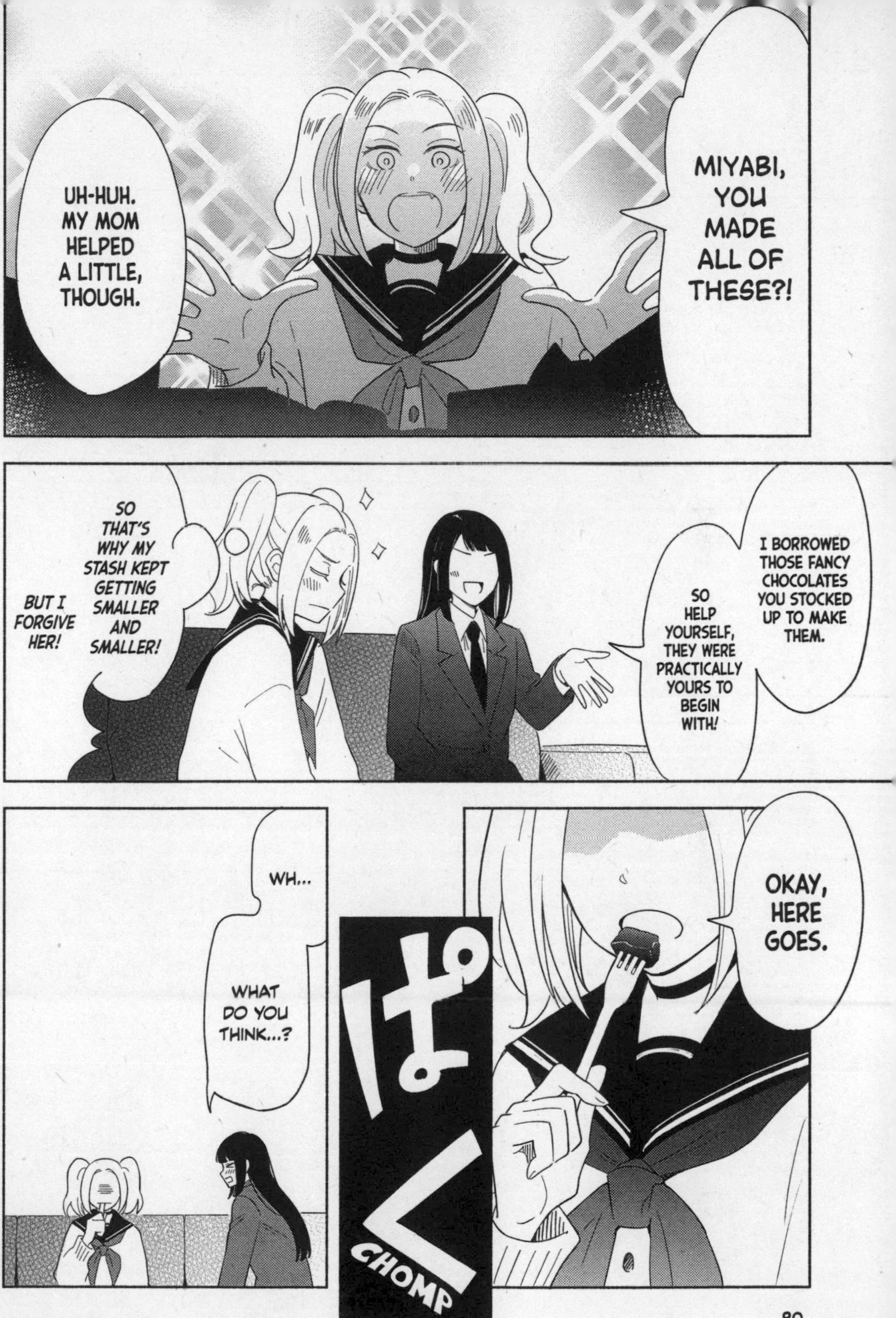
MIYABI, YOU MADE ALL OF THESE?!
UH-HUH. MY MOM HELPED A LITTLE, THOUGH.
I BORROWED THOSE FANCY CHOCOLATES YOU STOCKED UP TO MAKE THEM.
SO HELP YOURSELF, THEY WERE PRACTICALLY YOURS TO BEGIN WITH!
SO THAT'S WHY MY STASH KEPT GETTING SMALLER AND SMALLER!
BUT I FORGIVE HER!
OKAY, HERE GOES.
ぱく
CHOMP
WH...
WHAT DO YOU THINK...?

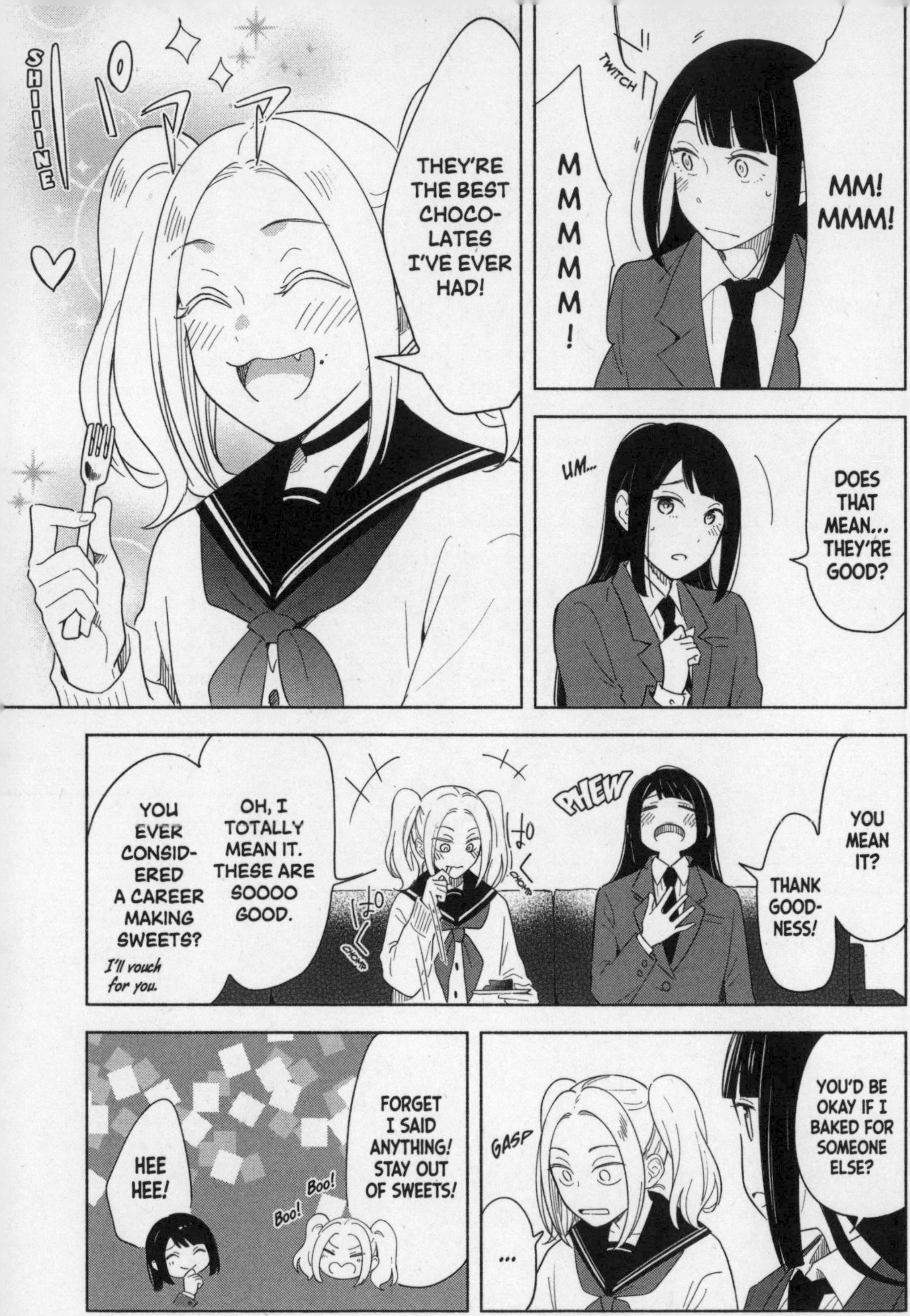
TWITCH
MM! MMM!
MMMMMM!
UM...
DOES THAT MEAN... THEY'RE GOOD?
SHIIINE
THEY'RE THE BEST CHOCOLATES I'VE EVER HAD!
YOU MEAN IT?
THANK GOODNESS!
PHEW
CHOMP
CHOMP
OH, I TOTALLY MEAN IT. THESE ARE SOOOO GOOD.
YOU EVER CONSIDERED A CAREER MAKING SWEETS?
I'll vouch for you.
YOU'D BE OKAY IF I BAKED FOR SOMEONE ELSE?
GASP
...
FORGET I SAID ANYTHING! STAY OUT OF SWEETS!
Boo!
Boo!
HEE HEE!

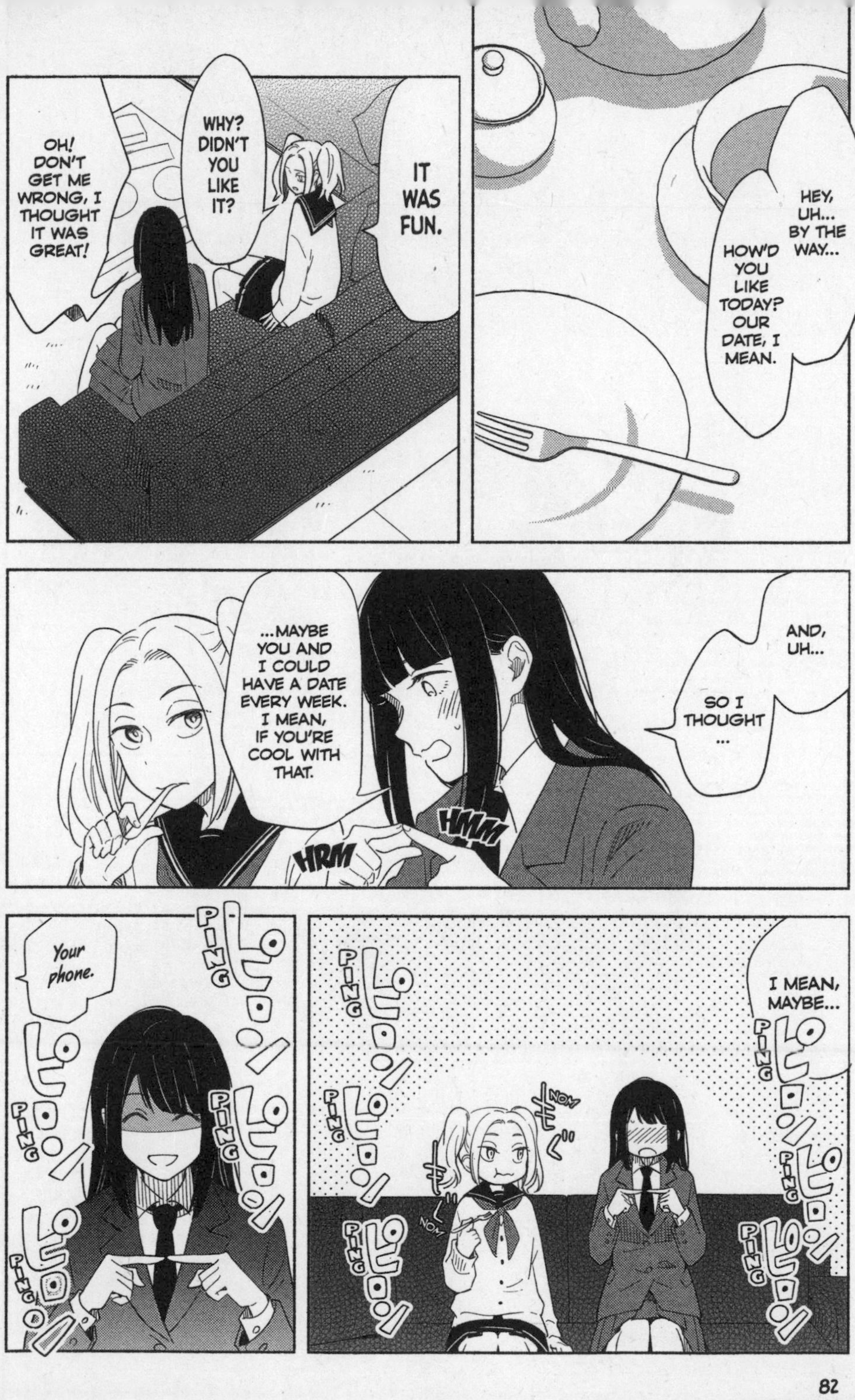
HEY, UH... BY THE WAY...
HOW'D YOU LIKE TODAY? OUR DATE, I MEAN.
IT WAS FUN.
WHY? DIDN'T YOU LIKE IT?
OH! DON'T GET ME WRONG, I THOUGHT IT WAS GREAT!
AND, UH...
SO I THOUGHT...
...MAYBE YOU AND I COULD HAVE A DATE EVERY WEEK. I MEAN, IF YOU'RE COOL WITH THAT.
HMM
HRM
I MEAN, MAYBE...
PING
PING
PING
PING
NOM
NOM
PING
PING
Your phone.
PING
PING
PING
PING

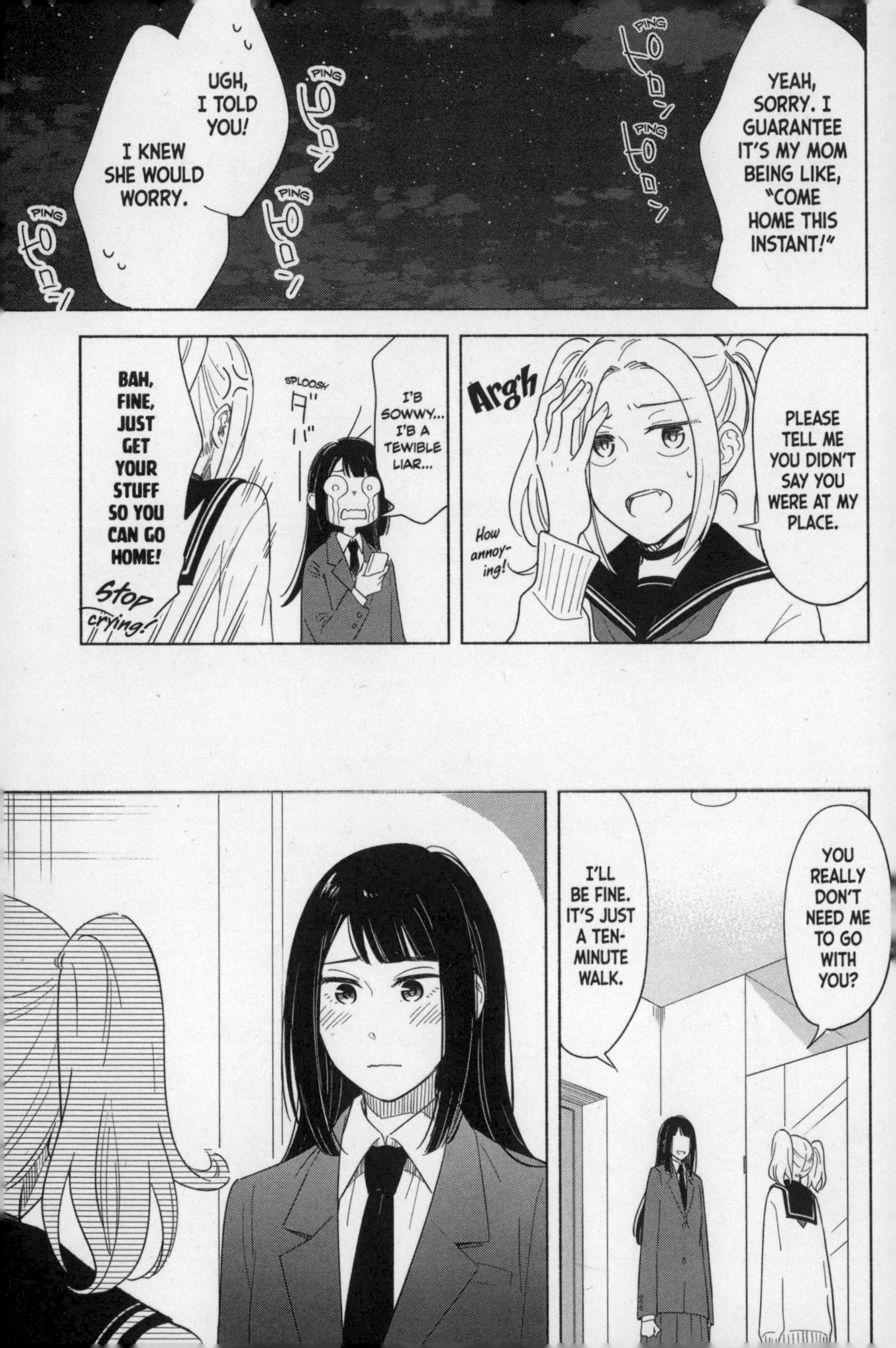
PING
PING
YEAH, SORRY. I GUARANTEE IT'S MY MOM BEING LIKE, "COME HOME THIS INSTANT!"
PING
PING
UGH, I TOLD YOU!
I KNEW SHE WOULD WORRY.
PING
PLEASE TELL ME YOU DIDN'T SAY YOU WERE AT MY PLACE.
Argh
How annoy-ing!
I'B SOWWY... I'B A TEWIBLE LIAR...
SPLOOSH
BAH, FINE, JUST GET YOUR STUFF SO YOU CAN GO HOME!
Stop crying!
YOU REALLY DON'T NEED ME TO GO WITH YOU?
I'LL BE FINE. IT'S JUST A TEN-MINUTE WALK.

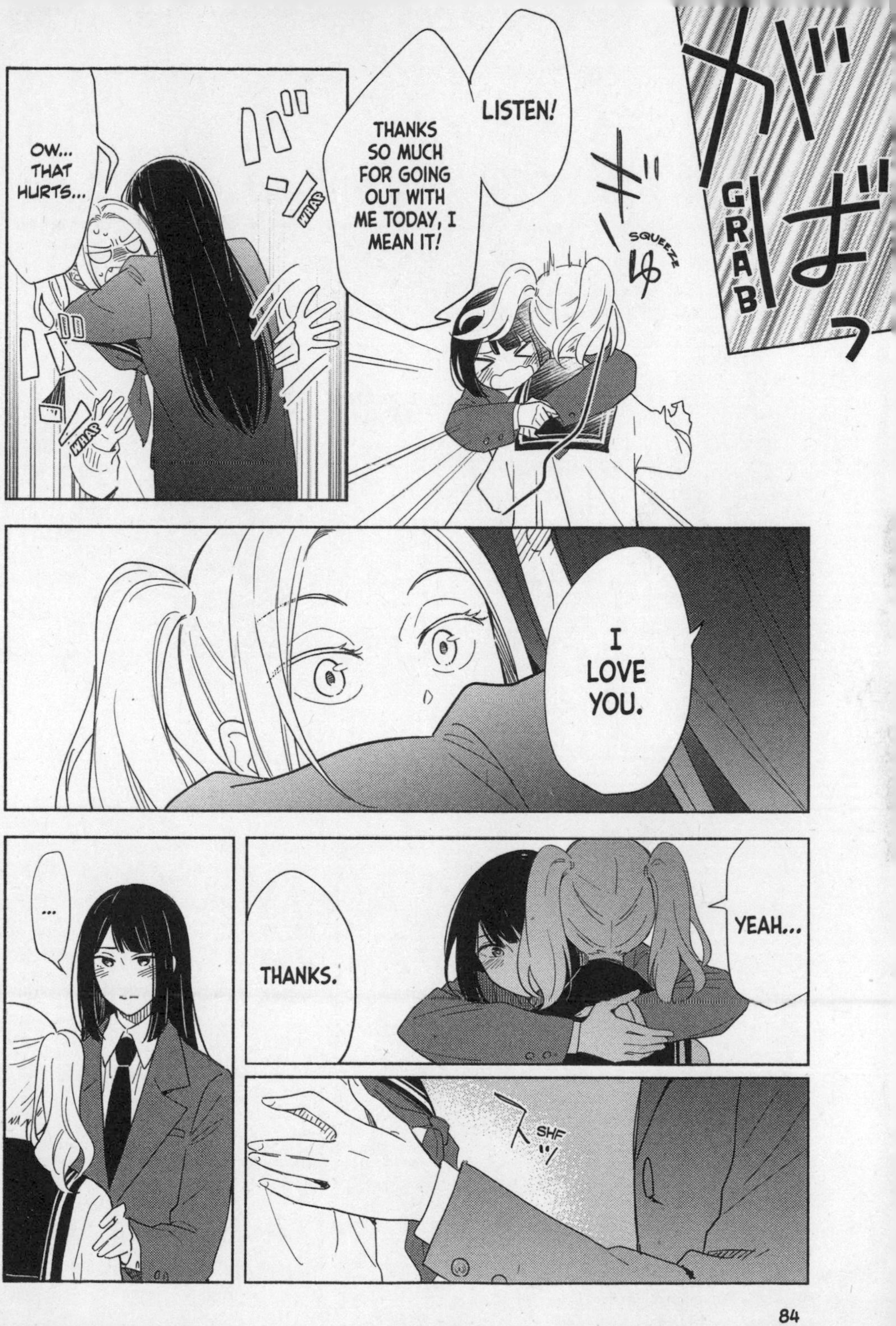
がばっ
GRAB
LISTEN!
THANKS SO MUCH FOR GOING OUT WITH ME TODAY, I MEAN IT!
SQUEEZE
OW... THAT HURTS...
WHAP
WHAP
I LOVE YOU.
YEAH...
THANKS.
SHF
...

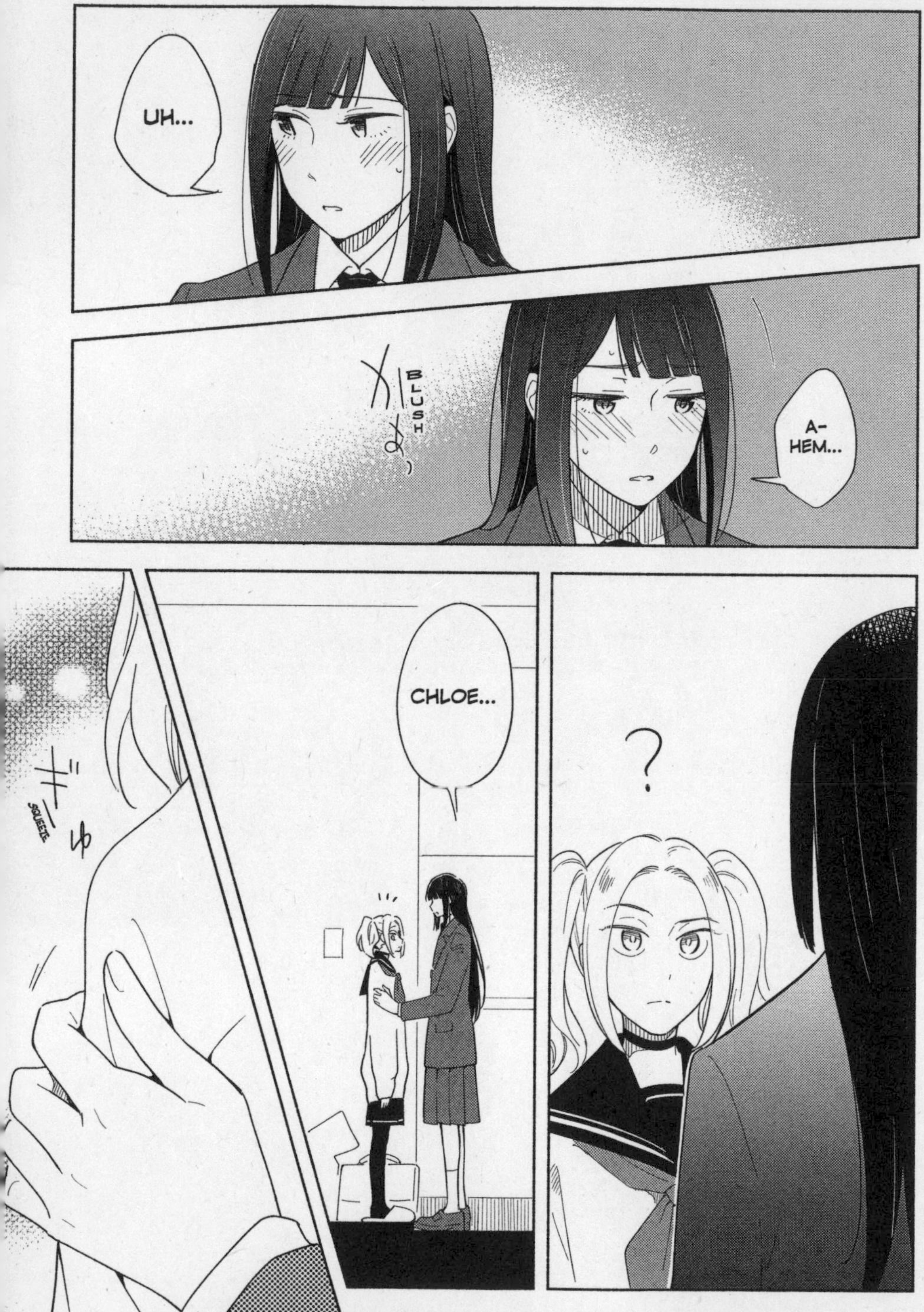
UH...
A-HEM...
BLUSH
?
CHLOE...
SQUEEZE

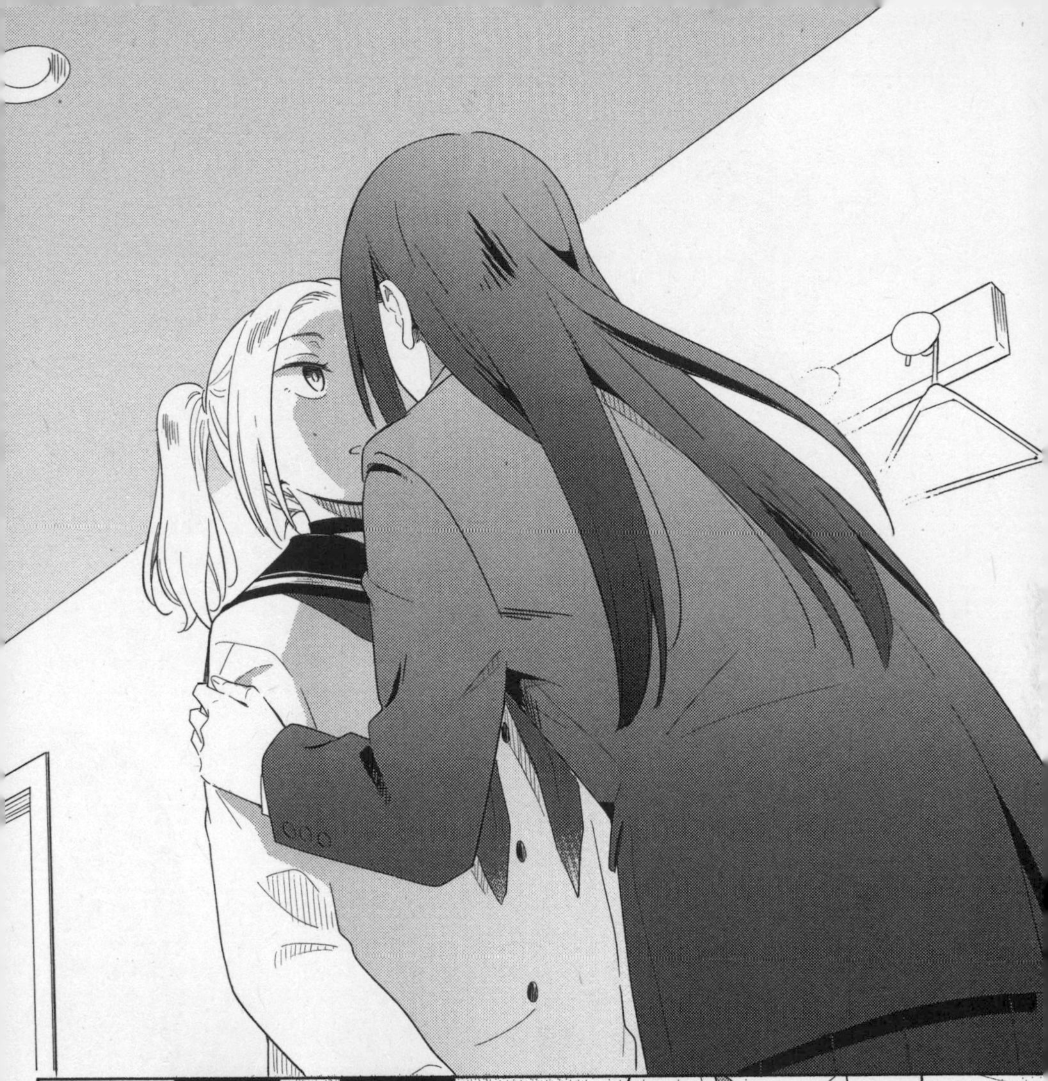
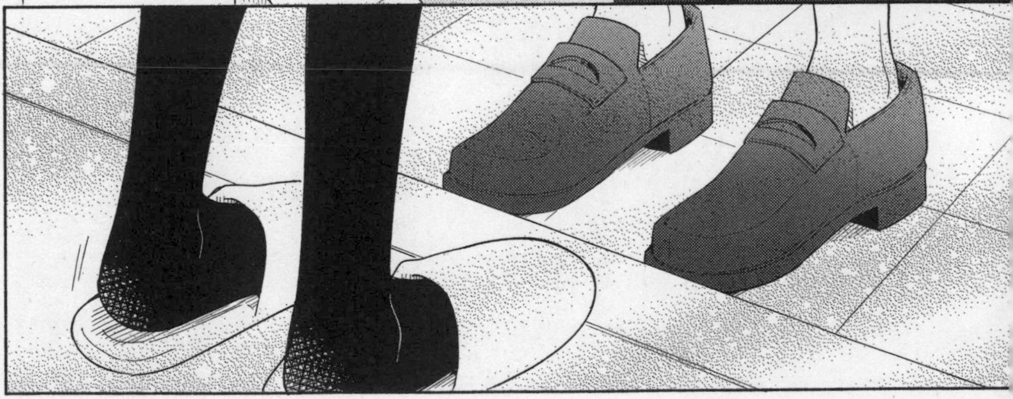

If I Could
Reach You

If I Could
Reach You

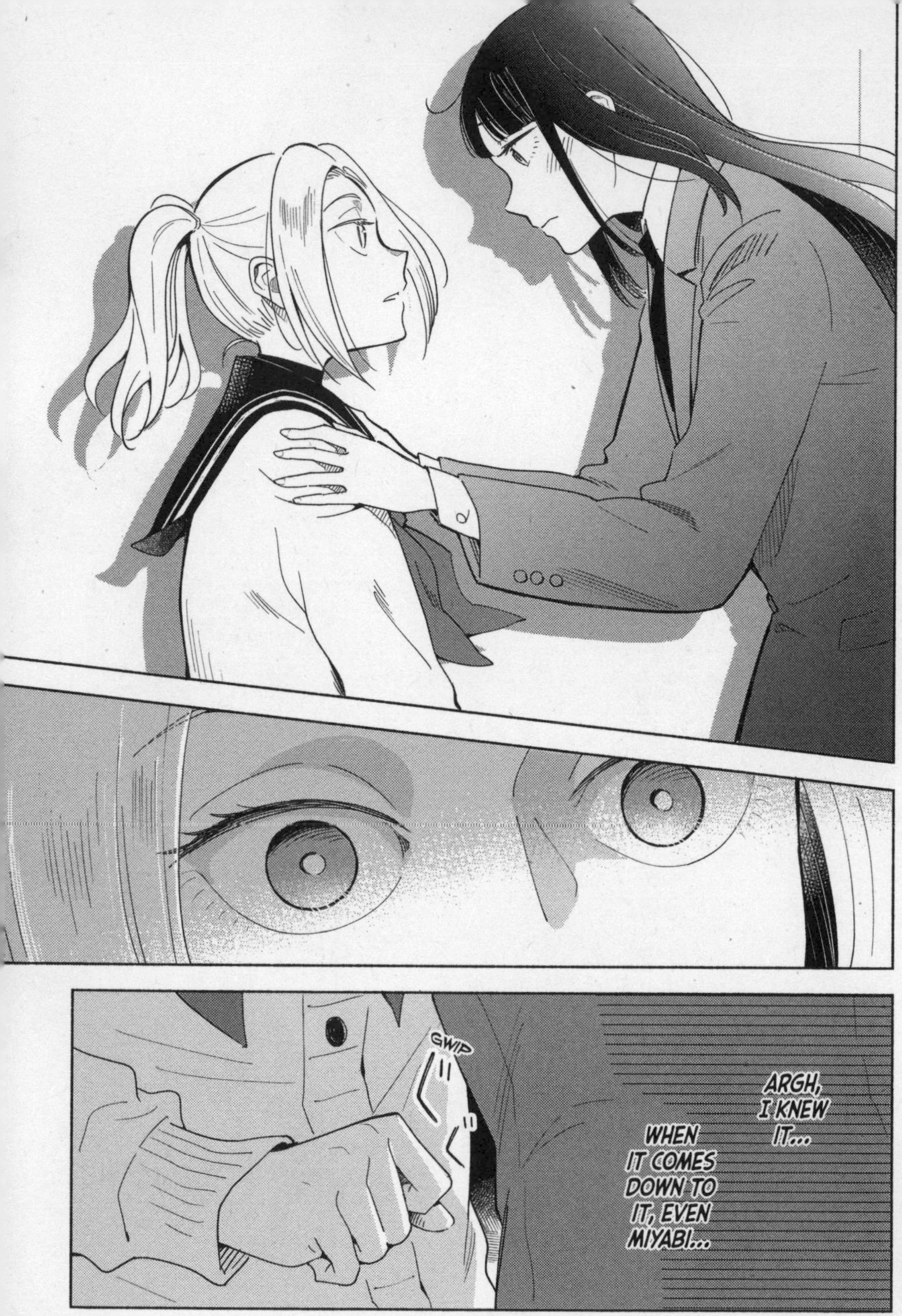
GWIP
ARGH, I KNEW IT...
WHEN IT COMES DOWN TO IT, EVEN MIYABI...

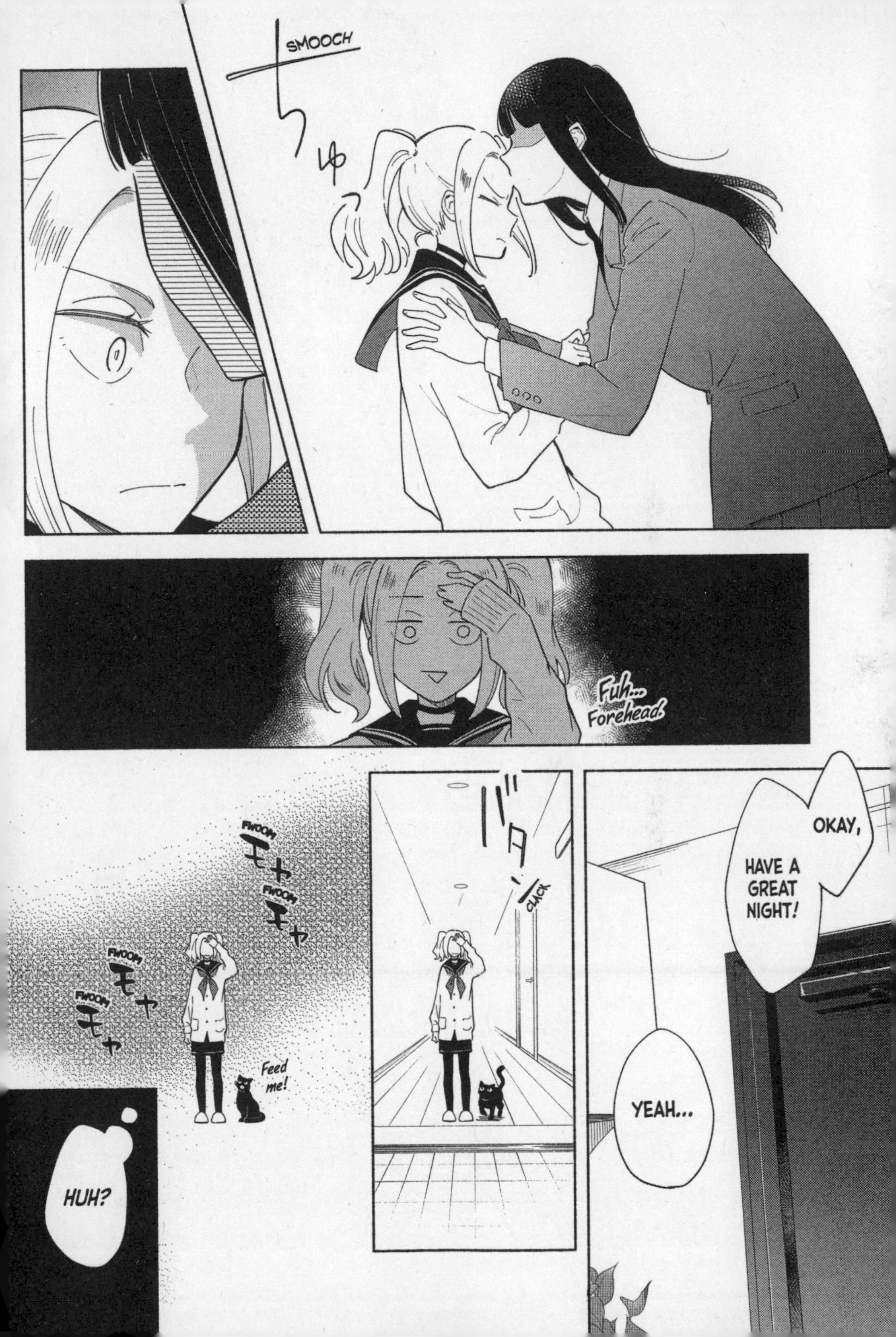
SMOOCH
Fuh... Forehead.
OKAY, HAVE A GREAT NIGHT!
YEAH...
CLACK
FWOOM
FWOOM
FWOOM
FWOOM
Feed me!
HUH?

Chapter 24

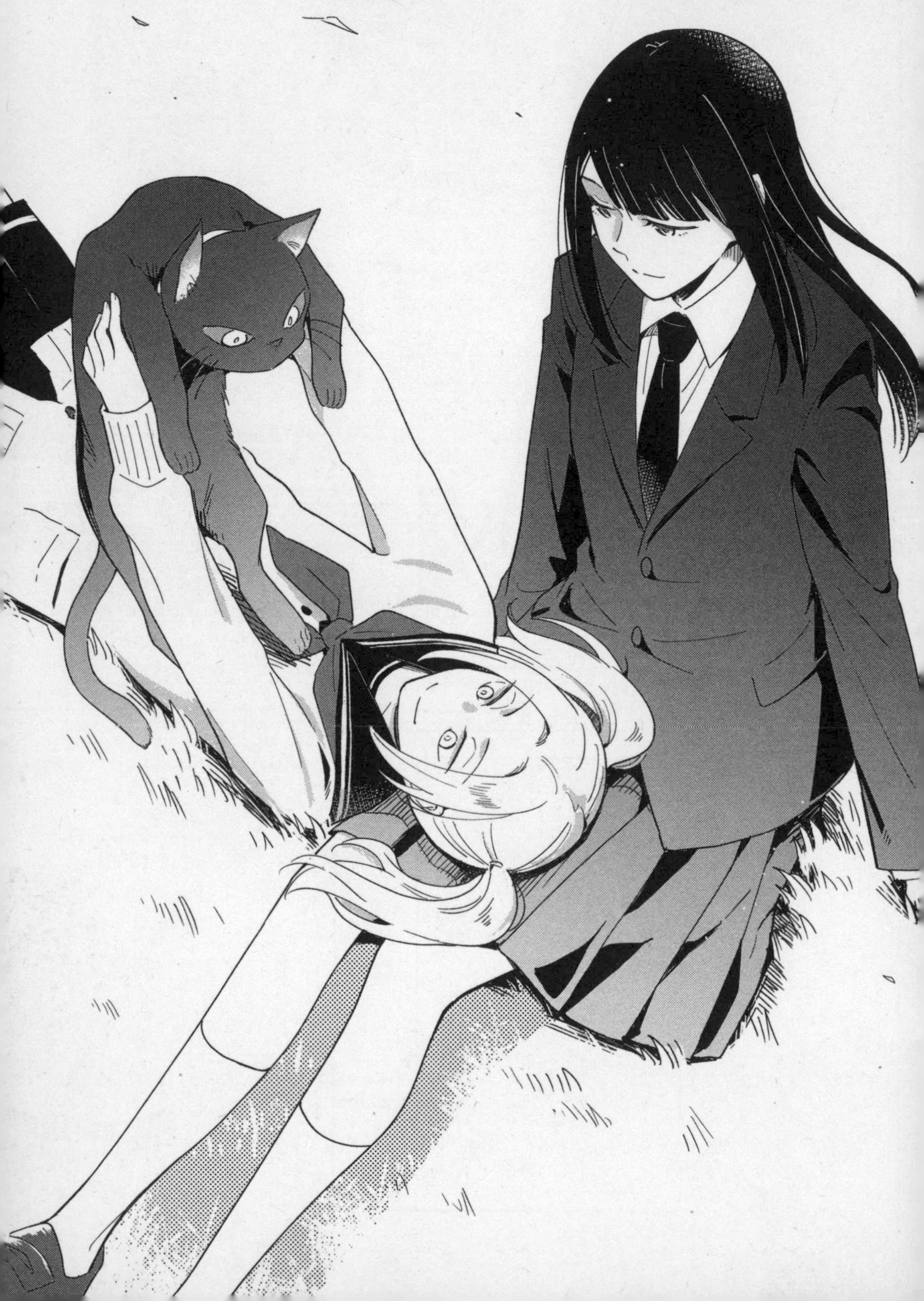

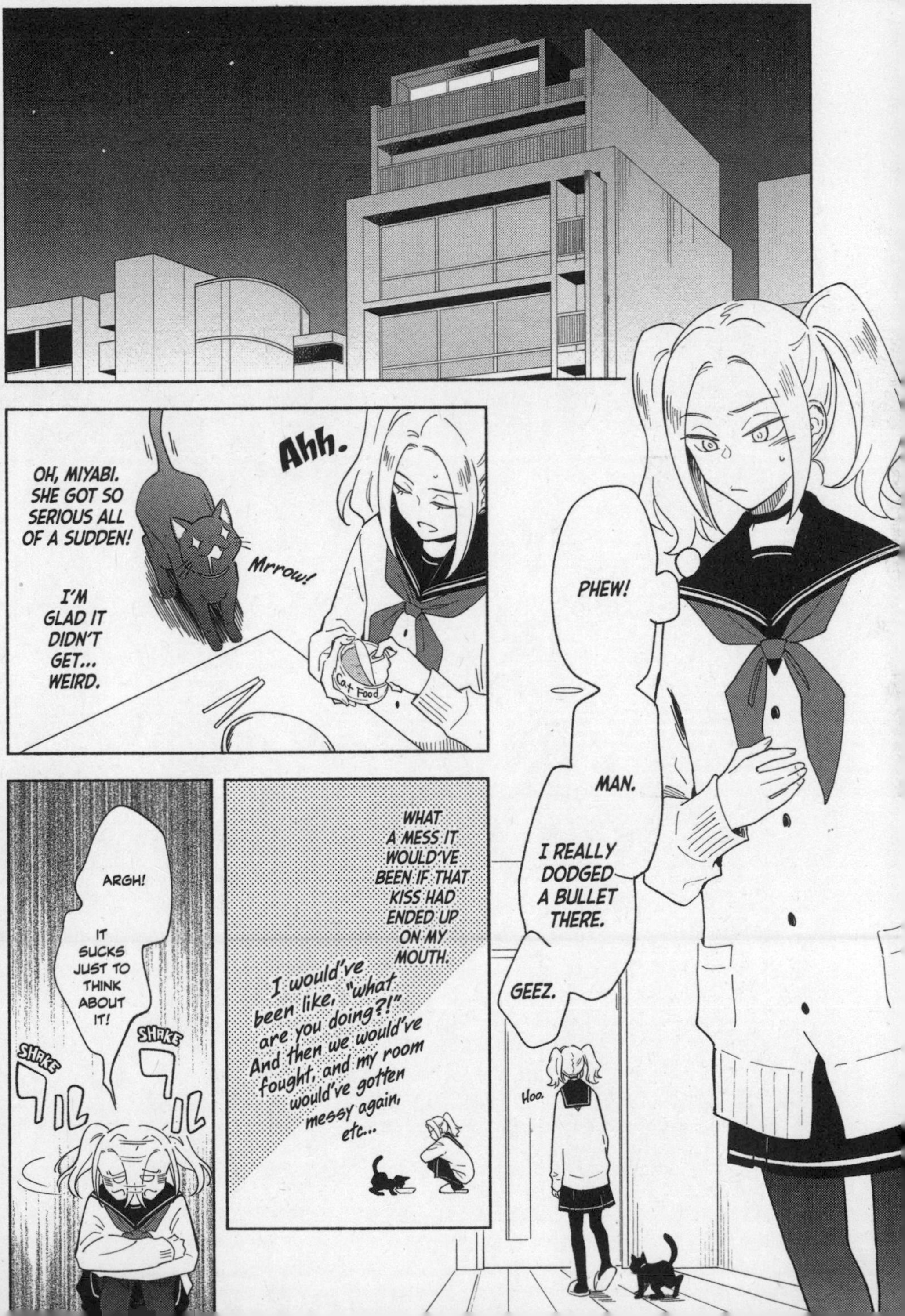
PHEW!
MAN.
I REALLY DODGED A BULLET THERE.
GEEZ.
Hoo.
Ahh.
OH, MIYABI. SHE GOT SO SERIOUS ALL OF A SUDDEN!
Mrrow!
I'M GLAD IT DIDN'T GET... WEIRD.
Cat Food
WHAT A MESS IT WOULD'VE BEEN IF THAT KISS HAD ENDED UP ON MY MOUTH.
I would've been like, "what are you doing?!" And then we would've fought, and my room would've gotten messy again, etc...
ARGH!
IT SUCKS JUST TO THINK ABOUT IT!
SHAKE
SHAKE

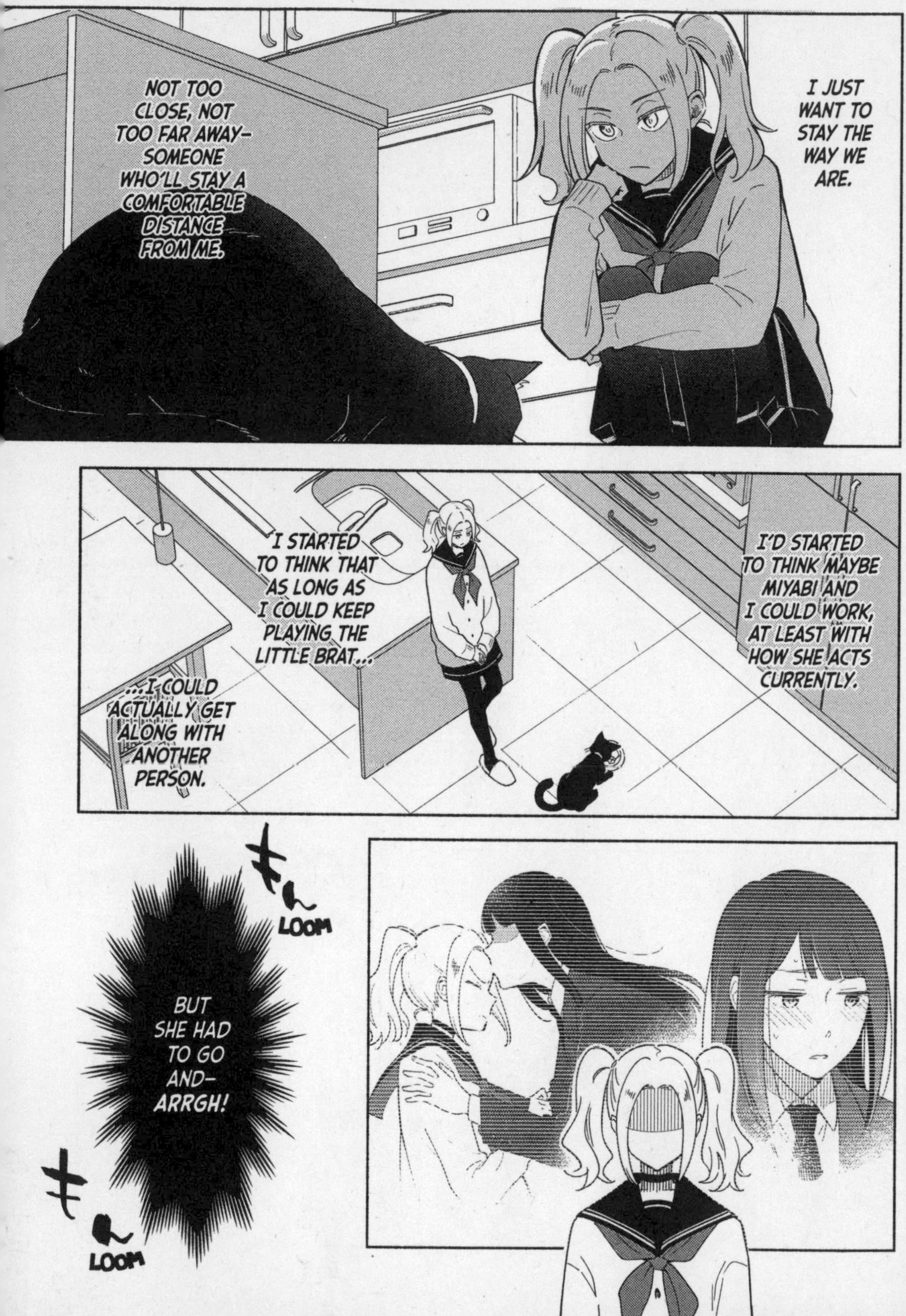
I JUST WANT TO STAY THE WAY WE ARE.
NOT TOO CLOSE, NOT TOO FAR AWAY—SOMEONE WHO'LL STAY A COMFORTABLE DISTANCE FROM ME.
I'D STARTED TO THINK MAYBE MIYABI AND I COULD WORK, AT LEAST WITH HOW SHE ACTS CURRENTLY.
I STARTED TO THINK THAT AS LONG AS I COULD KEEP PLAYING THE LITTLE BRAT...
...I COULD ACTUALLY GET ALONG WITH ANOTHER PERSON.
LOOM
BUT SHE HAD TO GO AND—ARRGH!
LOOM

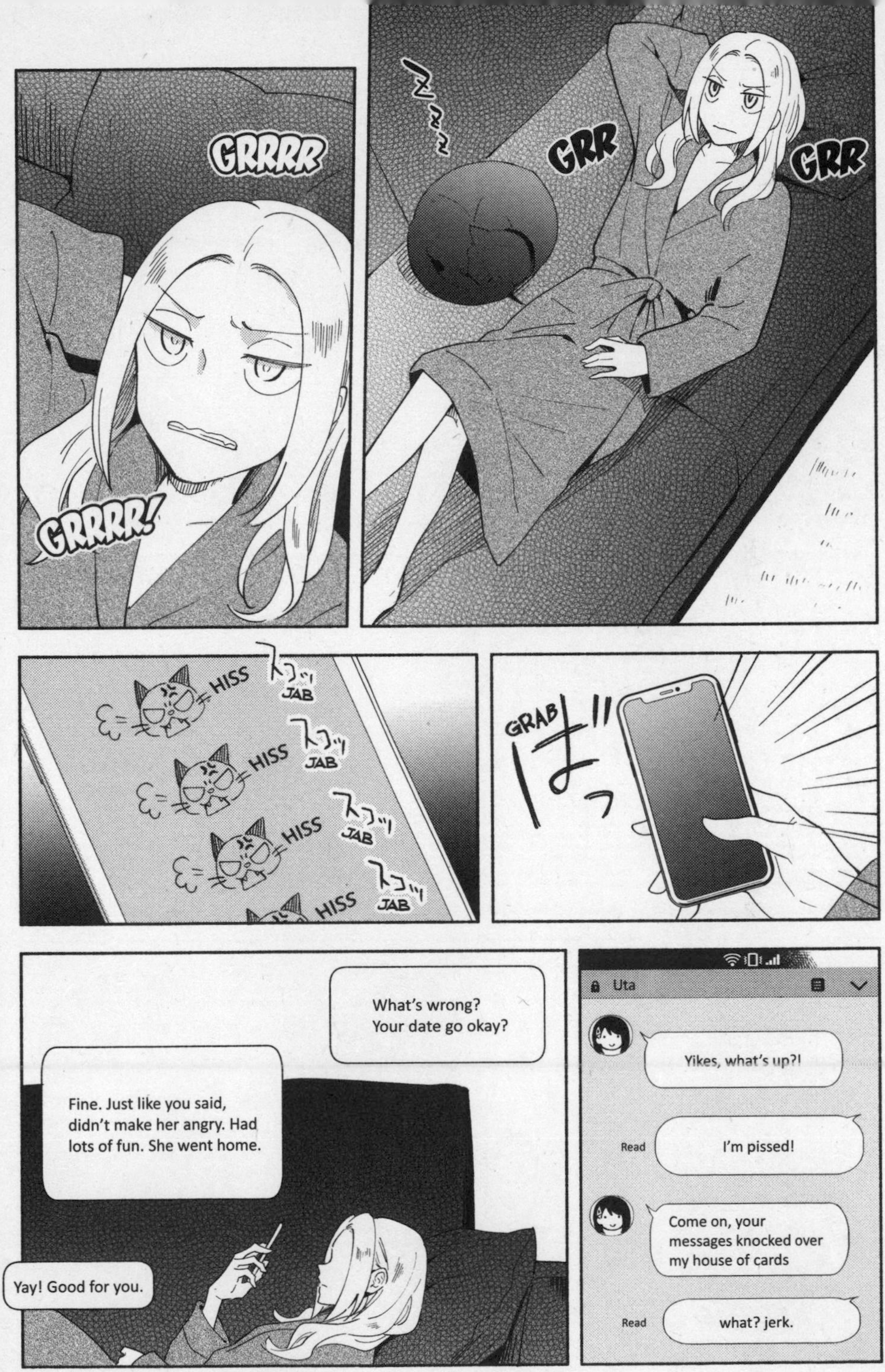
GRR
Z z z z
GRR
GRRRR
GRRRR!
GRAB
ばっ
HISS
ズコッ
JAB
HISS
ズコッ
JAB
HISS
ズコッ
JAB
HISS
ズコッ
JAB
Uta
Yikes, what's up?!
Read
I'm pissed!
Come on, your messages knocked over my house of cards
Read
what? jerk.
What's wrong? Your date go okay?
Fine. Just like you said, didn't make her angry. Had lots of fun. She went home.
Yay! Good for you.

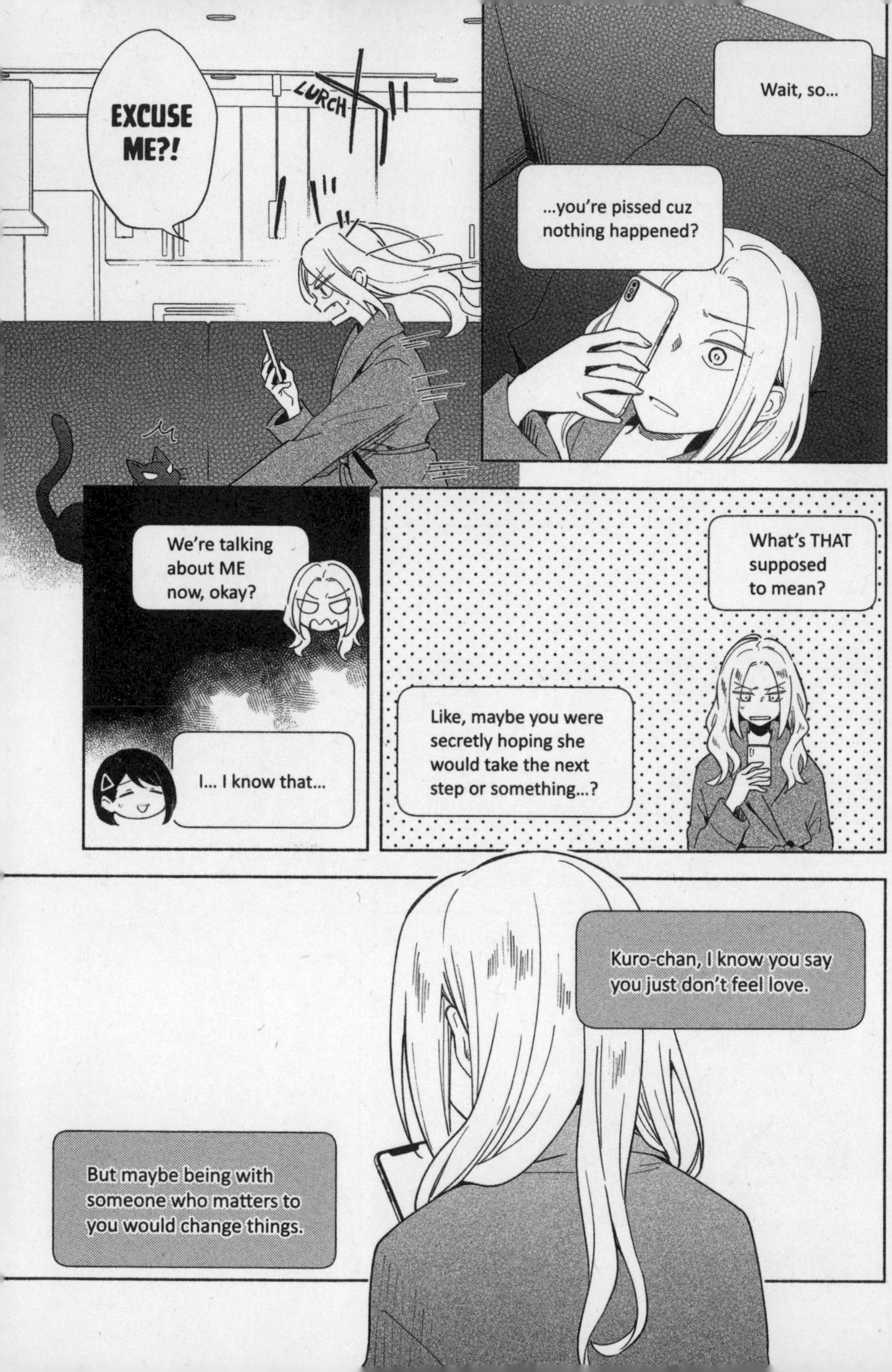
Wait, so...
...you're pissed cuz nothing happened?
EXCUSE ME?!
LURCH
What's THAT supposed to mean?
Like, maybe you were secretly hoping she would take the next step or something...?
We're talking about ME now, okay?
I... I know that...
Kuro-chan, I know you say you just don't feel love.
But maybe being with someone who matters to you would change things.

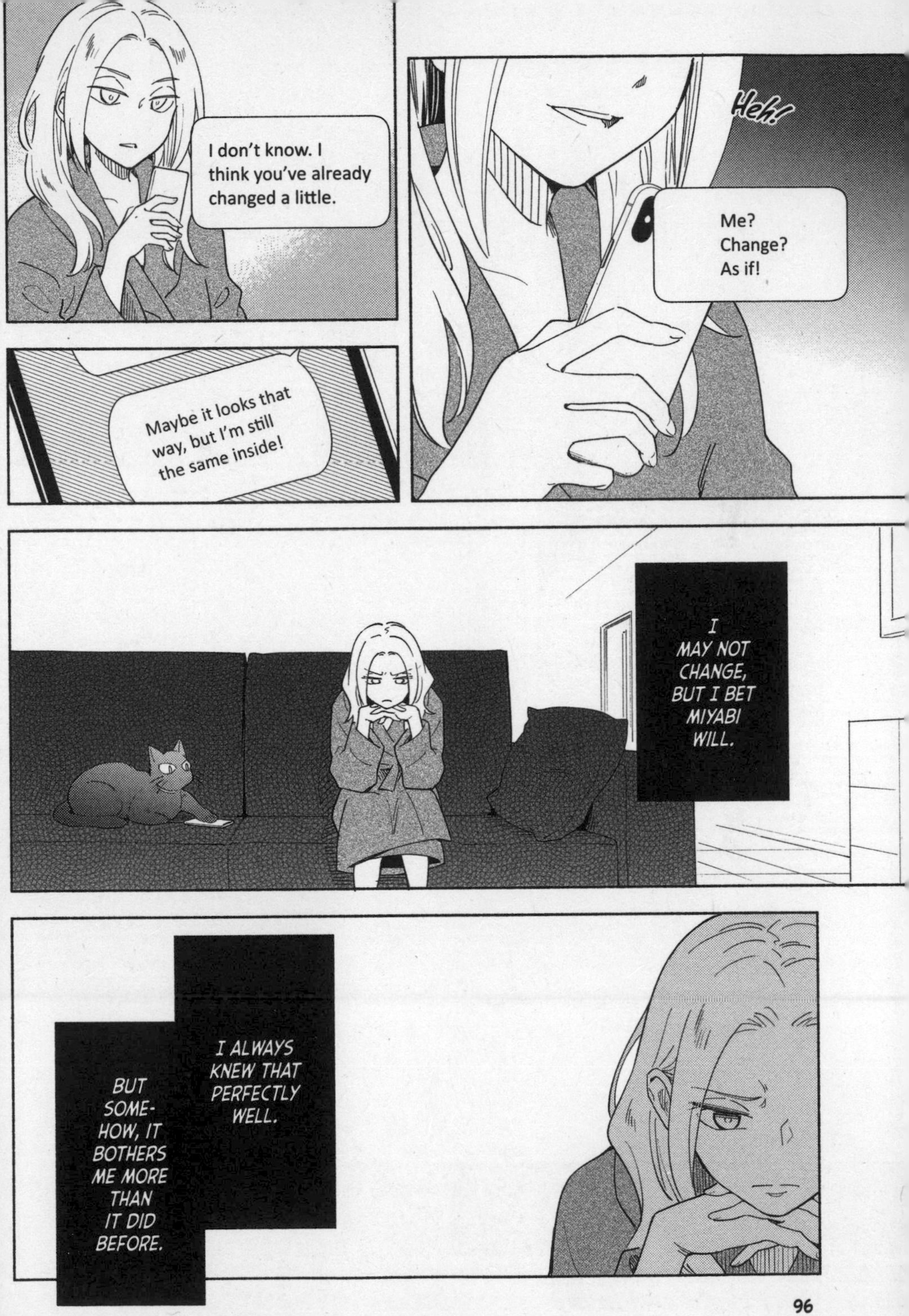
Heh!
Me? Change? As if!
I don't know. I think you've already changed a little.
Maybe it looks that way, but I'm still the same inside!
I MAY NOT CHANGE, BUT I BET MIYABI WILL.
I ALWAYS KNEW THAT PERFECTLY WELL.
BUT SOME-HOW, IT BOTHERS ME MORE THAN IT DID BEFORE.

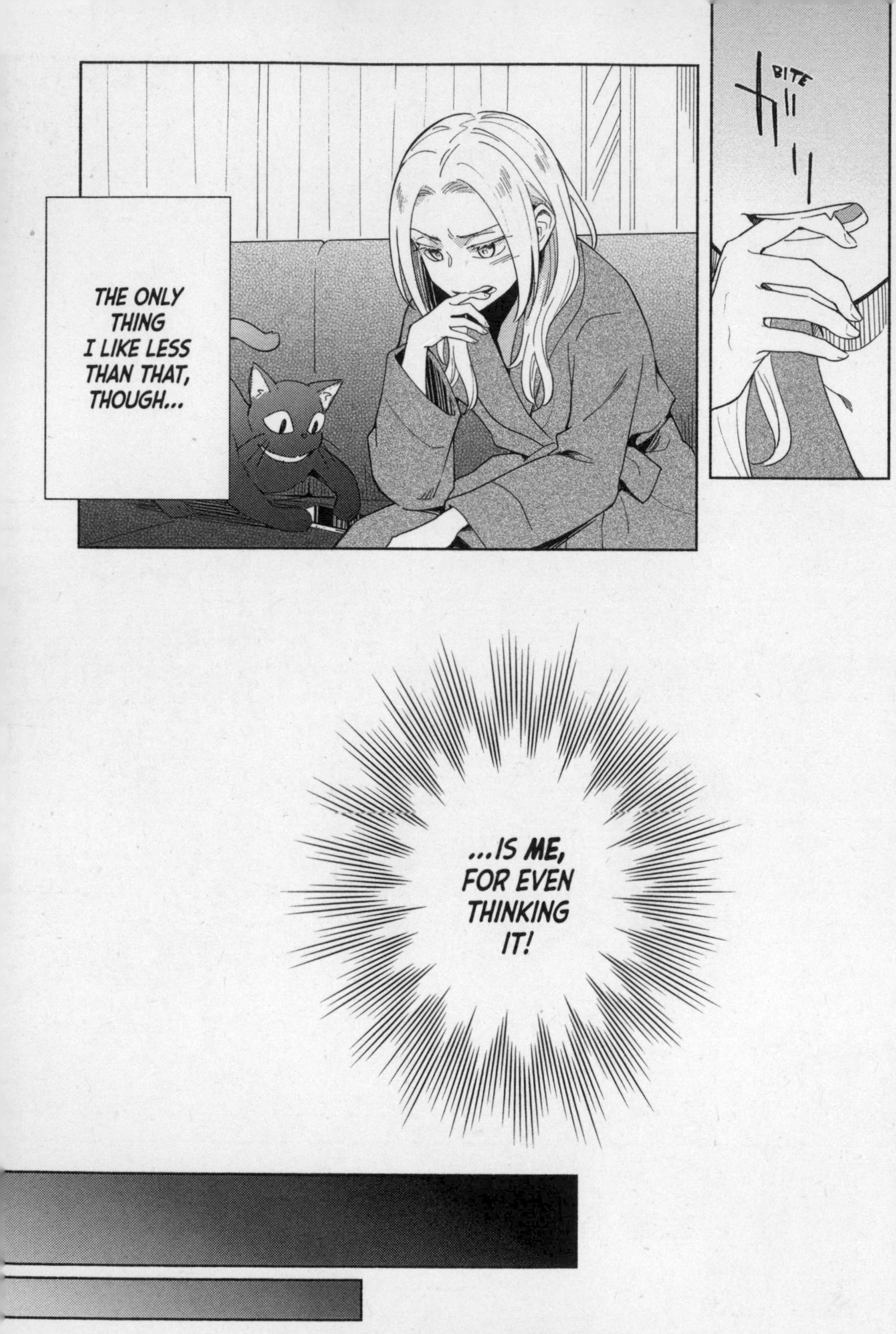
BITE
THE ONLY THING I LIKE LESS THAN THAT, THOUGH...
...IS ME, FOR EVEN THINKING IT!

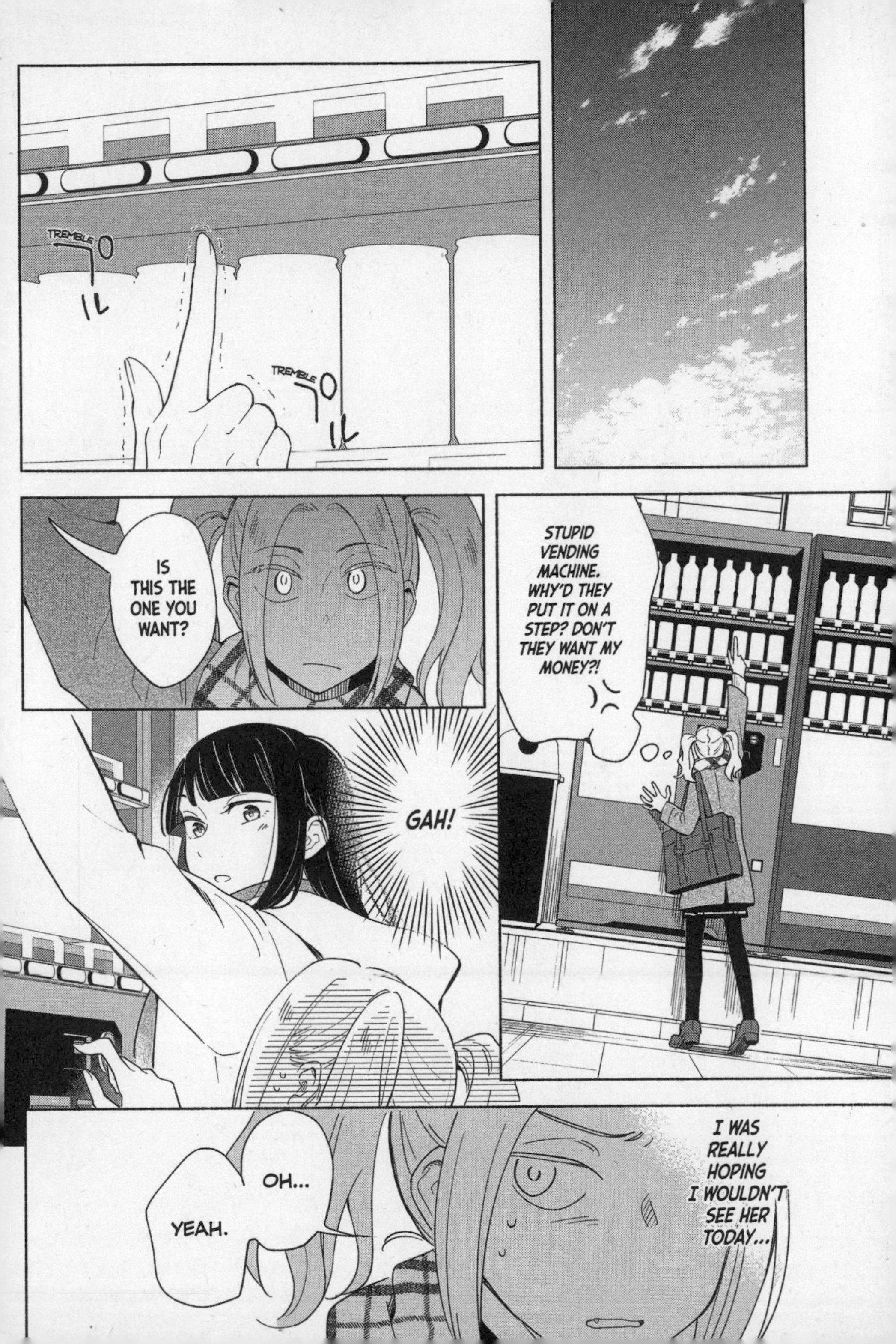
TREMBLE
TREMBLE
STUPID VENDING MACHINE. WHY'D THEY PUT IT ON A STEP? DON'T THEY WANT MY MONEY?!
IS THIS THE ONE YOU WANT?
GAH!
I WAS REALLY HOPING I WOULDN'T SEE HER TODAY...
OH...
YEAH.

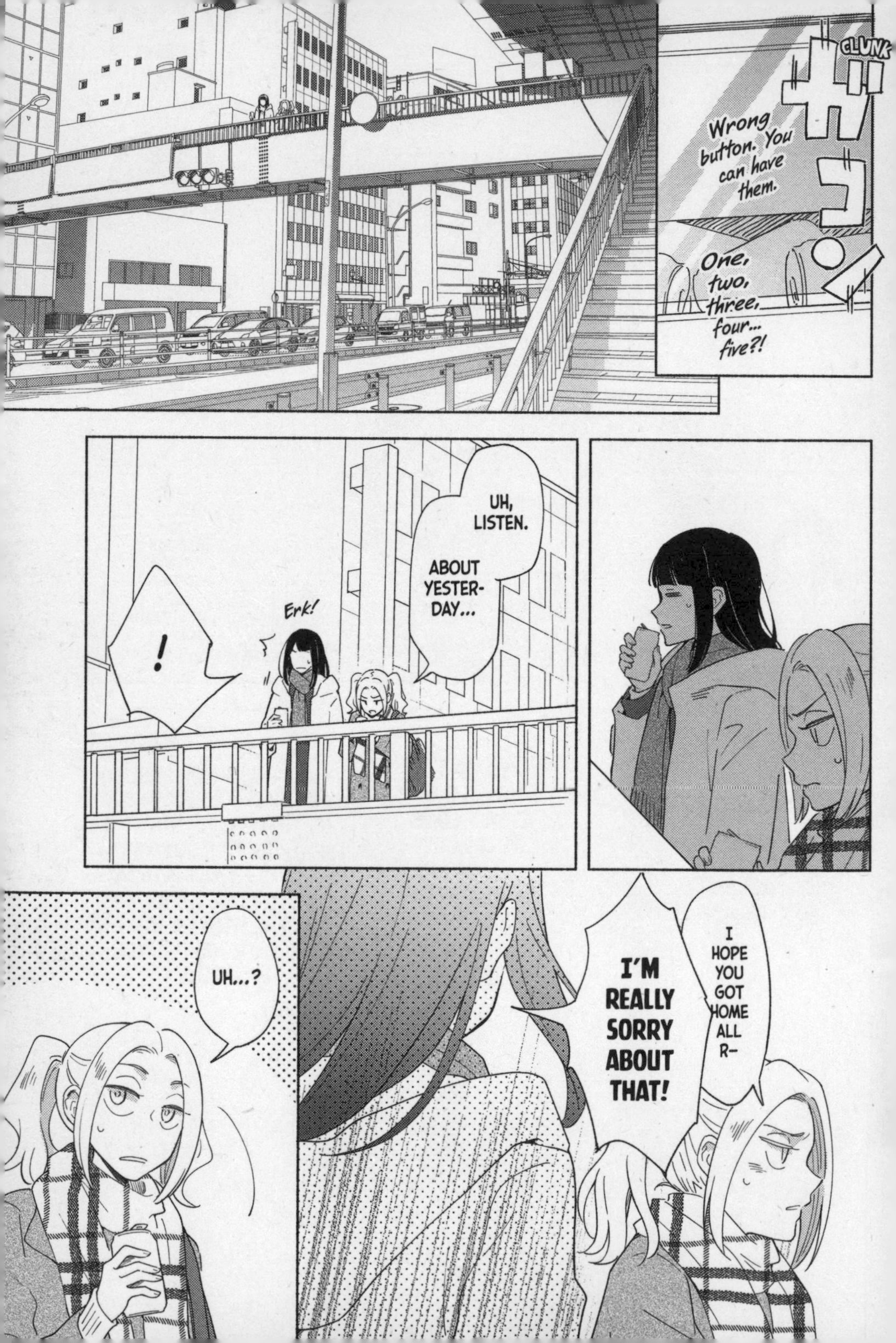
CLUNK
Wrong button. You can have them.
One, two, three, four... five?!
UH, LISTEN.
ABOUT YESTER-DAY...
Erk!
!
I HOPE YOU GOT HOME ALL R–
I'M REALLY SORRY ABOUT THAT!
UH...?

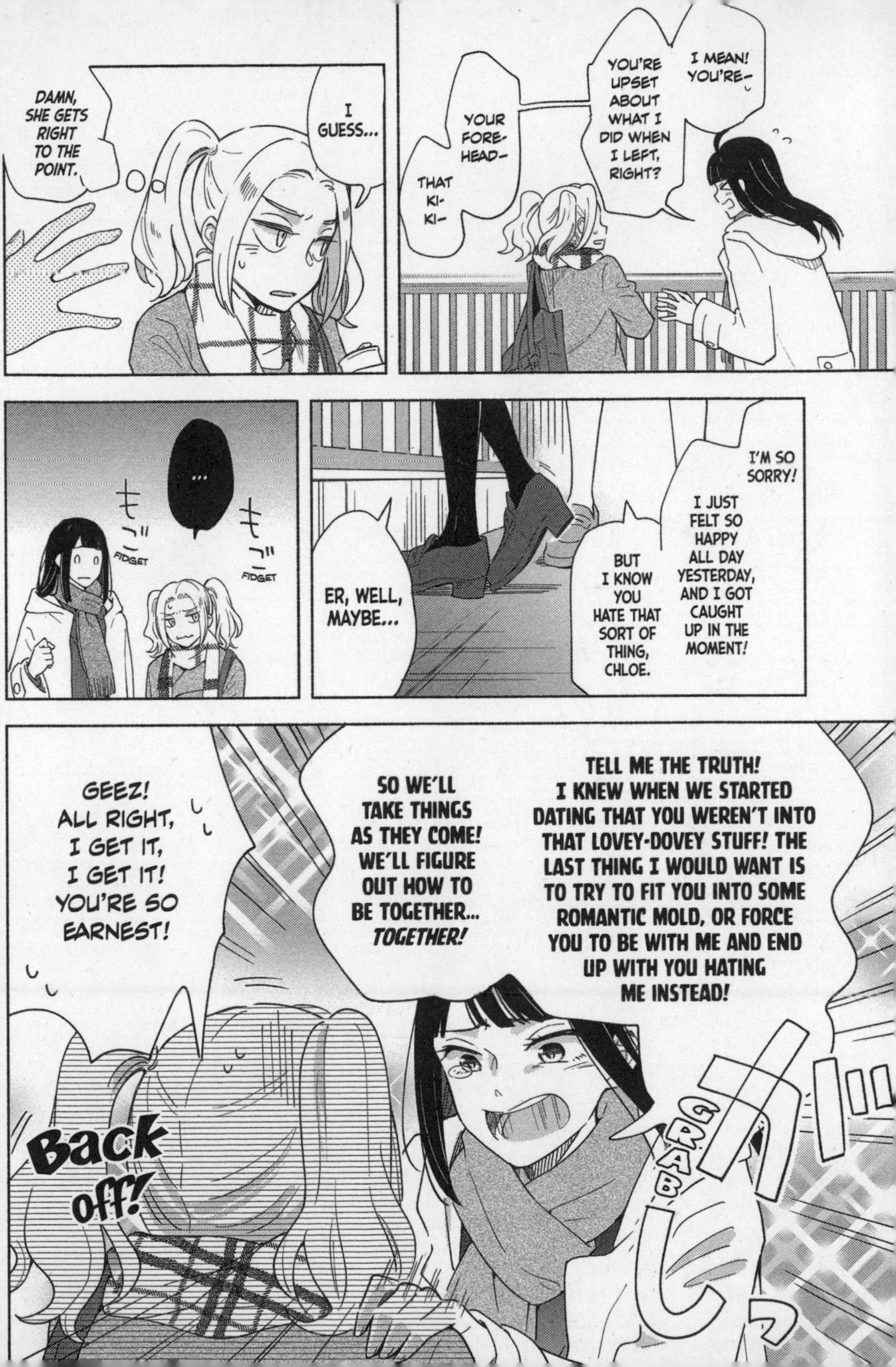
I MEAN! YOU'RE-
YOU'RE UPSET ABOUT WHAT I DID WHEN I LEFT, RIGHT?
YOUR FORE-HEAD- THAT KI-KI-
I GUESS...
DAMN, SHE GETS RIGHT TO THE POINT.
I'M SO SORRY!
I JUST FELT SO HAPPY ALL DAY YESTERDAY, AND I GOT CAUGHT UP IN THE MOMENT!
BUT I KNOW YOU HATE THAT SORT OF THING, CHLOE.
ER, WELL, MAYBE...
...
FIDGET
FIDGET
TELL ME THE TRUTH! I KNEW WHEN WE STARTED DATING THAT YOU WEREN'T INTO THAT LOVEY-DOVEY STUFF! THE LAST THING I WOULD WANT IS TO TRY TO FIT YOU INTO SOME ROMANTIC MOLD, OR FORCE YOU TO BE WITH ME AND END UP WITH YOU HATING ME INSTEAD!
SO WE'LL TAKE THINGS AS THEY COME! WE'LL FIGURE OUT HOW TO BE TOGETHER... *TOGETHER!*
GRAB
GEEZ! ALL RIGHT, I GET IT, I GET IT! YOU'RE SO EARNEST!
Back off!

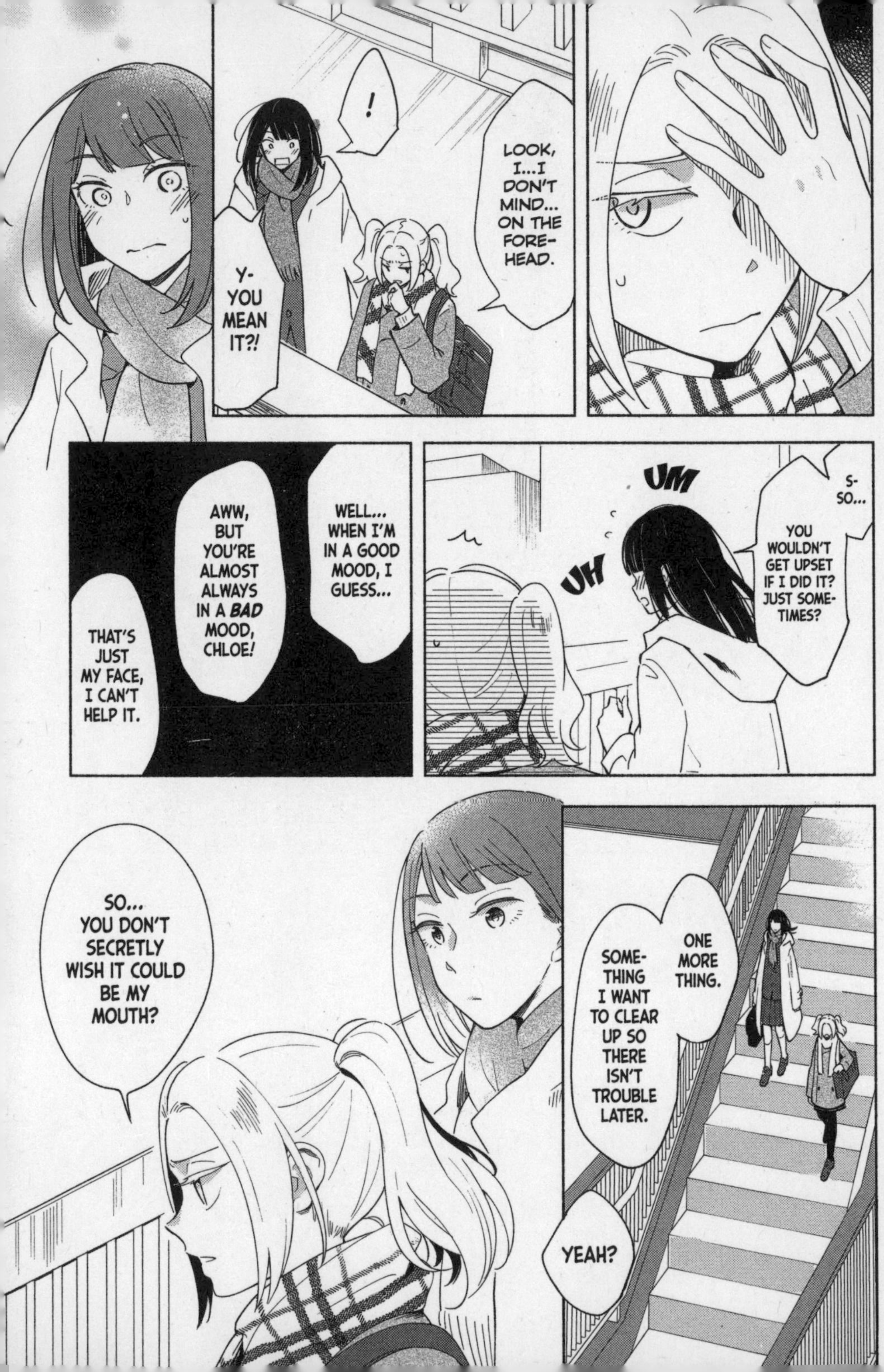
LOOK, I...I DON'T MIND... ON THE FORE-HEAD.
!
Y-YOU MEAN IT?!
S-SO...
YOU WOULDN'T GET UPSET IF I DID IT? JUST SOME-TIMES?
UM
UH
WELL... WHEN I'M IN A GOOD MOOD, I GUESS...
AWW, BUT YOU'RE ALMOST ALWAYS IN A *BAD* MOOD, CHLOE!
THAT'S JUST MY FACE, I CAN'T HELP IT.
ONE MORE THING.
SOME-THING I WANT TO CLEAR UP SO THERE ISN'T TROUBLE LATER.
YEAH?
SO... YOU DON'T SECRETLY WISH IT COULD BE MY MOUTH?

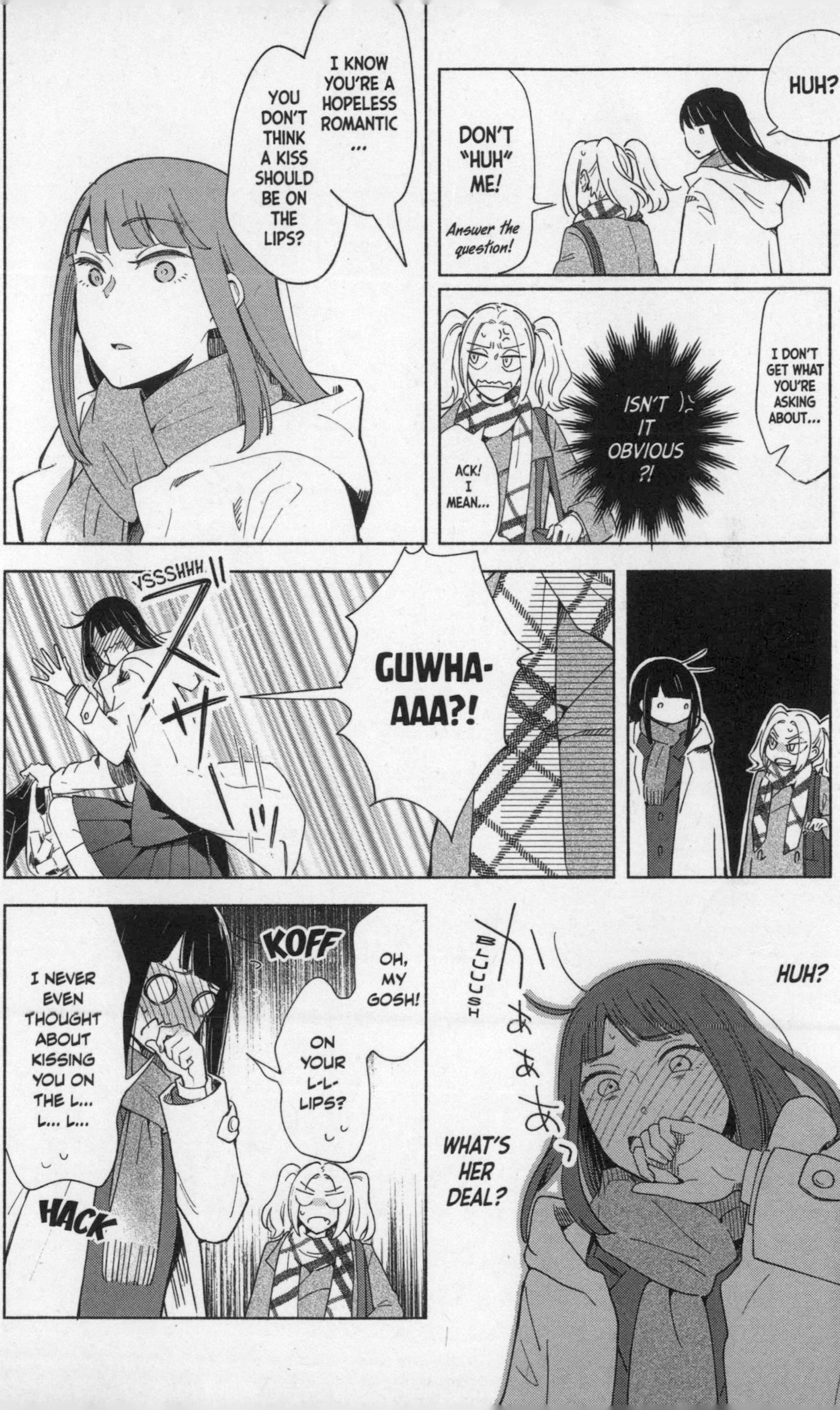
HUH?
DON'T "HUH" ME!
Answer the question!
I DON'T GET WHAT YOU'RE ASKING ABOUT...
ISN'T IT OBVIOUS?!
ACK! I MEAN...
I KNOW YOU'RE A HOPELESS ROMANTIC...
YOU DON'T THINK A KISS SHOULD BE ON THE LIPS?
YSSSHHH
GUWHA-AAA?!
BLUUUSH
あああっ
HUH?
WHAT'S HER DEAL?
KOFF
OH, MY GOSH!
ON YOUR L-L-LIPS?
I NEVER EVEN THOUGHT ABOUT KISSING YOU ON THE L... L... L...
HACK

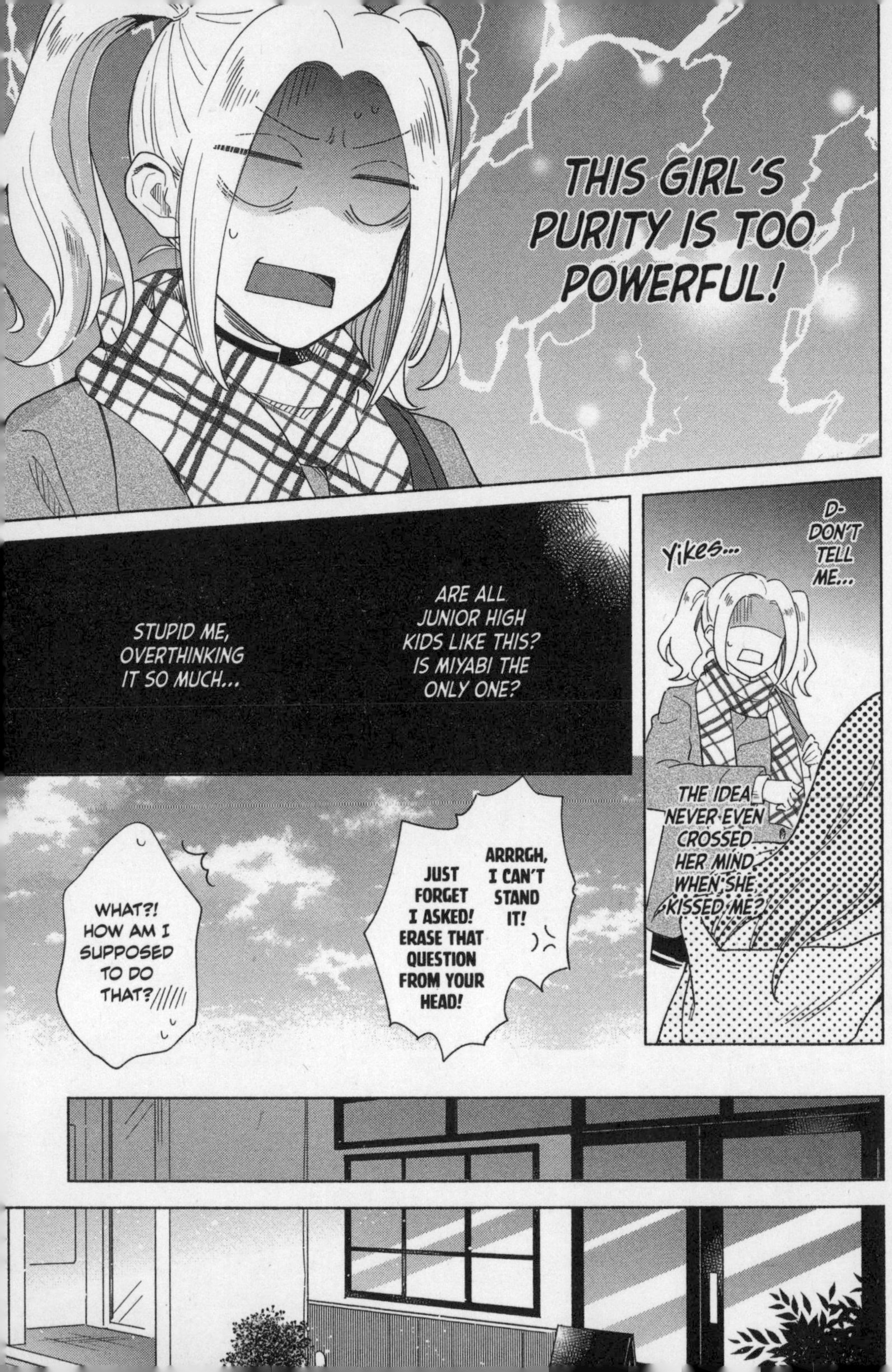
THIS GIRL'S PURITY IS TOO POWERFUL!
D-DON'T TELL ME...
Yikes...
THE IDEA NEVER EVEN CROSSED HER MIND WHEN SHE KISSED ME?
ARE ALL JUNIOR HIGH KIDS LIKE THIS? IS MIYABI THE ONLY ONE?
STUPID ME, OVERTHINKING IT SO MUCH...
ARRRGH, I CAN'T STAND IT!
JUST FORGET I ASKED! ERASE THAT QUESTION FROM YOUR HEAD!
WHAT?! HOW AM I SUPPOSED TO DO THAT?

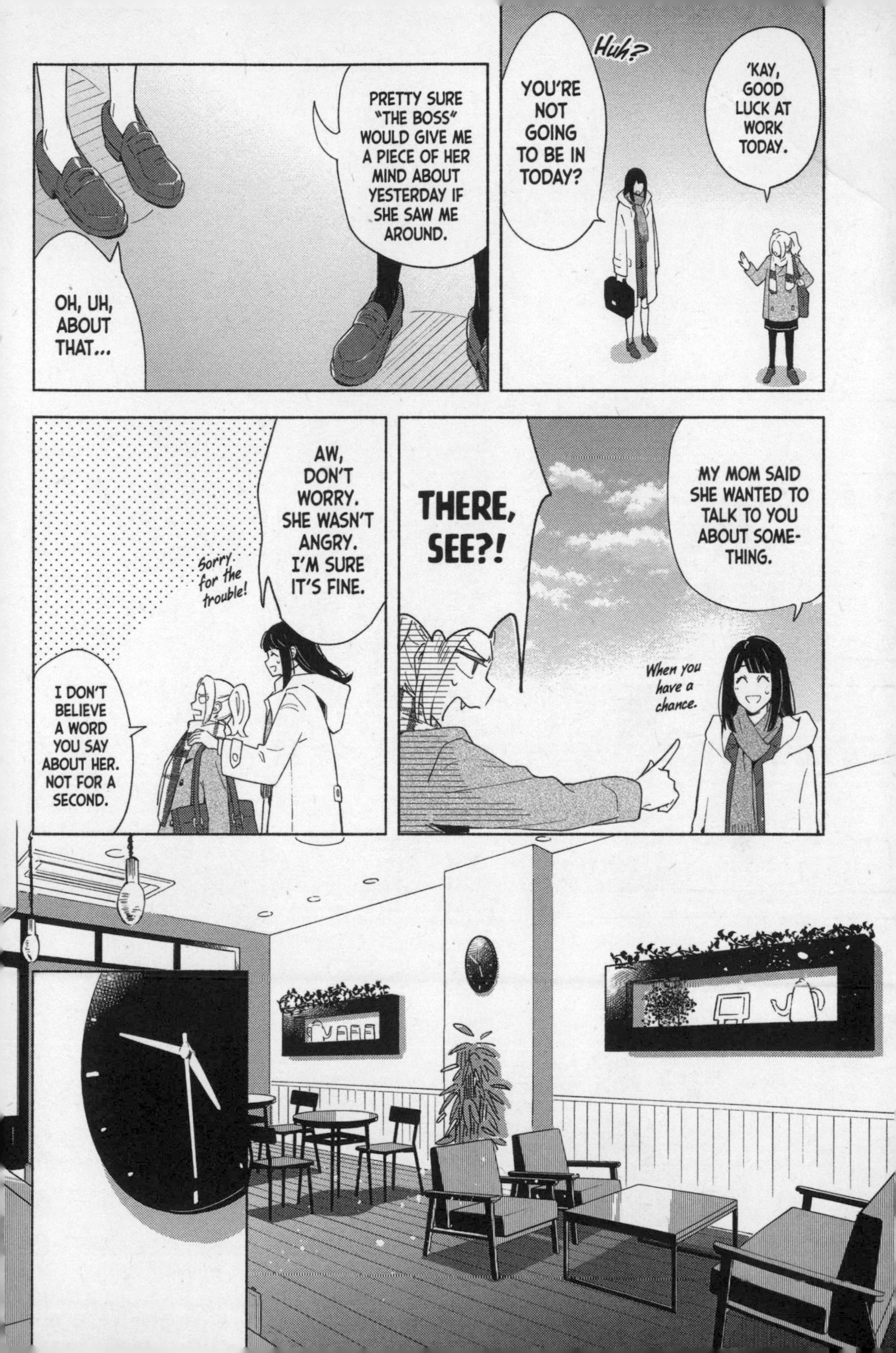
'KAY, GOOD LUCK AT WORK TODAY.
Huh?
YOU'RE NOT GOING TO BE IN TODAY?
PRETTY SURE "THE BOSS" WOULD GIVE ME A PIECE OF HER MIND ABOUT YESTERDAY IF SHE SAW ME AROUND.
OH, UH, ABOUT THAT...
MY MOM SAID SHE WANTED TO TALK TO YOU ABOUT SOME-THING.
When you have a chance.
THERE, SEE?!
AW, DON'T WORRY. SHE WASN'T ANGRY. I'M SURE IT'S FINE.
Sorry for the trouble!
I DON'T BELIEVE A WORD YOU SAY ABOUT HER. NOT FOR A SECOND.

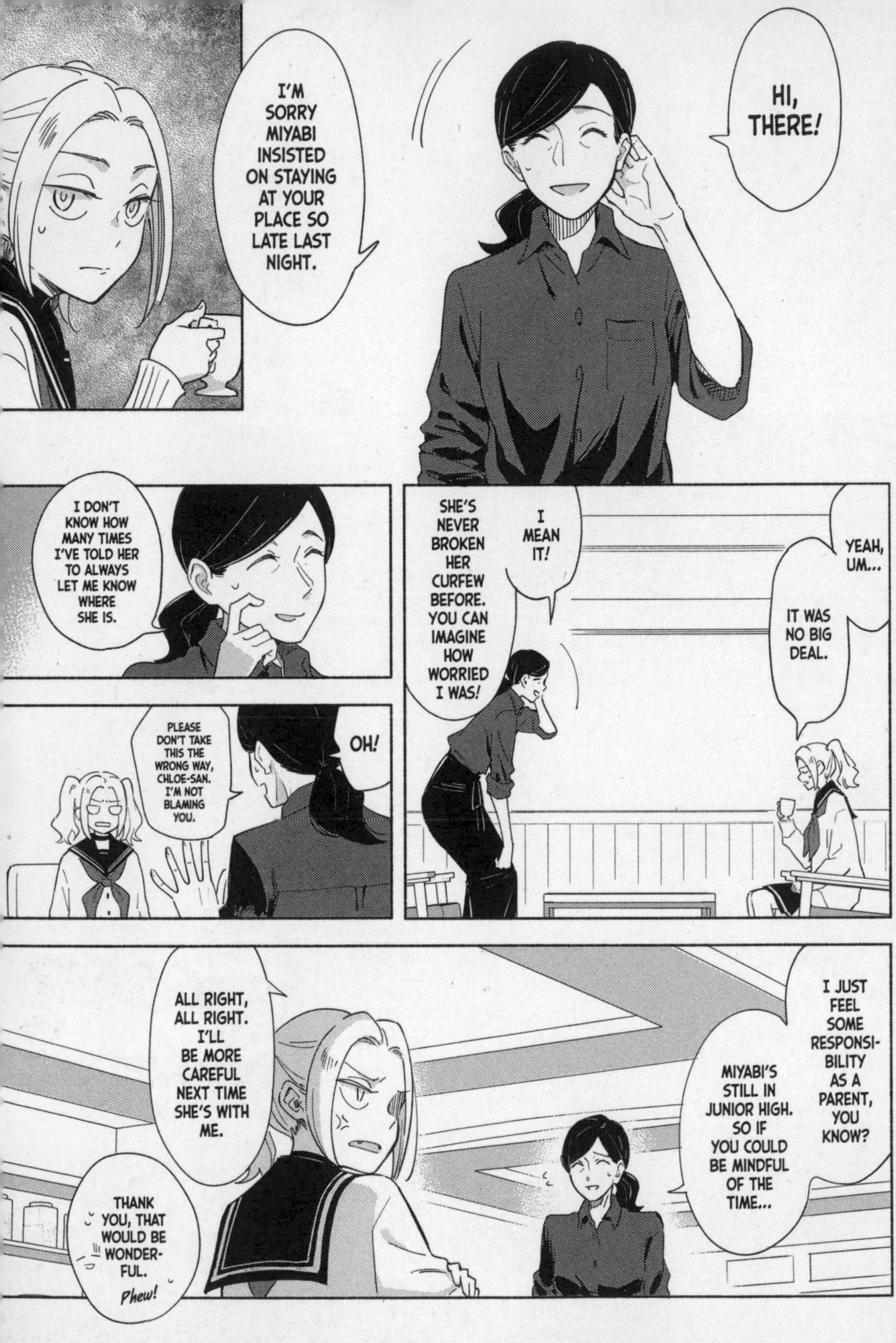
HI, THERE!
I'M SORRY MIYABI INSISTED ON STAYING AT YOUR PLACE SO LATE LAST NIGHT.
YEAH, UM...
IT WAS NO BIG DEAL.
I MEAN IT!
SHE'S NEVER BROKEN HER CURFEW BEFORE. YOU CAN IMAGINE HOW WORRIED I WAS!
I DON'T KNOW HOW MANY TIMES I'VE TOLD HER TO ALWAYS LET ME KNOW WHERE SHE IS.
OH!
PLEASE DON'T TAKE THIS THE WRONG WAY, CHLOE-SAN. I'M NOT BLAMING YOU.
I JUST FEEL SOME RESPONSI-BILITY AS A PARENT, YOU KNOW?
MIYABI'S STILL IN JUNIOR HIGH. SO IF YOU COULD BE MINDFUL OF THE TIME...
ALL RIGHT, ALL RIGHT. I'LL BE MORE CAREFUL NEXT TIME SHE'S WITH ME.
THANK YOU, THAT WOULD BE WONDER-FUL.
Phew!

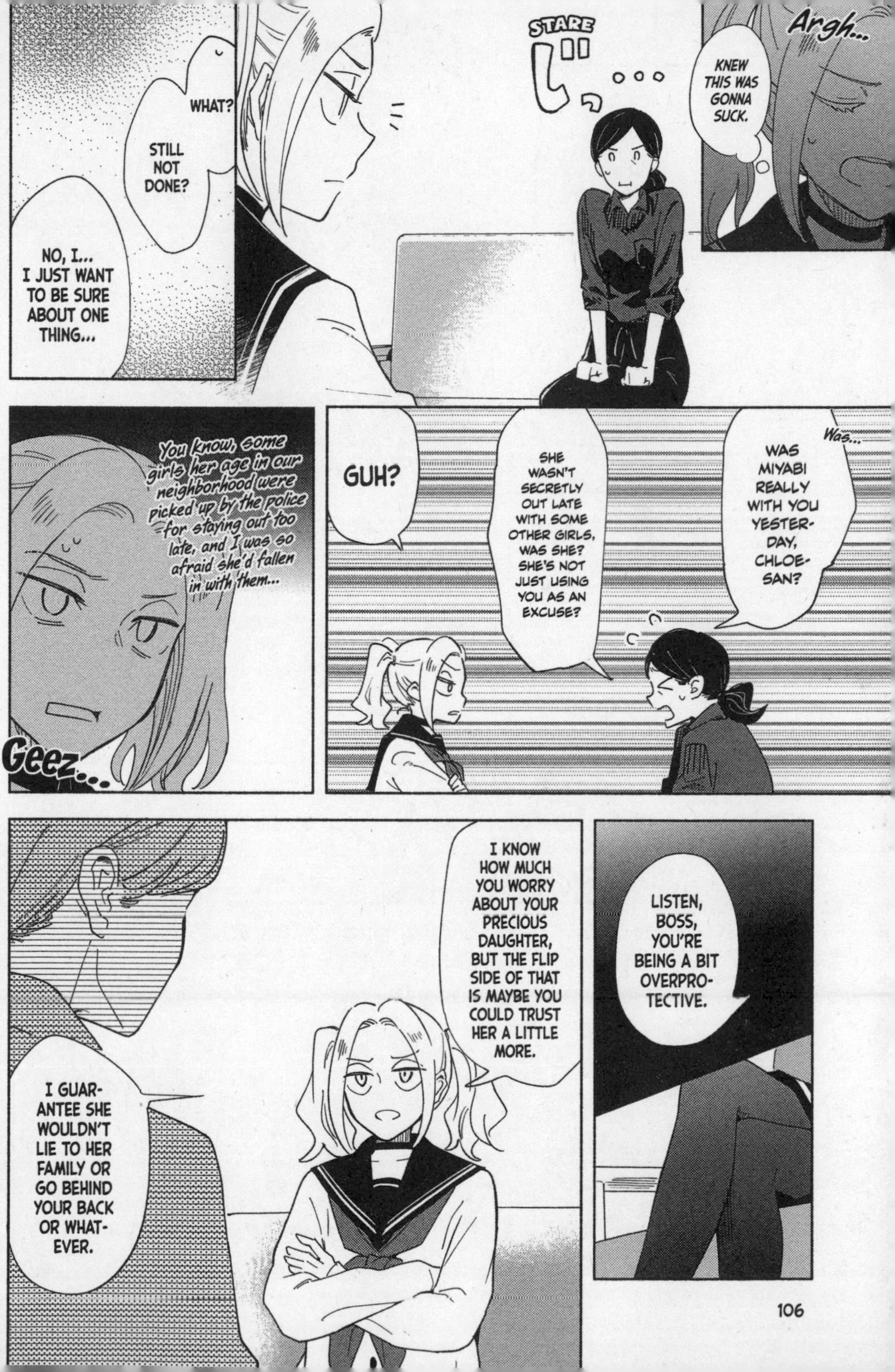
Argh...
KNEW THIS WAS GONNA SUCK.
STARE
WHAT?
STILL NOT DONE?
NO, I... I JUST WANT TO BE SURE ABOUT ONE THING...
Was...
WAS MIYABI REALLY WITH YOU YESTER-DAY, CHLOE-SAN?
SHE WASN'T SECRETLY OUT LATE WITH SOME OTHER GIRLS, WAS SHE? SHE'S NOT JUST USING YOU AS AN EXCUSE?
GUH?
You know, some girls her age in our neighborhood were picked up by the police for staying out too late, and I was so afraid she'd fallen in with them...
Geez...
LISTEN, BOSS, YOU'RE BEING A BIT OVERPRO-TECTIVE.
I KNOW HOW MUCH YOU WORRY ABOUT YOUR PRECIOUS DAUGHTER, BUT THE FLIP SIDE OF THAT IS MAYBE YOU COULD TRUST HER A LITTLE MORE.
I GUAR-ANTEE SHE WOULDN'T LIE TO HER FAMILY OR GO BEHIND YOUR BACK OR WHAT-EVER.

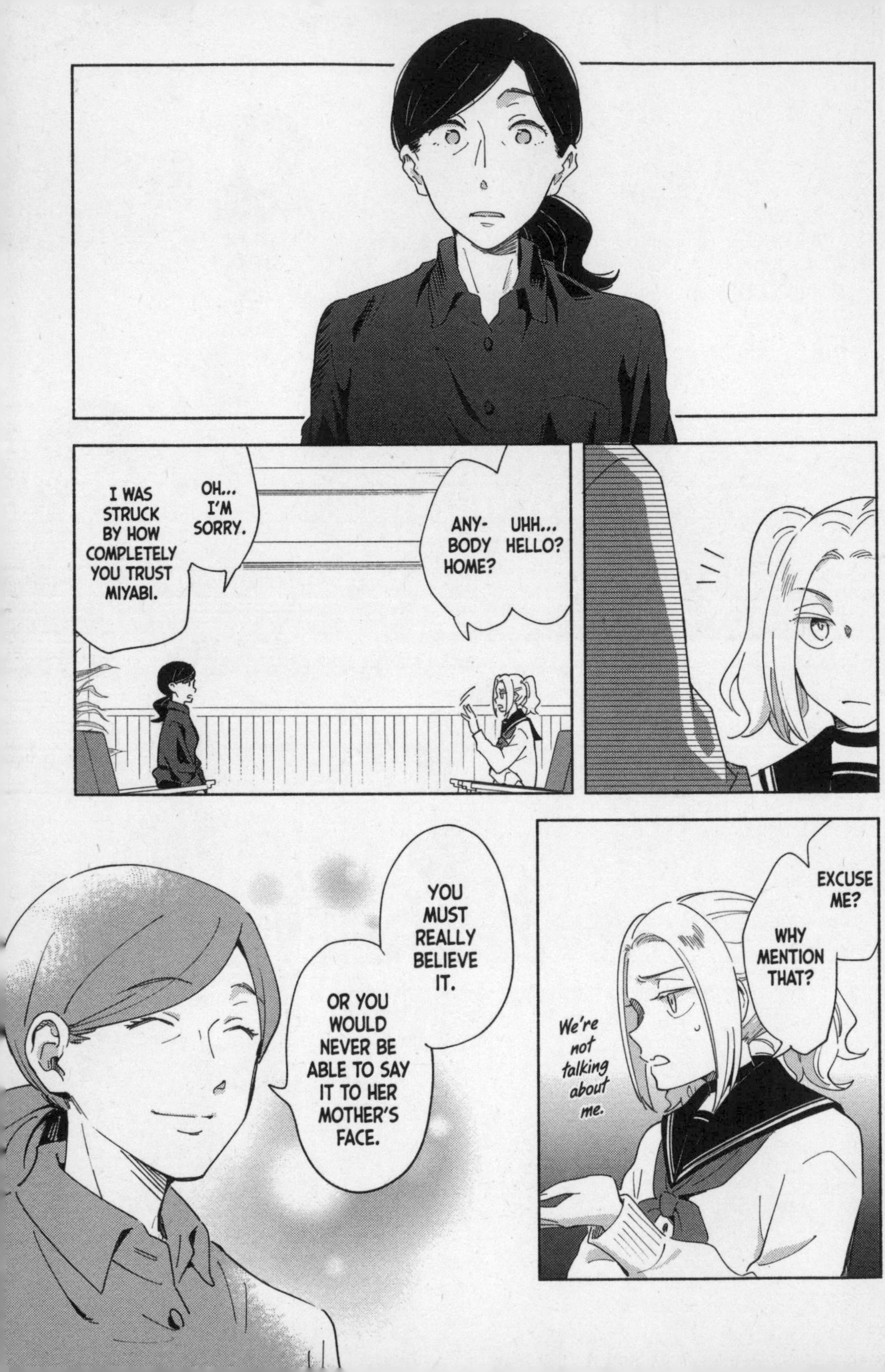
UHH... HELLO?
ANYBODY HOME?
OH... I'M SORRY.
I WAS STRUCK BY HOW COMPLETELY YOU TRUST MIYABI.
EXCUSE ME?
WHY MENTION THAT?
We're not talking about me.
YOU MUST REALLY BELIEVE IT.
OR YOU WOULD NEVER BE ABLE TO SAY IT TO HER MOTHER'S FACE.

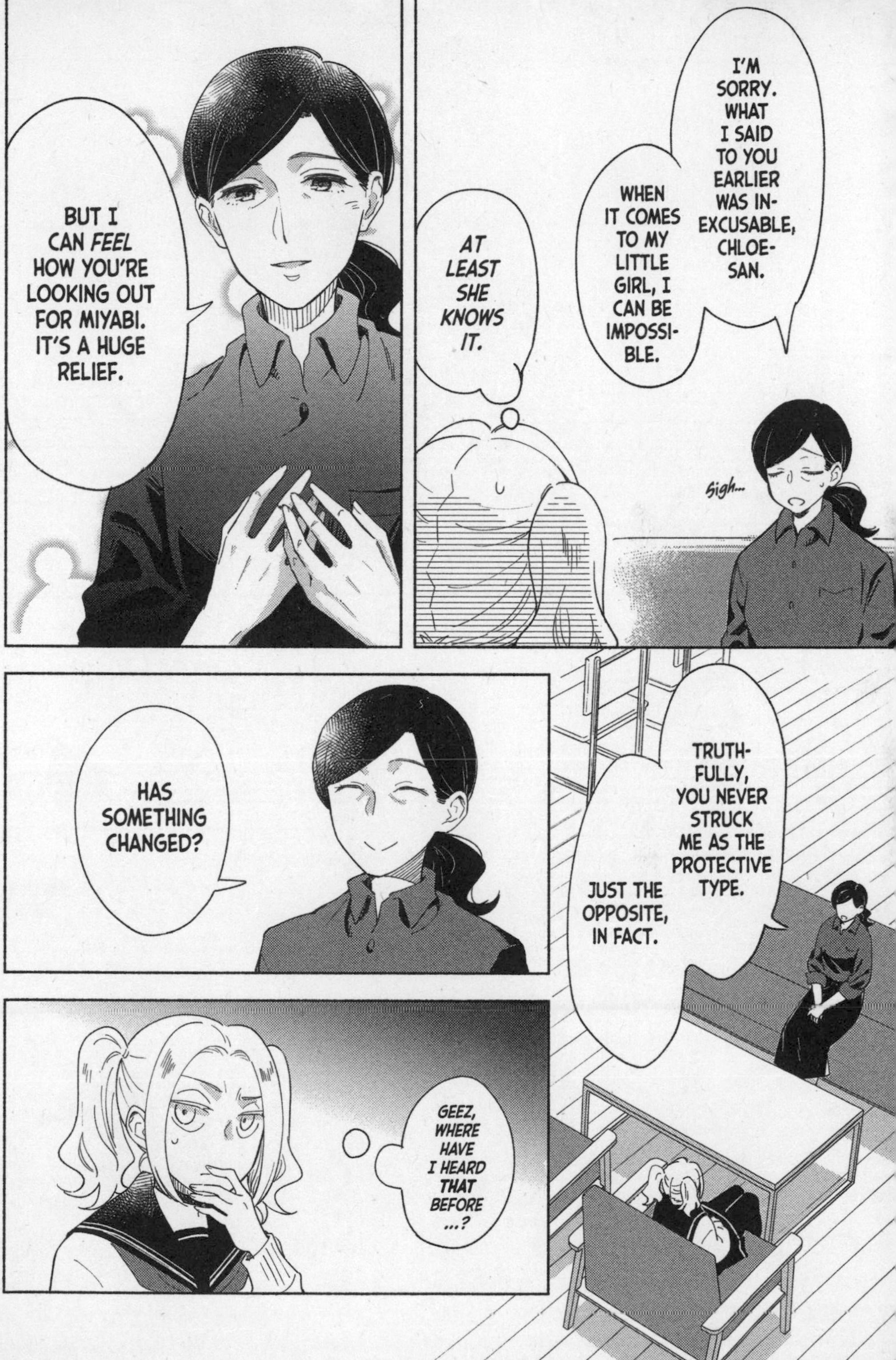
I'M SORRY. WHAT I SAID TO YOU EARLIER WAS IN-EXCUSABLE, CHLOE-SAN.
WHEN IT COMES TO MY LITTLE GIRL, I CAN BE IMPOSSI-BLE.
AT LEAST SHE KNOWS IT.
Sigh...
BUT I CAN *FEEL* HOW YOU'RE LOOKING OUT FOR MIYABI. IT'S A HUGE RELIEF.
TRUTH-FULLY, YOU NEVER STRUCK ME AS THE PROTECTIVE TYPE.
JUST THE OPPOSITE, IN FACT.
HAS SOMETHING CHANGED?
GEEZ, WHERE HAVE I HEARD **THAT** BEFORE ...?

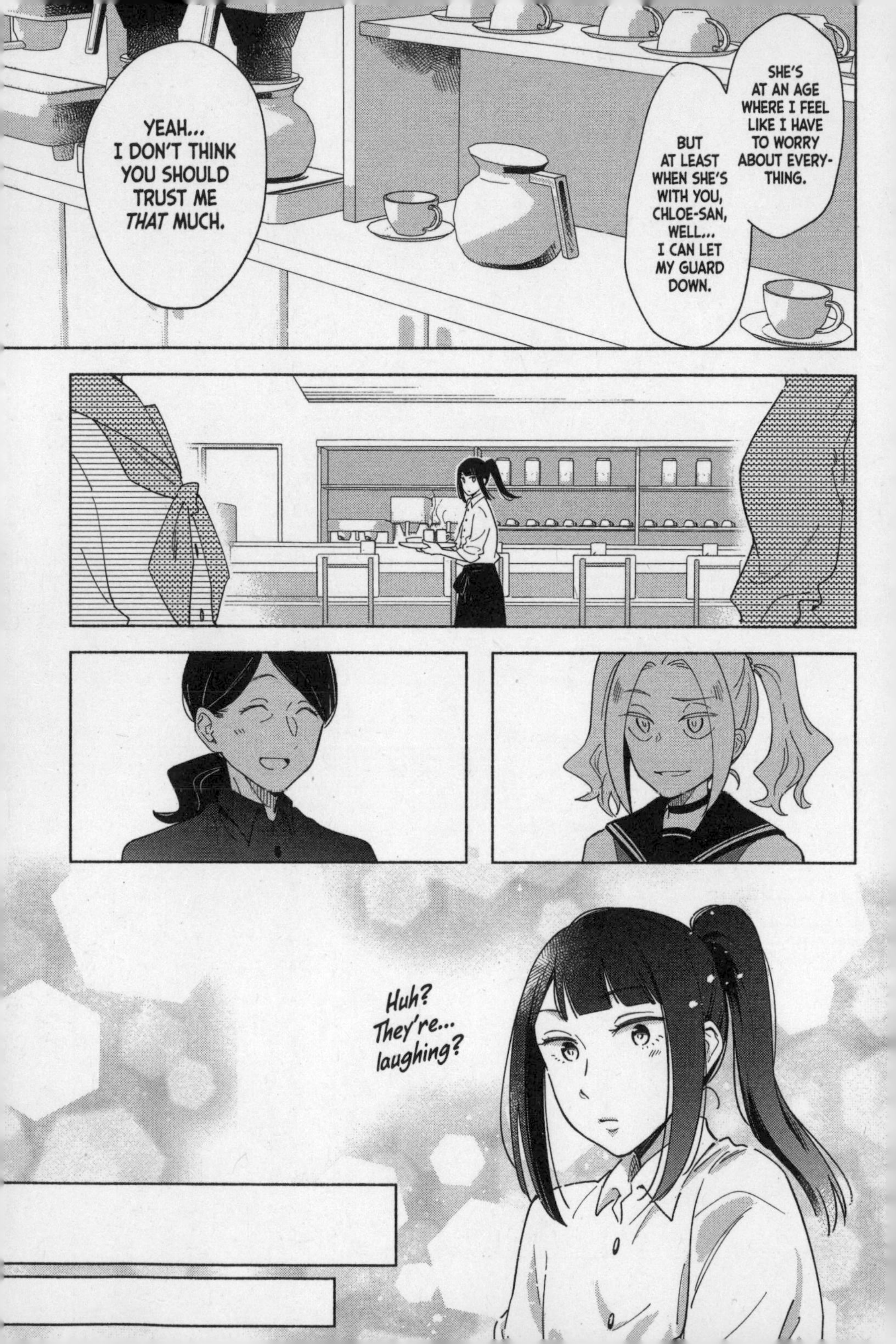
SHE'S AT AN AGE WHERE I FEEL LIKE I HAVE TO WORRY ABOUT EVERY-THING.
BUT AT LEAST WHEN SHE'S WITH YOU, CHLOE-SAN, WELL... I CAN LET MY GUARD DOWN.
YEAH... I DON'T THINK YOU SHOULD TRUST ME *THAT* MUCH.
Huh? They're... laughing?

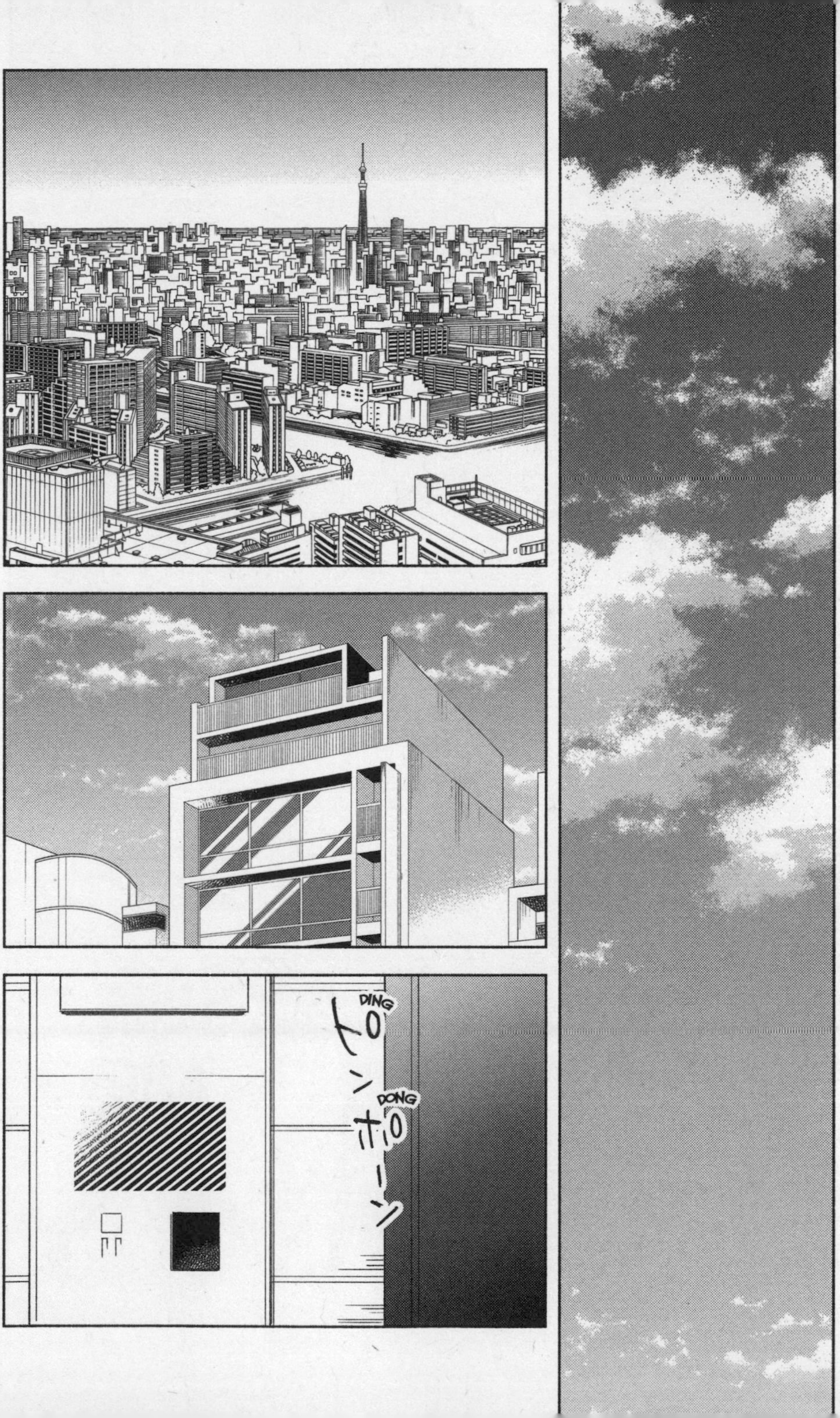
ピンポーン
DING
DONG

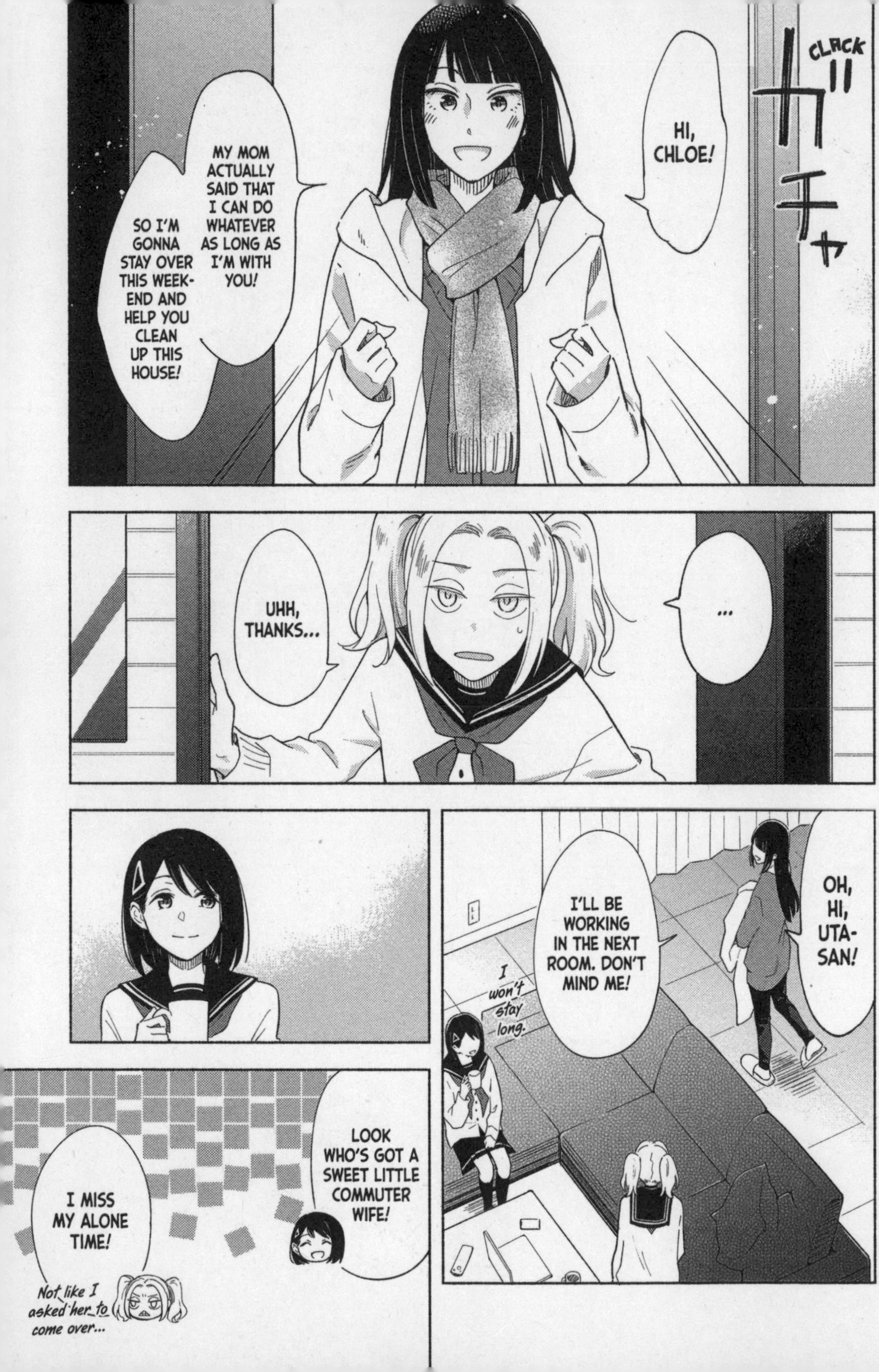
CLACK
ガチャ
HI, CHLOE!
MY MOM ACTUALLY SAID THAT I CAN DO WHATEVER AS LONG AS I'M WITH YOU!
SO I'M GONNA STAY OVER THIS WEEK-END AND HELP YOU CLEAN UP THIS HOUSE!
...
UHH, THANKS...
OH, HI, UTA-SAN!
I'LL BE WORKING IN THE NEXT ROOM. DON'T MIND ME!
I won't stay long.
LOOK WHO'S GOT A SWEET LITTLE COMMUTER WIFE!
I MISS MY ALONE TIME!
Not like I asked her to come over...

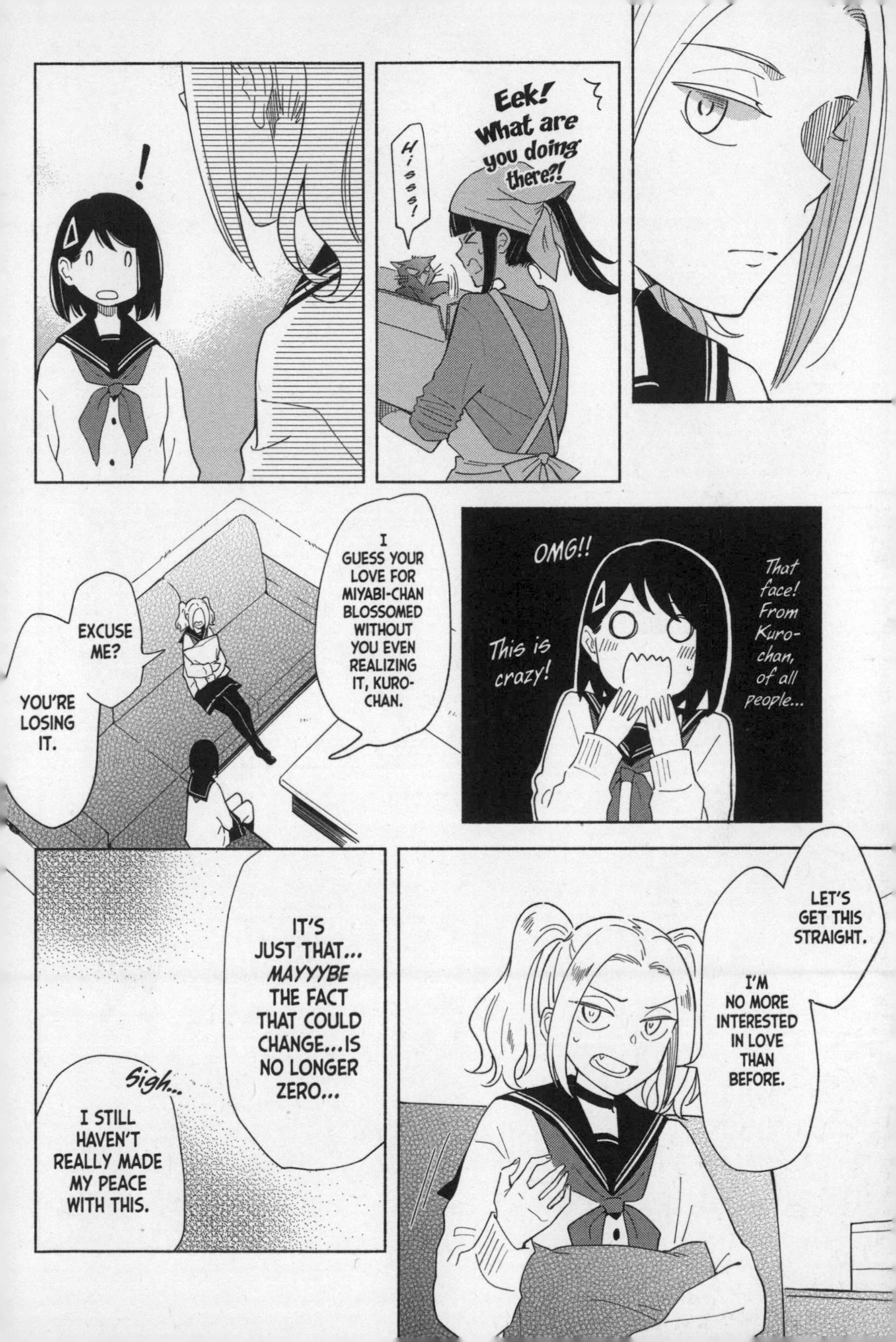
Eek! What are you doing there?!
Hisss!
!
OMG!!
That face! From Kuro-chan, of all people...
This is crazy!
I GUESS YOUR LOVE FOR MIYABI-CHAN BLOSSOMED WITHOUT YOU EVEN REALIZING IT, KURO-CHAN.
EXCUSE ME?
YOU'RE LOSING IT.
LET'S GET THIS STRAIGHT.
I'M NO MORE INTERESTED IN LOVE THAN BEFORE.
IT'S JUST THAT... *MAYYYBE* THE FACT THAT COULD CHANGE...IS NO LONGER ZERO...
Sigh...
I STILL HAVEN'T REALLY MADE MY PEACE WITH THIS.

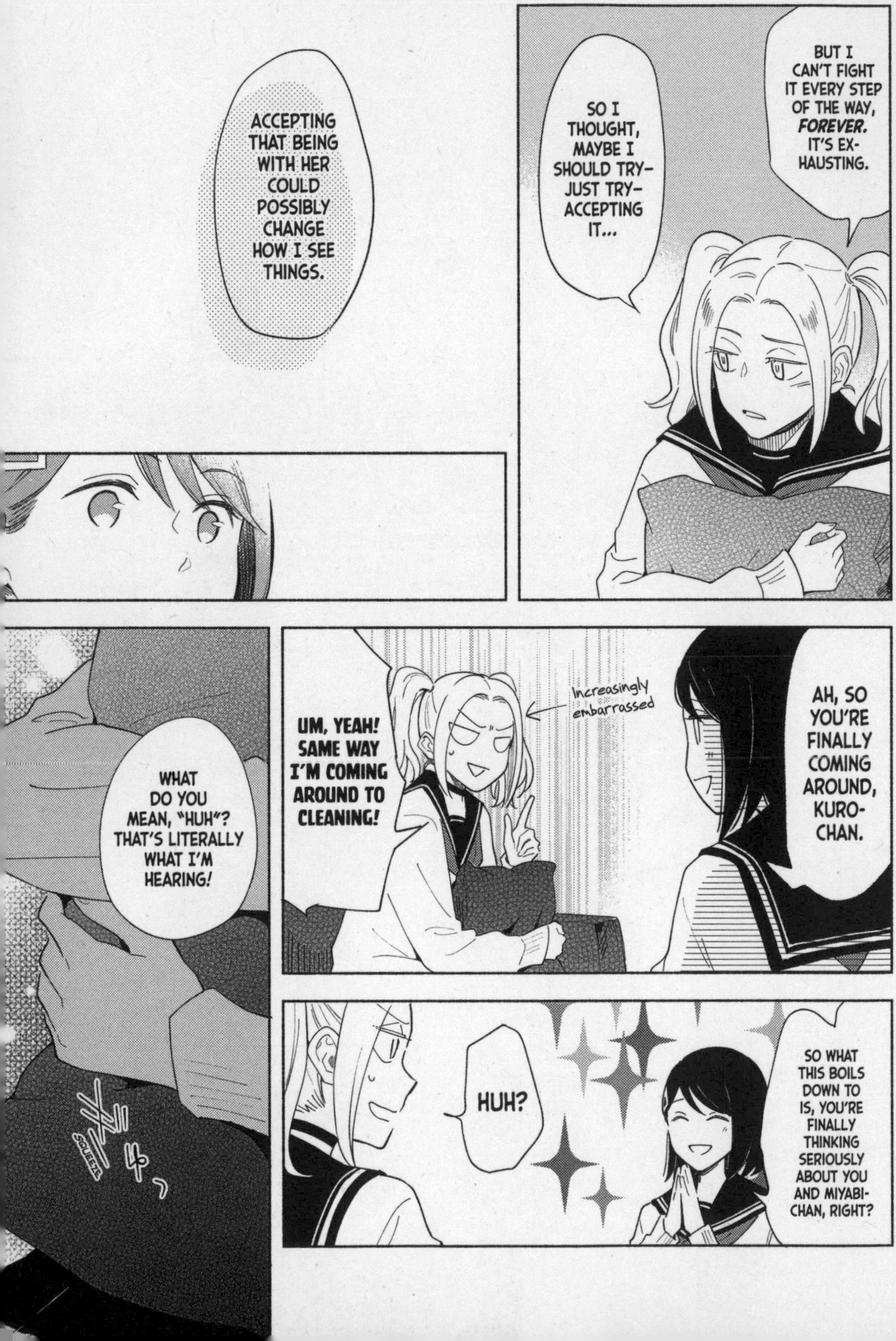
BUT I CAN'T FIGHT IT EVERY STEP OF THE WAY, ***FOREVER.*** IT'S EX-HAUSTING.
SO I THOUGHT, MAYBE I SHOULD TRY– JUST TRY– ACCEPTING IT...
ACCEPTING THAT BEING WITH HER COULD POSSIBLY CHANGE HOW I SEE THINGS.
AH, SO YOU'RE FINALLY COMING AROUND, KURO-CHAN.
UM, YEAH! SAME WAY I'M COMING AROUND TO CLEANING!
Increasingly embarrassed
SO WHAT THIS BOILS DOWN TO IS, YOU'RE FINALLY THINKING SERIOUSLY ABOUT YOU AND MIYABI-CHAN, RIGHT?
HUH?
WHAT DO YOU MEAN, "HUH"? THAT'S LITERALLY WHAT I'M HEARING!
SQUEEZE

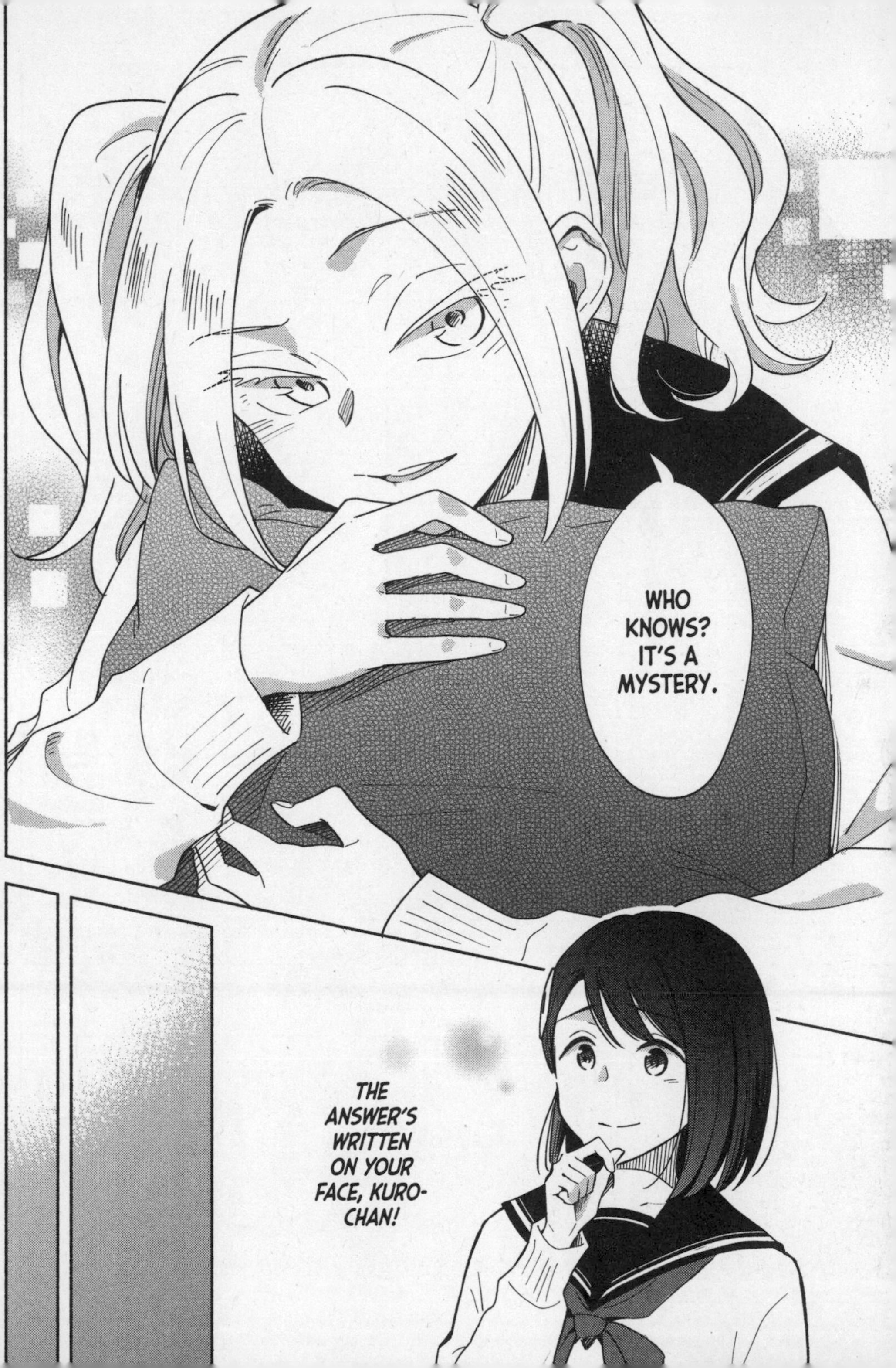
WHO KNOWS? IT'S A MYSTERY.
THE ANSWER'S WRITTEN ON YOUR FACE, KURO-CHAN!

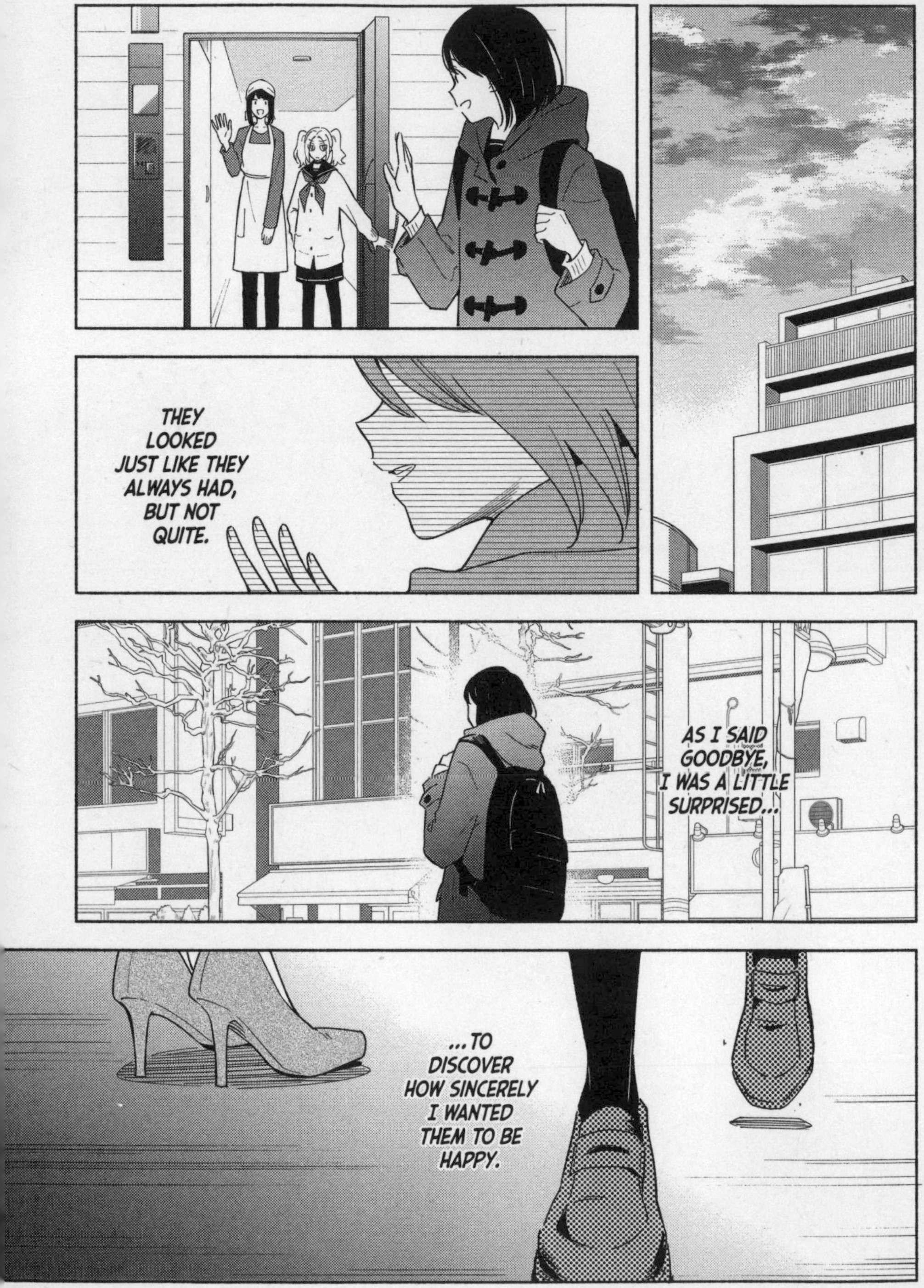
THEY LOOKED JUST LIKE THEY ALWAYS HAD, BUT NOT QUITE.
AS I SAID GOODBYE, I WAS A LITTLE SURPRISED...
...TO DISCOVER HOW SINCERELY I WANTED THEM TO BE HAPPY.

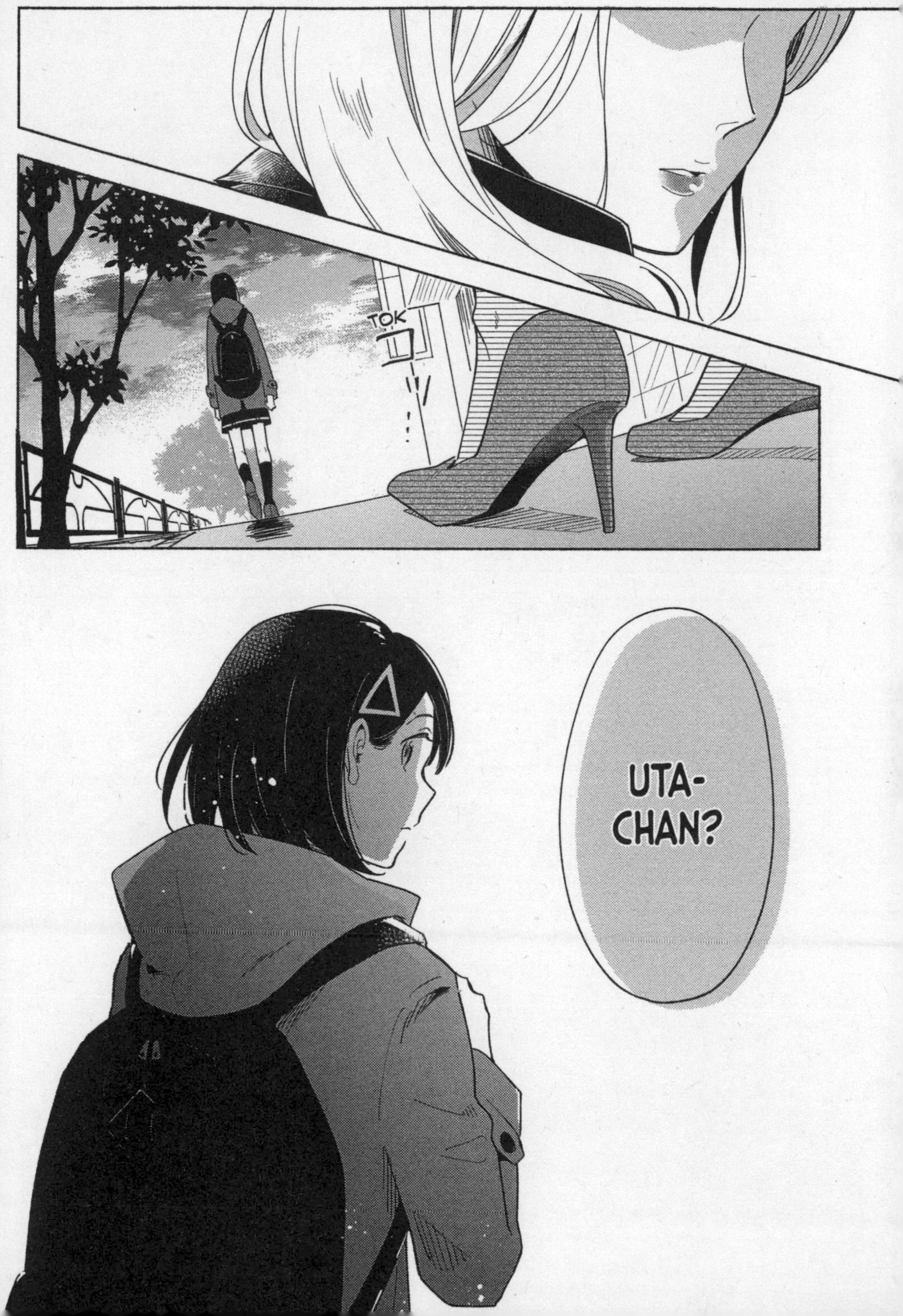
TOK
UTA-
CHAN?

If I Could Reach You

If I Could
Reach You

Chapter 25

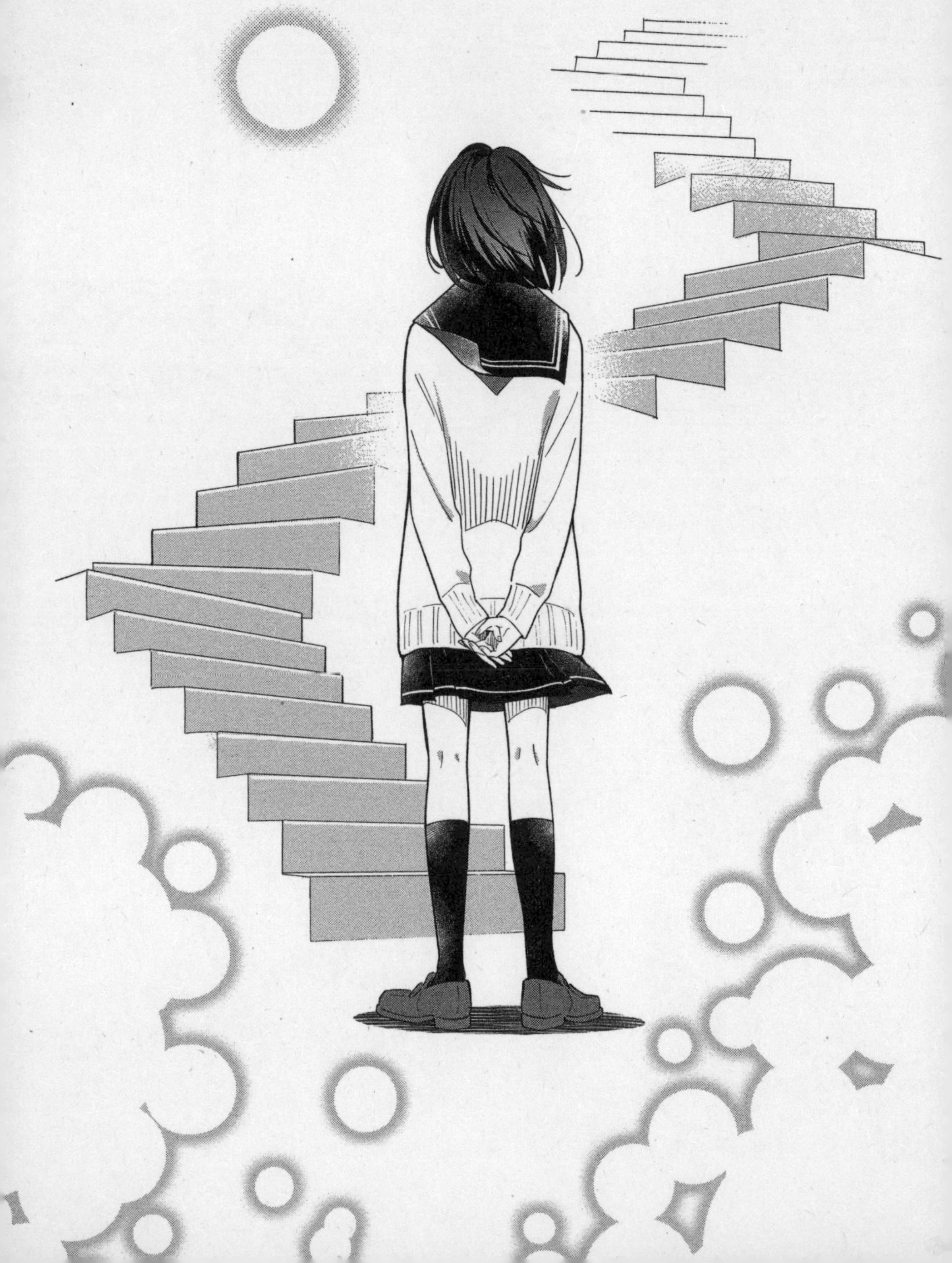

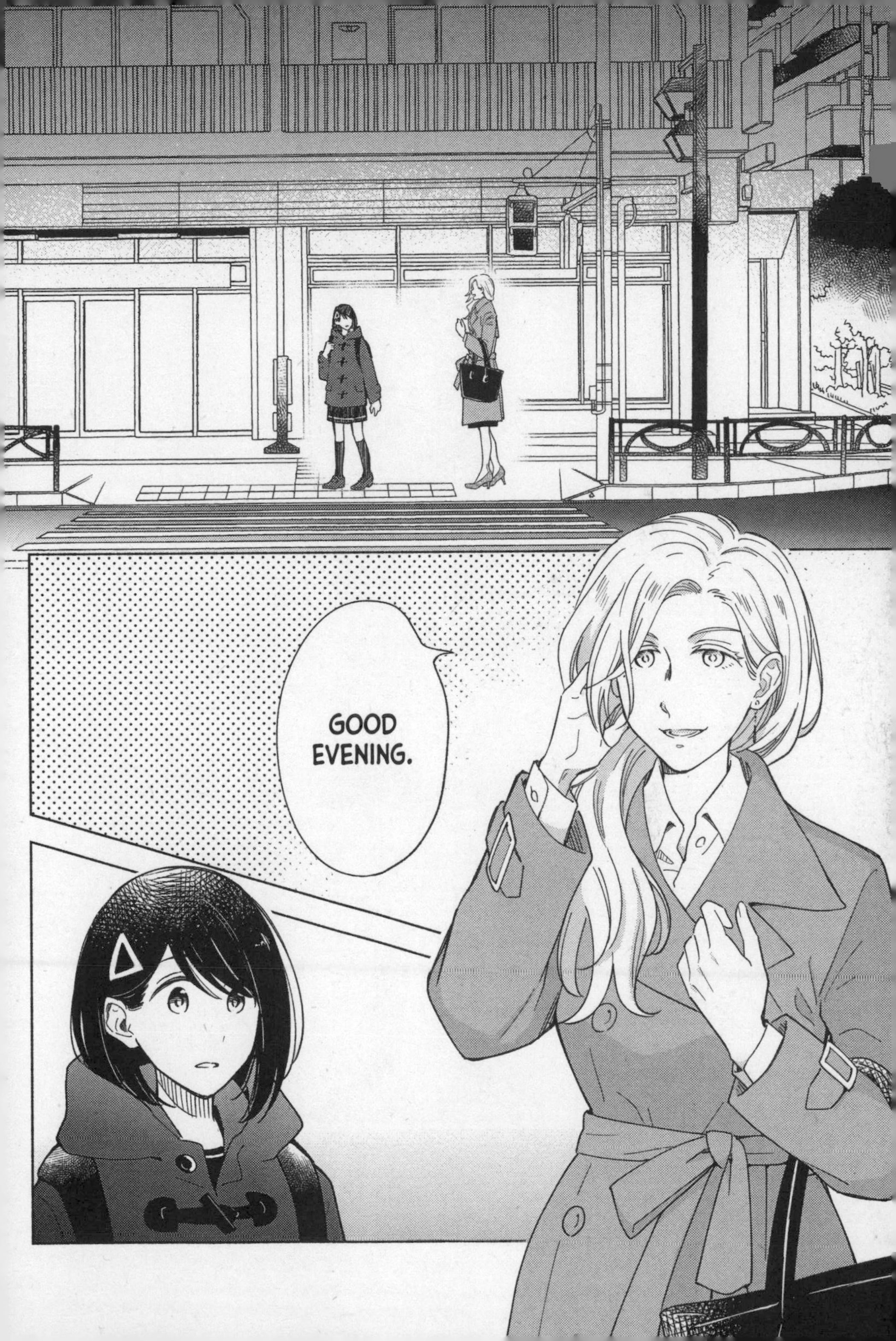
GOOD EVENING.

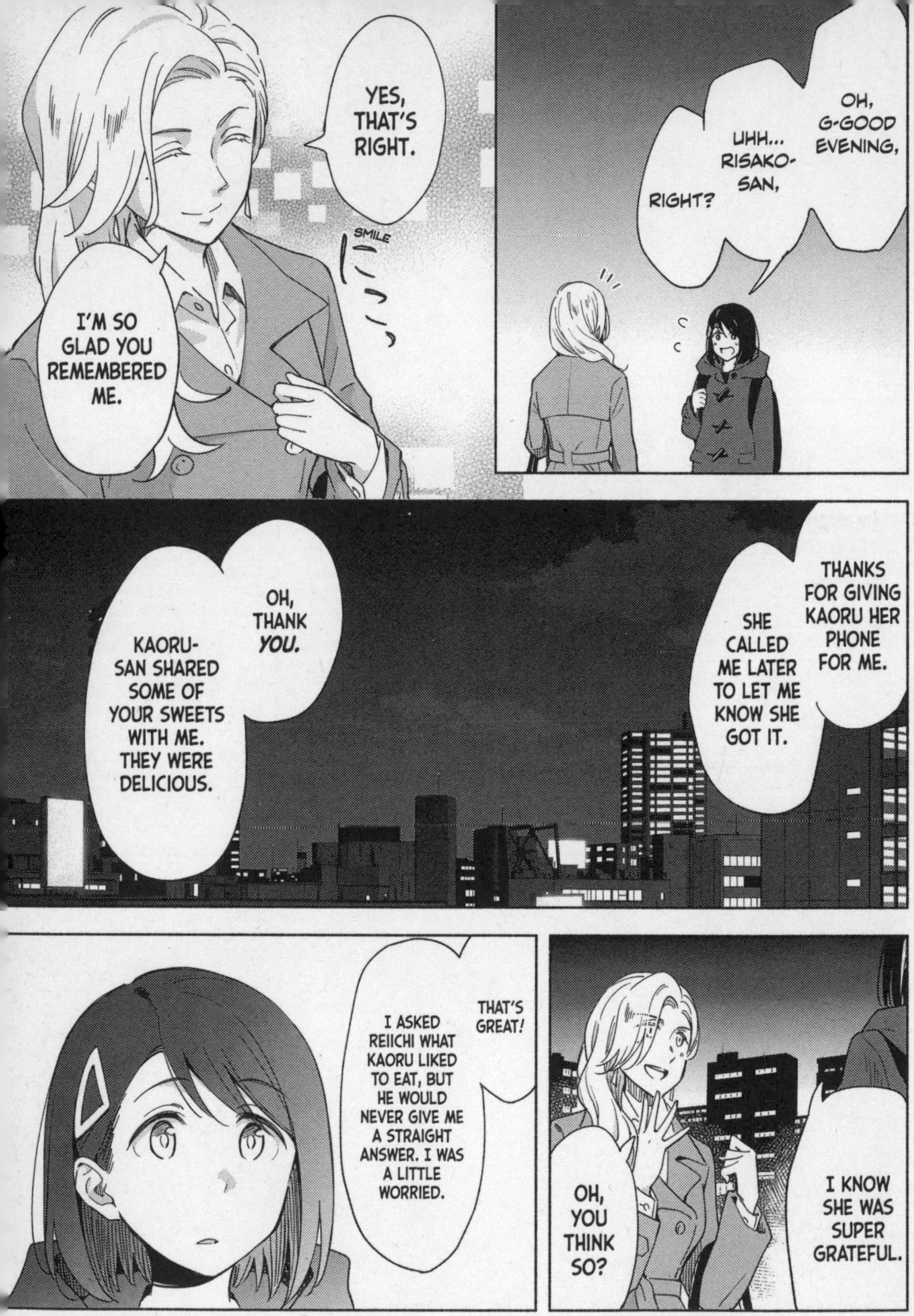
OH, G-GOOD EVENING,
UHH... RISAKO-SAN, RIGHT?
YES, THAT'S RIGHT.
SMILE
I'M SO GLAD YOU REMEMBERED ME.
THANKS FOR GIVING KAORU HER PHONE FOR ME.
SHE CALLED ME LATER TO LET ME KNOW SHE GOT IT.
OH, THANK *YOU.*
KAORU-SAN SHARED SOME OF YOUR SWEETS WITH ME. THEY WERE DELICIOUS.
I KNOW SHE WAS SUPER GRATEFUL.
OH, YOU THINK SO?
THAT'S GREAT!
I ASKED REIICHI WHAT KAORU LIKED TO EAT, BUT HE WOULD NEVER GIVE ME A STRAIGHT ANSWER. I WAS A LITTLE WORRIED.

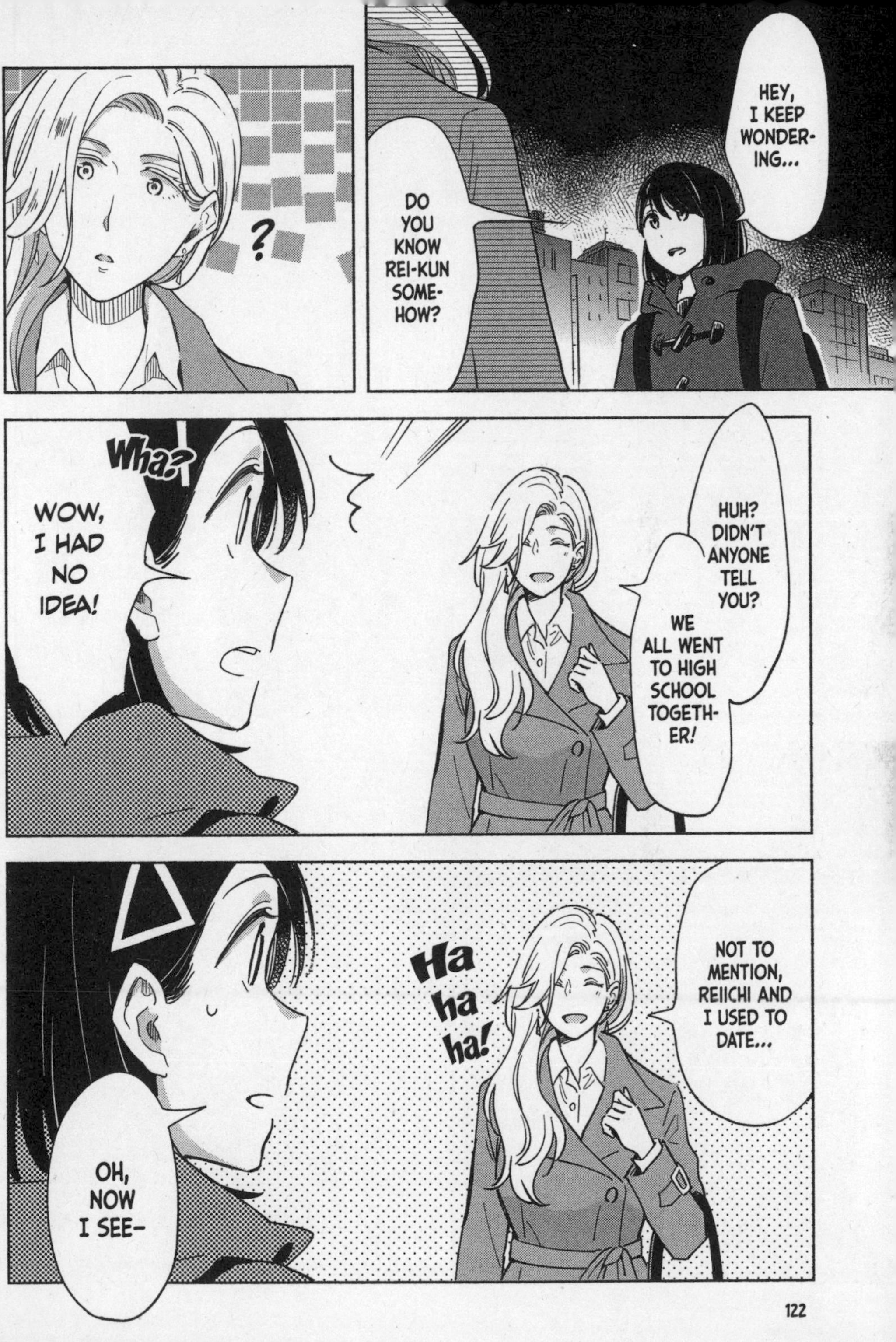
HEY, I KEEP WONDER-ING...
DO YOU KNOW REI-KUN SOME-HOW?
?
HUH? DIDN'T ANYONE TELL YOU?
WE ALL WENT TO HIGH SCHOOL TOGETH-ER!
Wha?
WOW, I HAD NO IDEA!
NOT TO MENTION, REIICHI AND I USED TO DATE...
Ha ha ha!
OH, NOW I SEE-

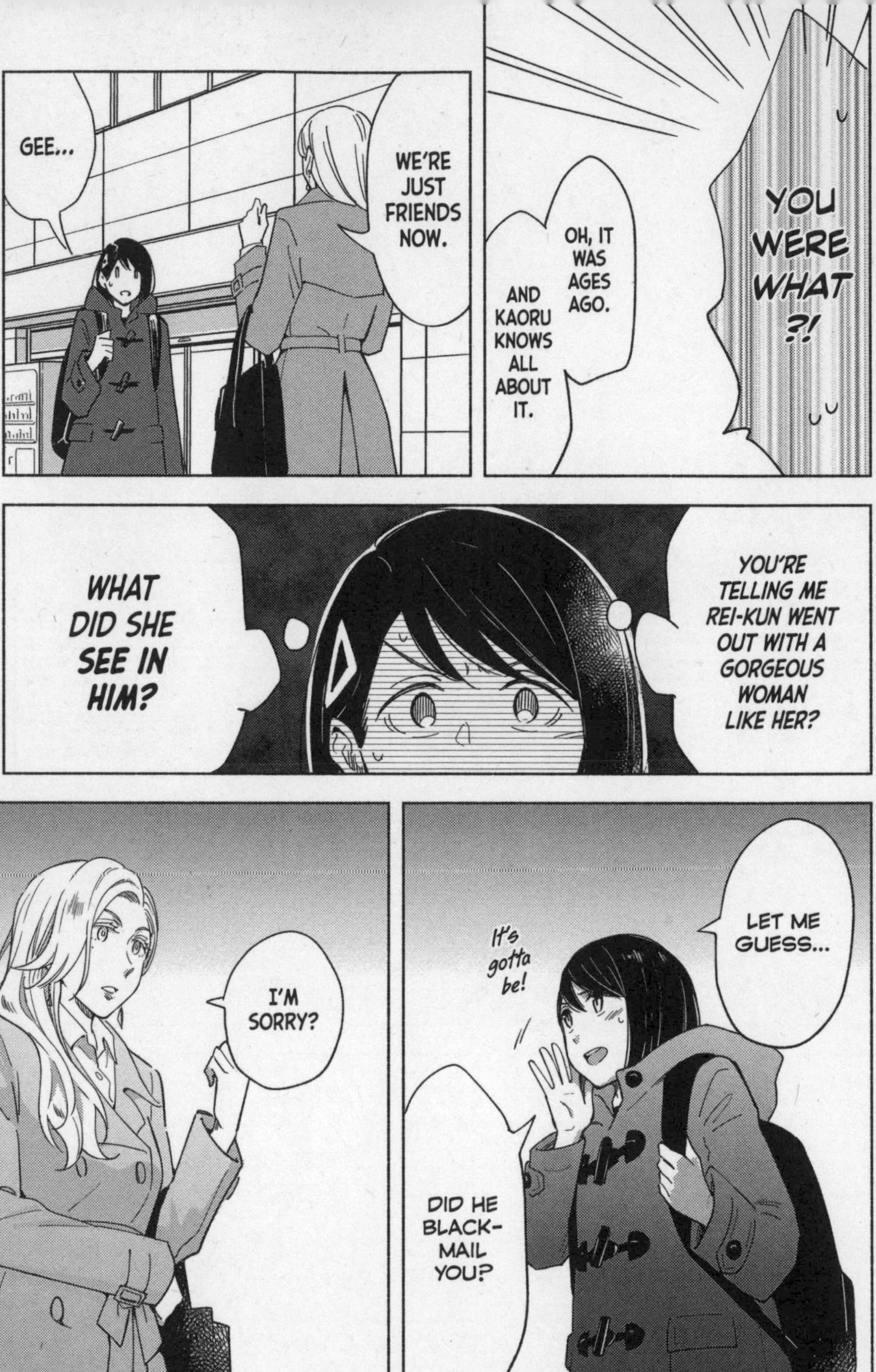
YOU WERE WHAT?!
OH, IT WAS AGES AGO.
AND KAORU KNOWS ALL ABOUT IT.
WE'RE JUST FRIENDS NOW.
GEE...
YOU'RE TELLING ME REI-KUN WENT OUT WITH A GORGEOUS WOMAN LIKE HER?
WHAT DID SHE SEE IN HIM?
LET ME GUESS...
It's gotta be!
DID HE BLACK-MAIL YOU?
I'M SORRY?

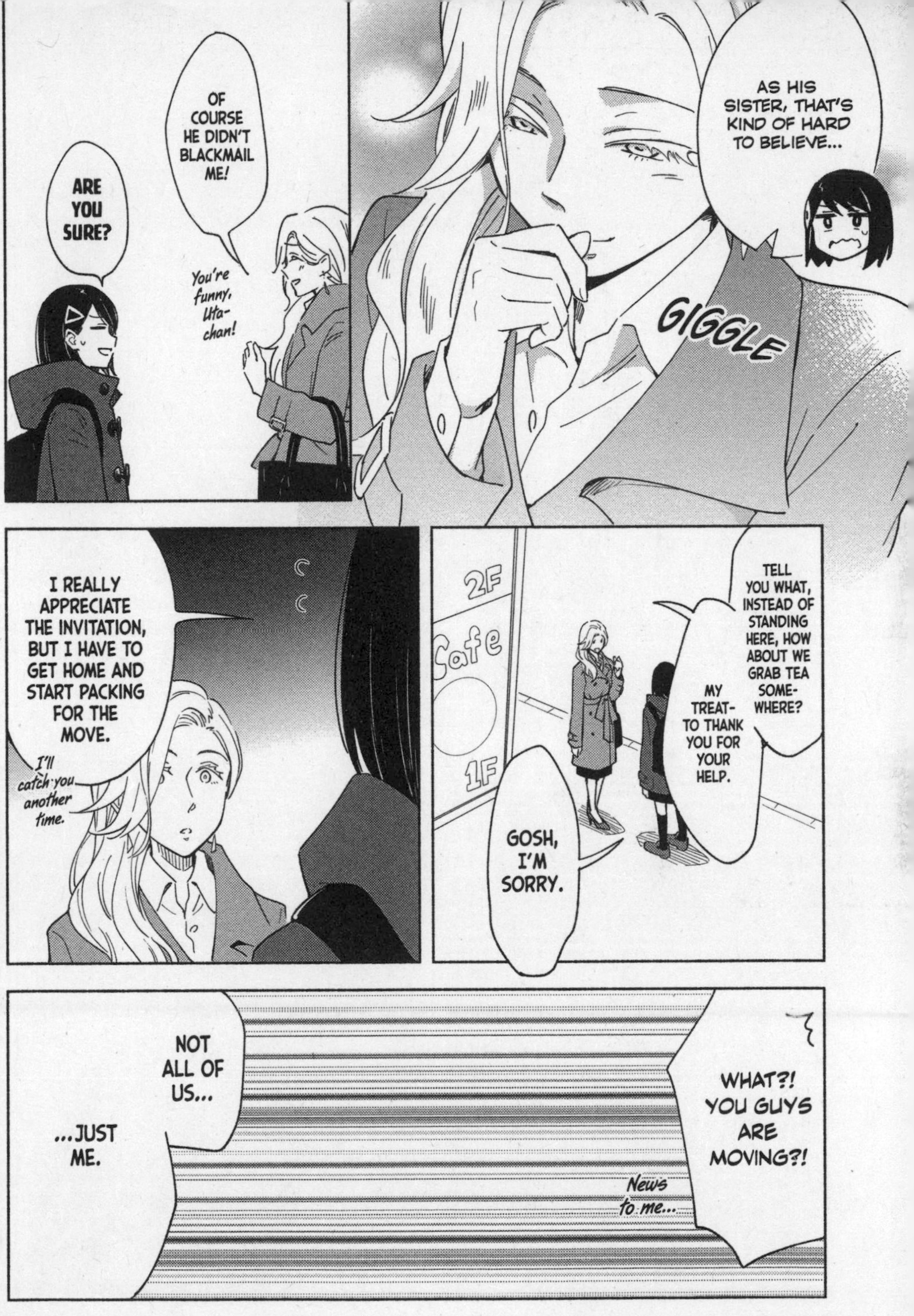
AS HIS SISTER, THAT'S KIND OF HARD TO BELIEVE...
GIGGLE
OF COURSE HE DIDN'T BLACKMAIL ME!
You're funny, Uta-chan!
ARE YOU SURE?
TELL YOU WHAT, INSTEAD OF STANDING HERE, HOW ABOUT WE GRAB TEA SOME-WHERE?
MY TREAT-TO THANK YOU FOR YOUR HELP.
GOSH, I'M SORRY.
I REALLY APPRECIATE THE INVITATION, BUT I HAVE TO GET HOME AND START PACKING FOR THE MOVE.
I'll catch you another time.
WHAT?! YOU GUYS ARE MOVING?!
News to me...
NOT ALL OF US...
...JUST ME.

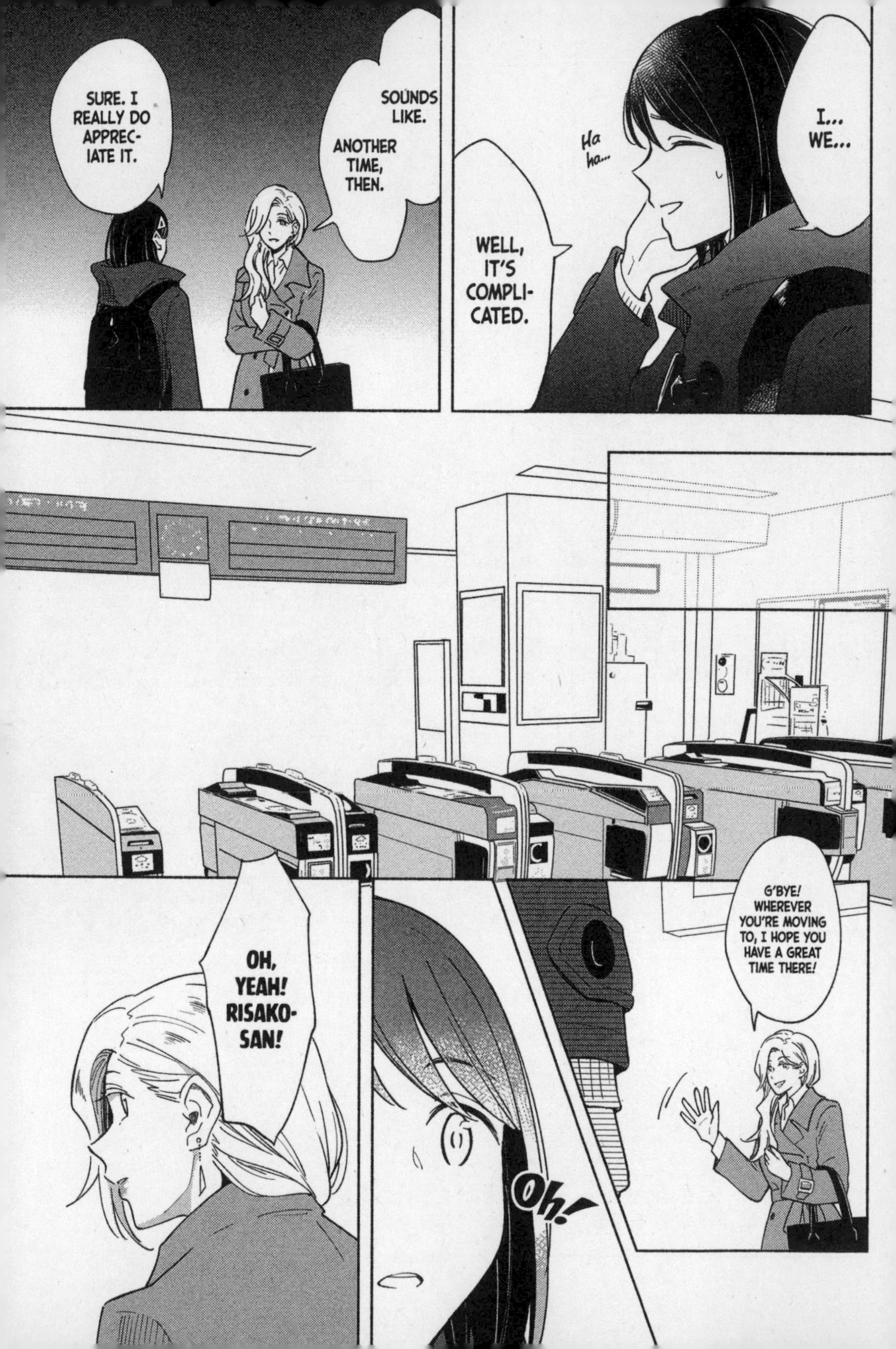
I... WE...
Ha ha...
WELL, IT'S COMPLICATED.
SOUNDS LIKE.
ANOTHER TIME, THEN.
SURE. I REALLY DO APPRECIATE IT.
G'BYE! WHEREVER YOU'RE MOVING TO, I HOPE YOU HAVE A GREAT TIME THERE!
Oh!
OH, YEAH! RISAKO-SAN!

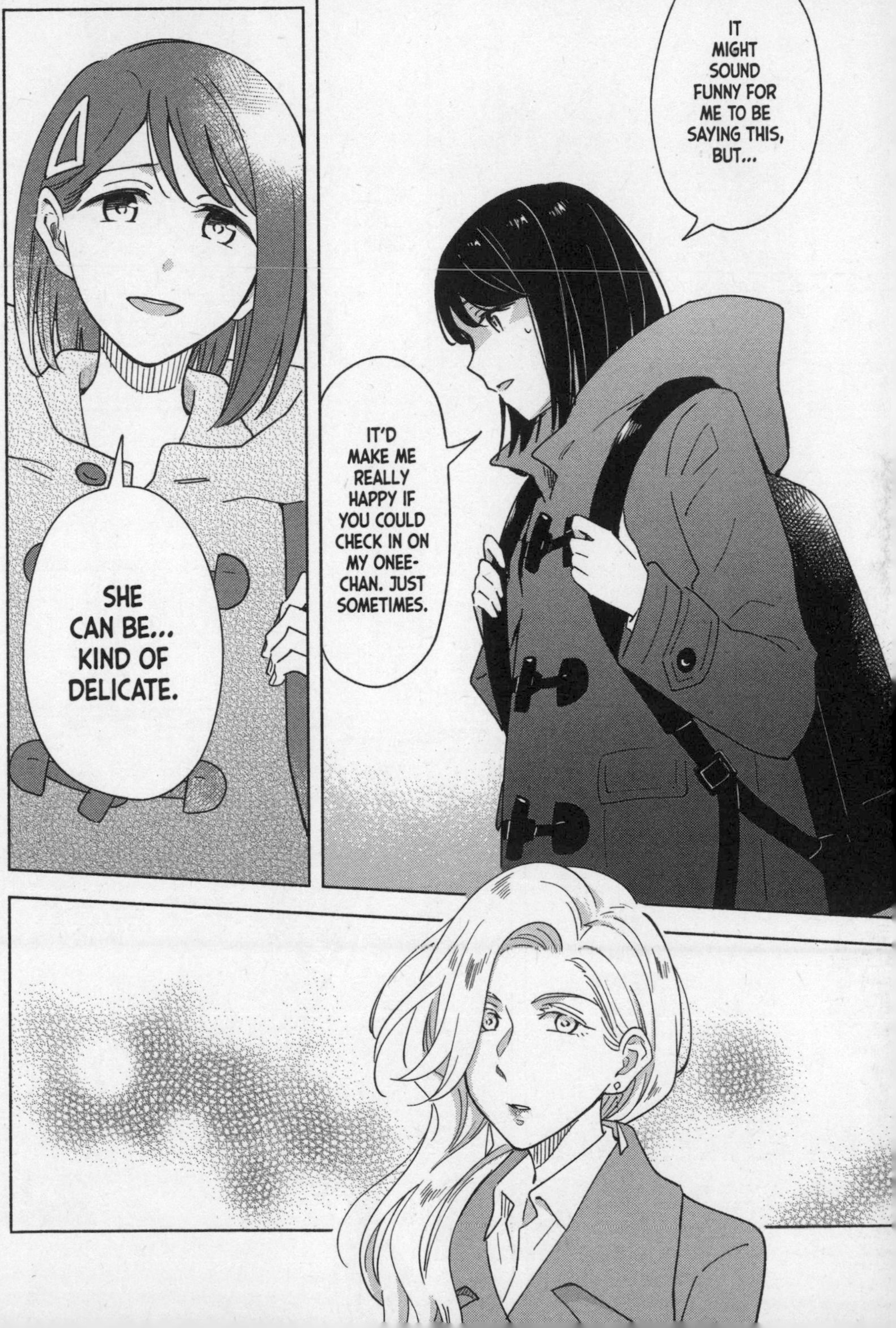
IT MIGHT SOUND FUNNY FOR ME TO BE SAYING THIS, BUT...
IT'D MAKE ME REALLY HAPPY IF YOU COULD CHECK IN ON MY ONEE-CHAN. JUST SOMETIMES.
SHE CAN BE... KIND OF DELICATE.

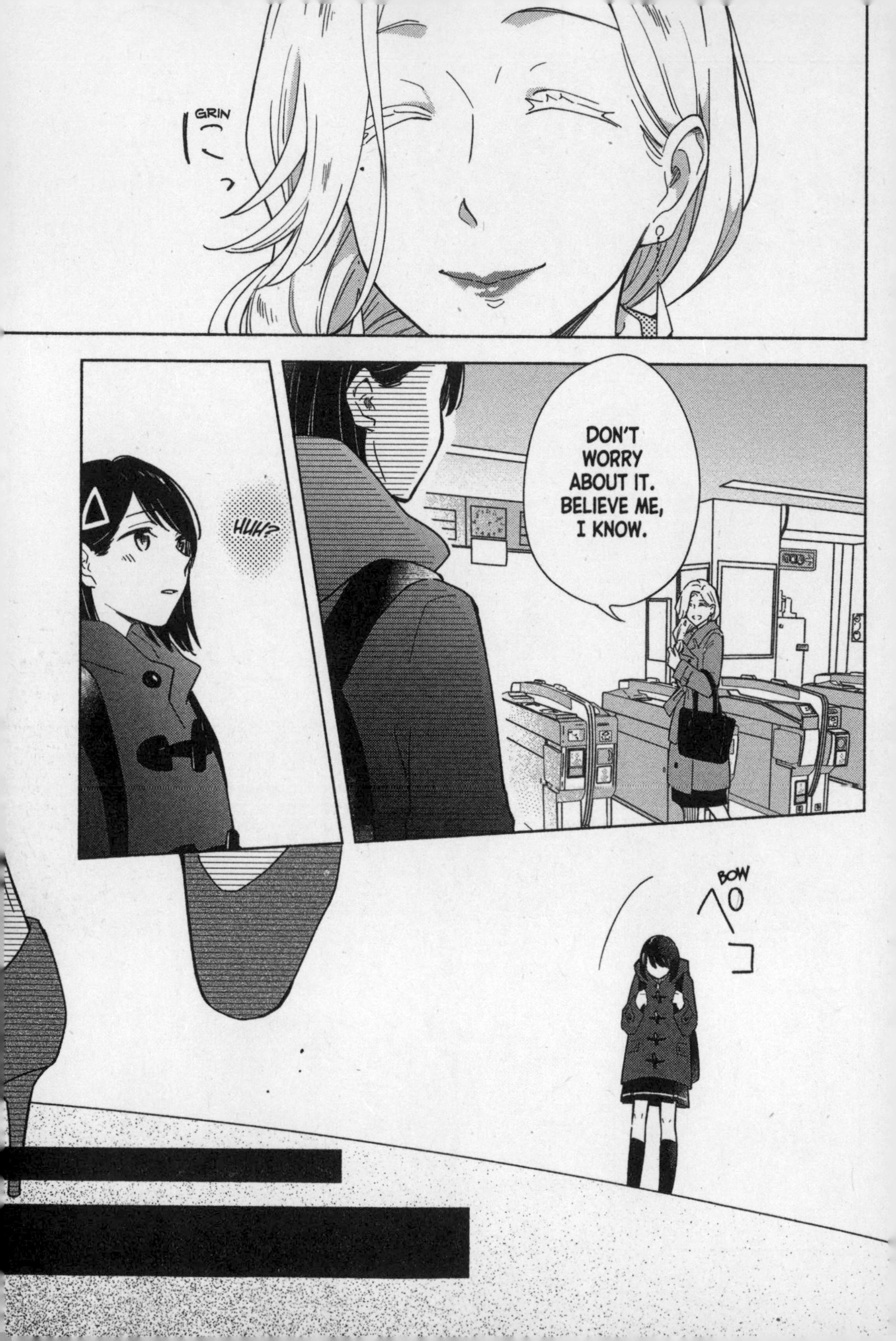
GRIN
DON'T WORRY ABOUT IT. BELIEVE ME, I KNOW.
HUH?
BOW

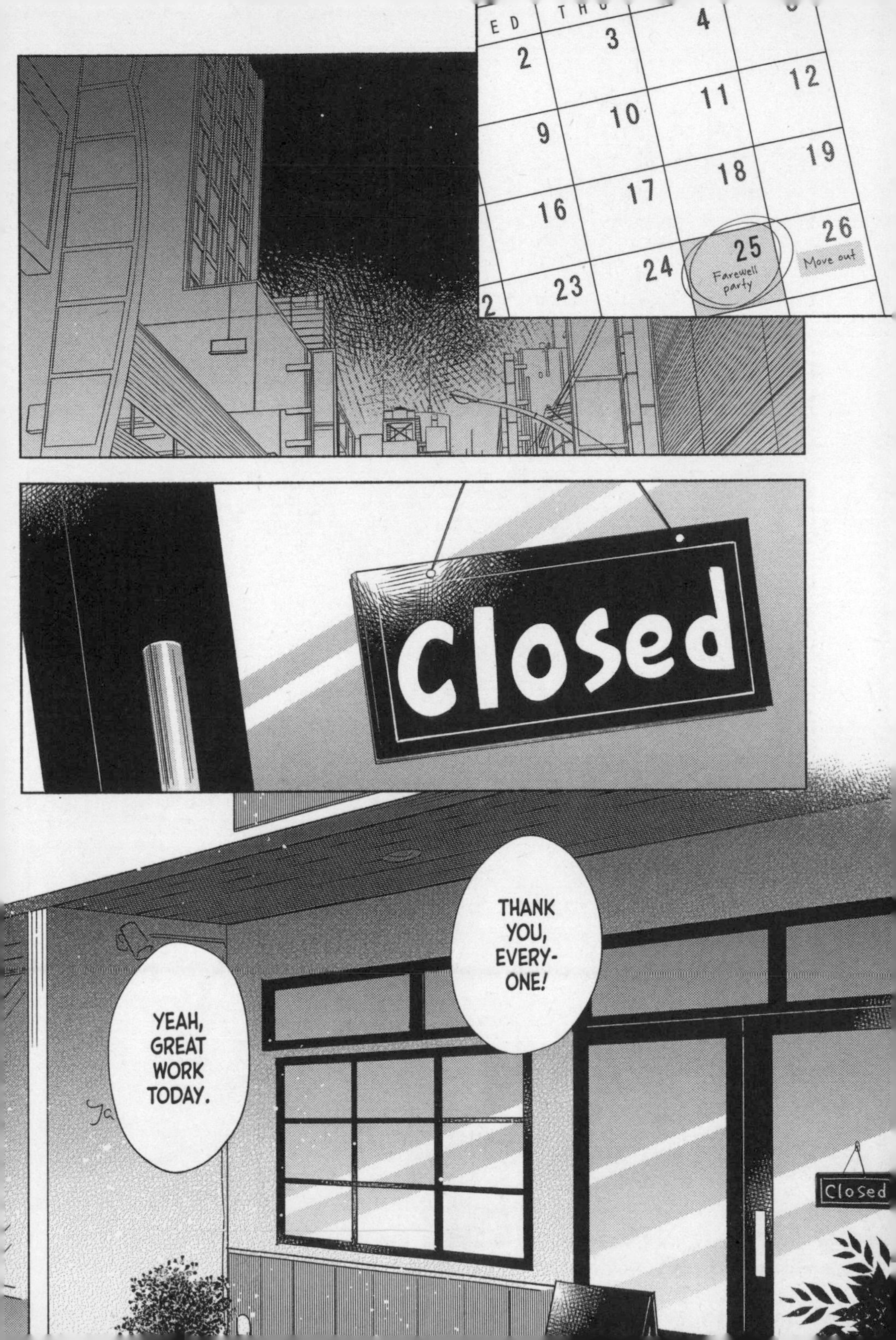
25 Farewell party
26 Move out
Closed
THANK YOU, EVERY-ONE!
YEAH, GREAT WORK TODAY.
Closed

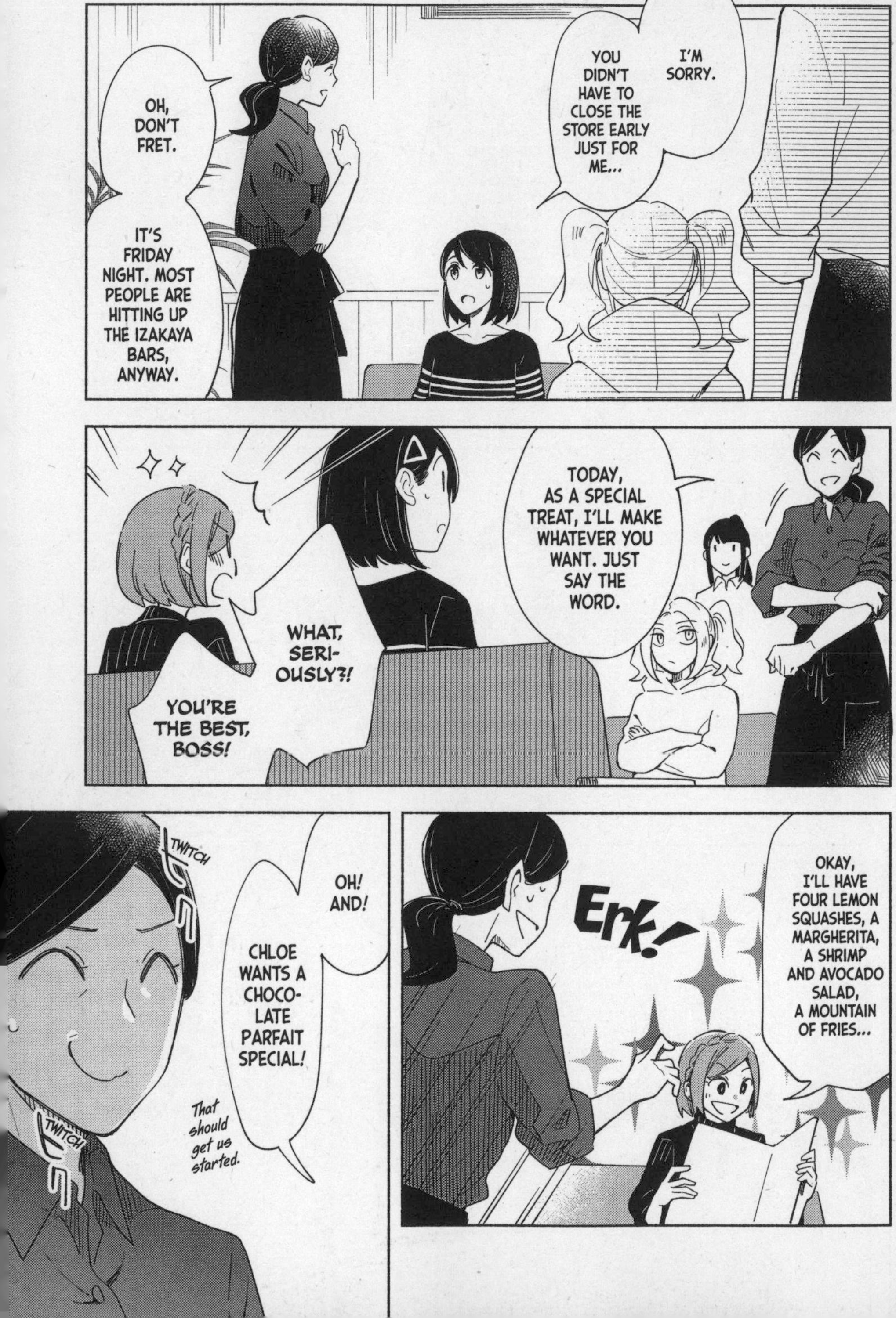
I'M SORRY.
YOU DIDN'T HAVE TO CLOSE THE STORE EARLY JUST FOR ME...
OH, DON'T FRET.
IT'S FRIDAY NIGHT. MOST PEOPLE ARE HITTING UP THE IZAKAYA BARS, ANYWAY.
TODAY, AS A SPECIAL TREAT, I'LL MAKE WHATEVER YOU WANT. JUST SAY THE WORD.
WHAT, SERI-OUSLY?!
YOU'RE THE BEST, BOSS!
OKAY, I'LL HAVE FOUR LEMON SQUASHES, A MARGHERITA, A SHRIMP AND AVOCADO SALAD, A MOUNTAIN OF FRIES...
Erk!
TWITCH
OH! AND!
CHLOE WANTS A CHOCO-LATE PARFAIT SPECIAL!
That should get us started.
TWITCH

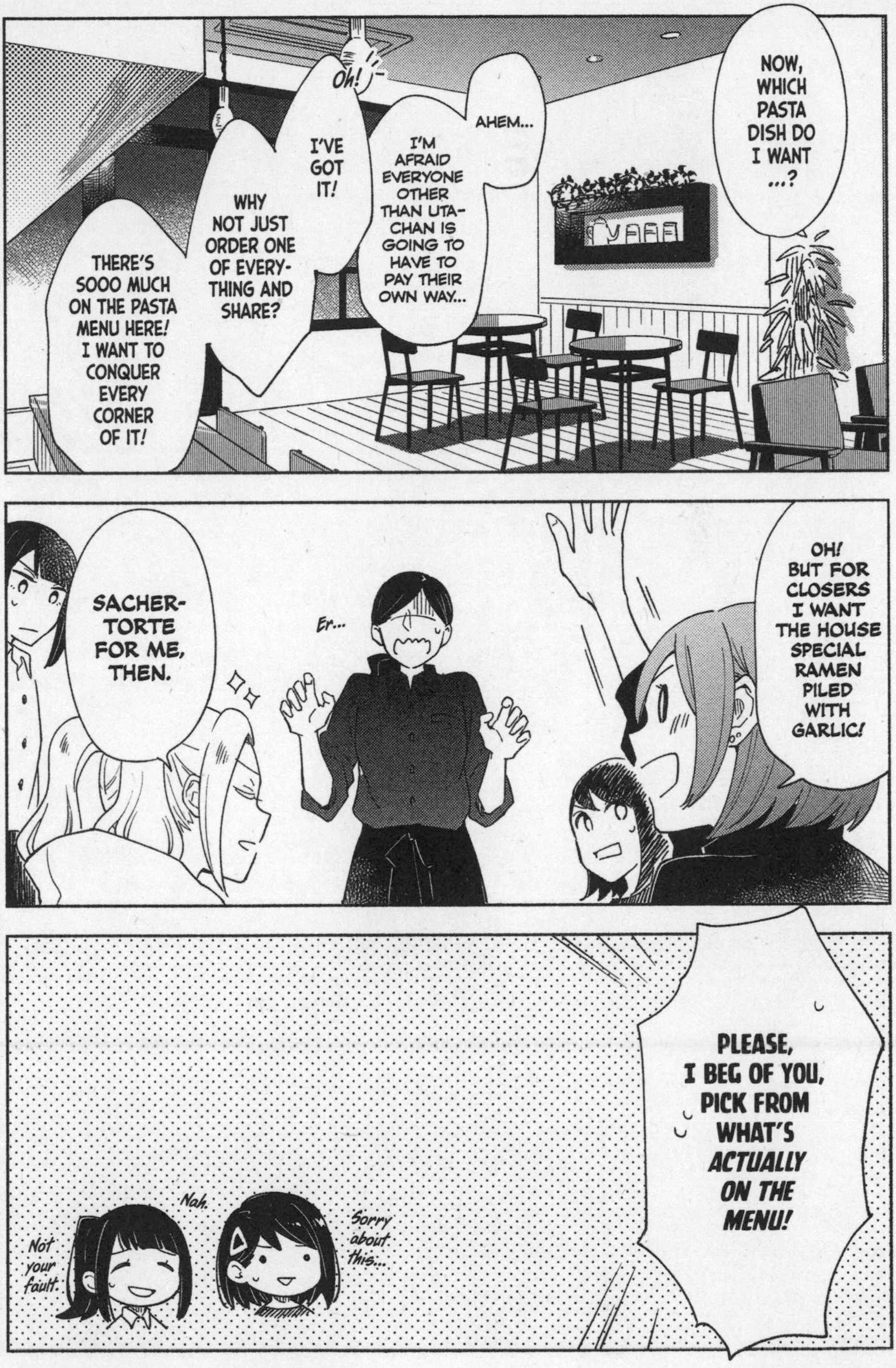
NOW, WHICH PASTA DISH DO I WANT ...?
AHEM...
I'M AFRAID EVERYONE OTHER THAN UTA-CHAN IS GOING TO HAVE TO PAY THEIR OWN WAY...
Oh!
I'VE GOT IT!
WHY NOT JUST ORDER ONE OF EVERY-THING AND SHARE?
THERE'S SOOO MUCH ON THE PASTA MENU HERE! I WANT TO CONQUER EVERY CORNER OF IT!
OH! BUT FOR CLOSERS I WANT THE HOUSE SPECIAL RAMEN PILED WITH GARLIC!
Er...
SACHER-TORTE FOR ME, THEN.
PLEASE, I BEG OF YOU, PICK FROM WHAT'S *ACTUALLY* ON THE MENU!
Sorry about this...
Nah.
Not your fault.

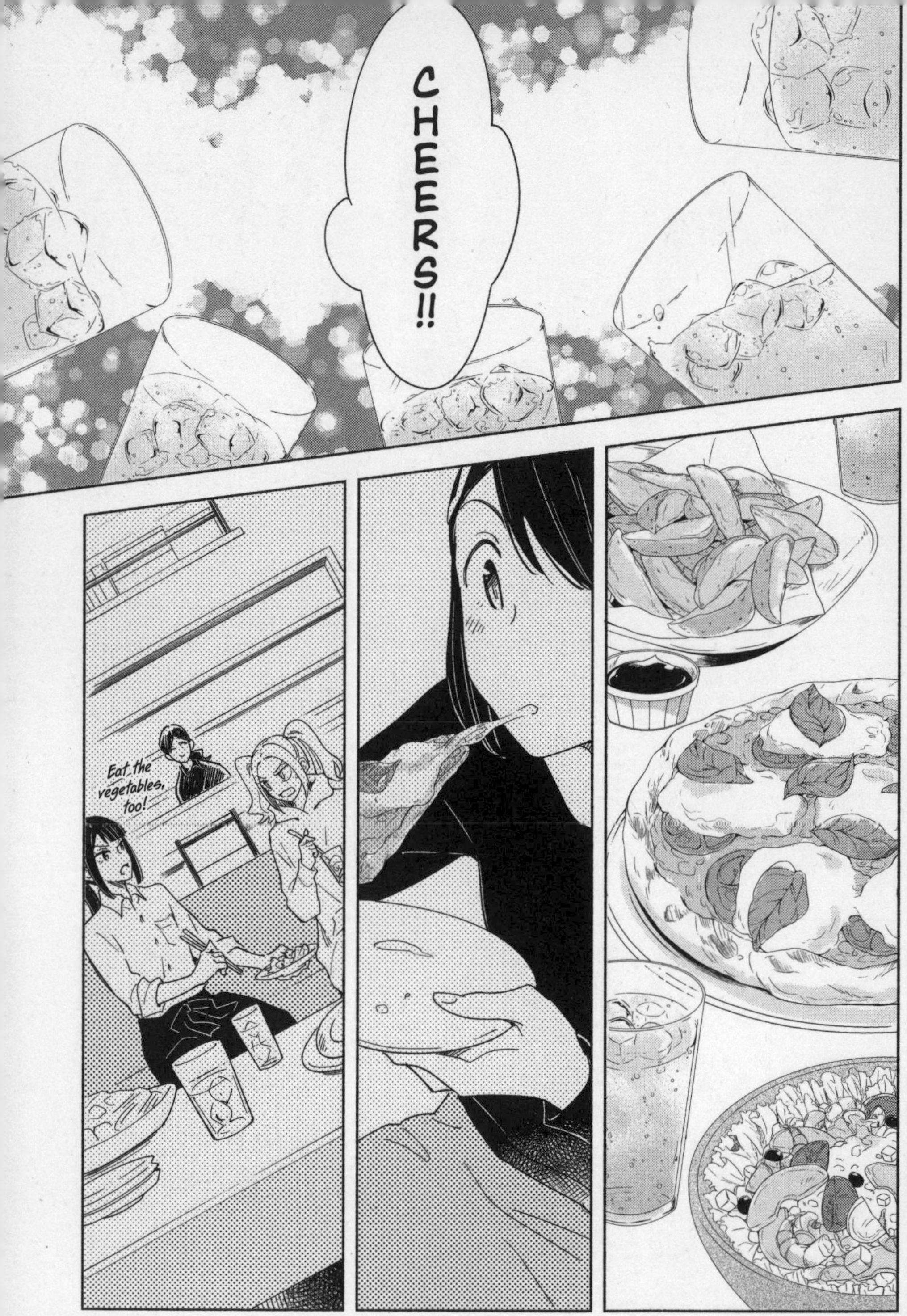
CHEERS!!
Eat the vegetables, too!

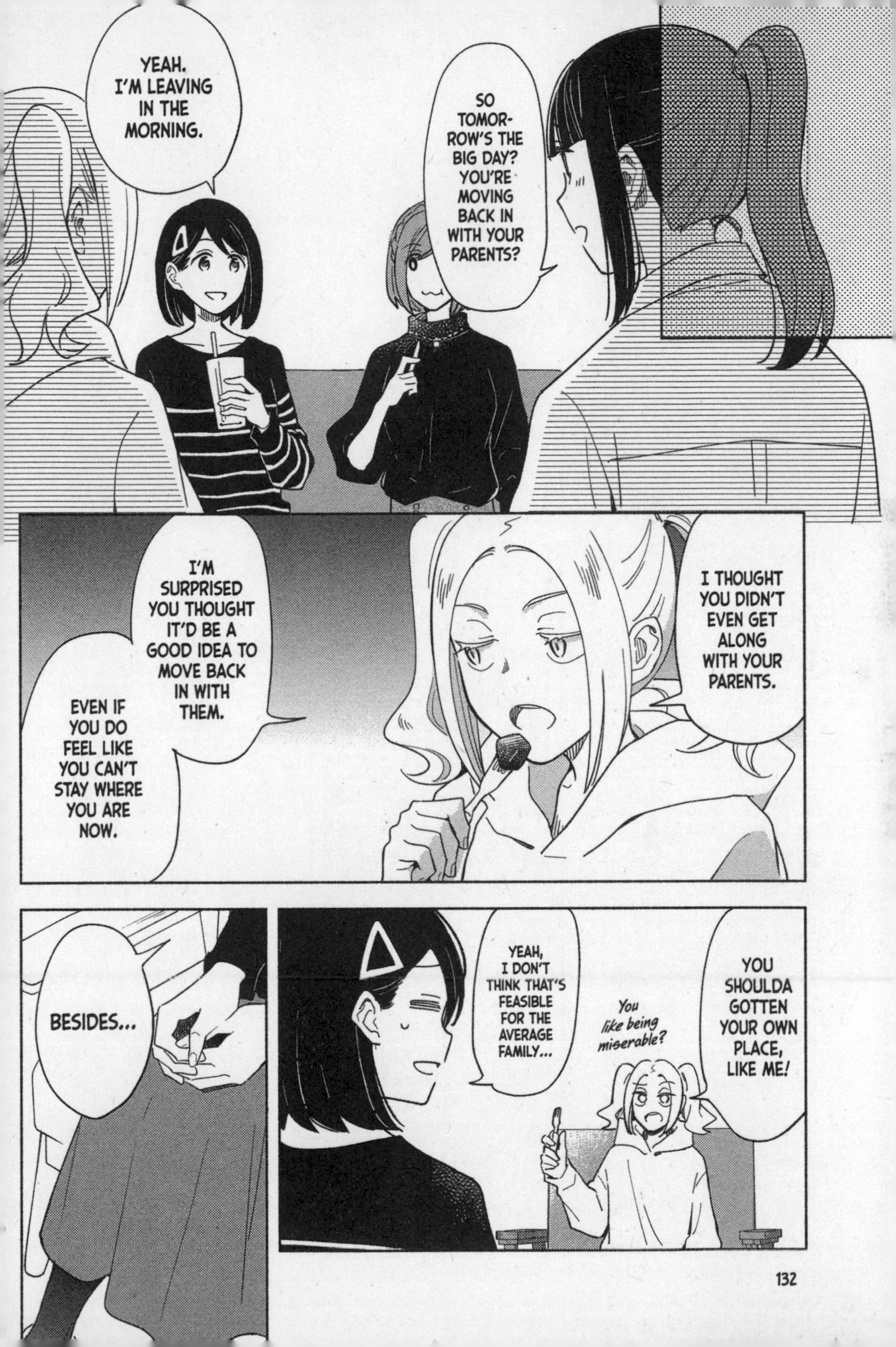
SO TOMORROW'S THE BIG DAY? YOU'RE MOVING BACK IN WITH YOUR PARENTS?
YEAH. I'M LEAVING IN THE MORNING.
I THOUGHT YOU DIDN'T EVEN GET ALONG WITH YOUR PARENTS.
I'M SURPRISED YOU THOUGHT IT'D BE A GOOD IDEA TO MOVE BACK IN WITH THEM.
EVEN IF YOU DO FEEL LIKE YOU CAN'T STAY WHERE YOU ARE NOW.
YOU SHOULDA GOTTEN YOUR OWN PLACE, LIKE ME!
You like being miserable?
YEAH, I DON'T THINK THAT'S FEASIBLE FOR THE AVERAGE FAMILY...
BESIDES...

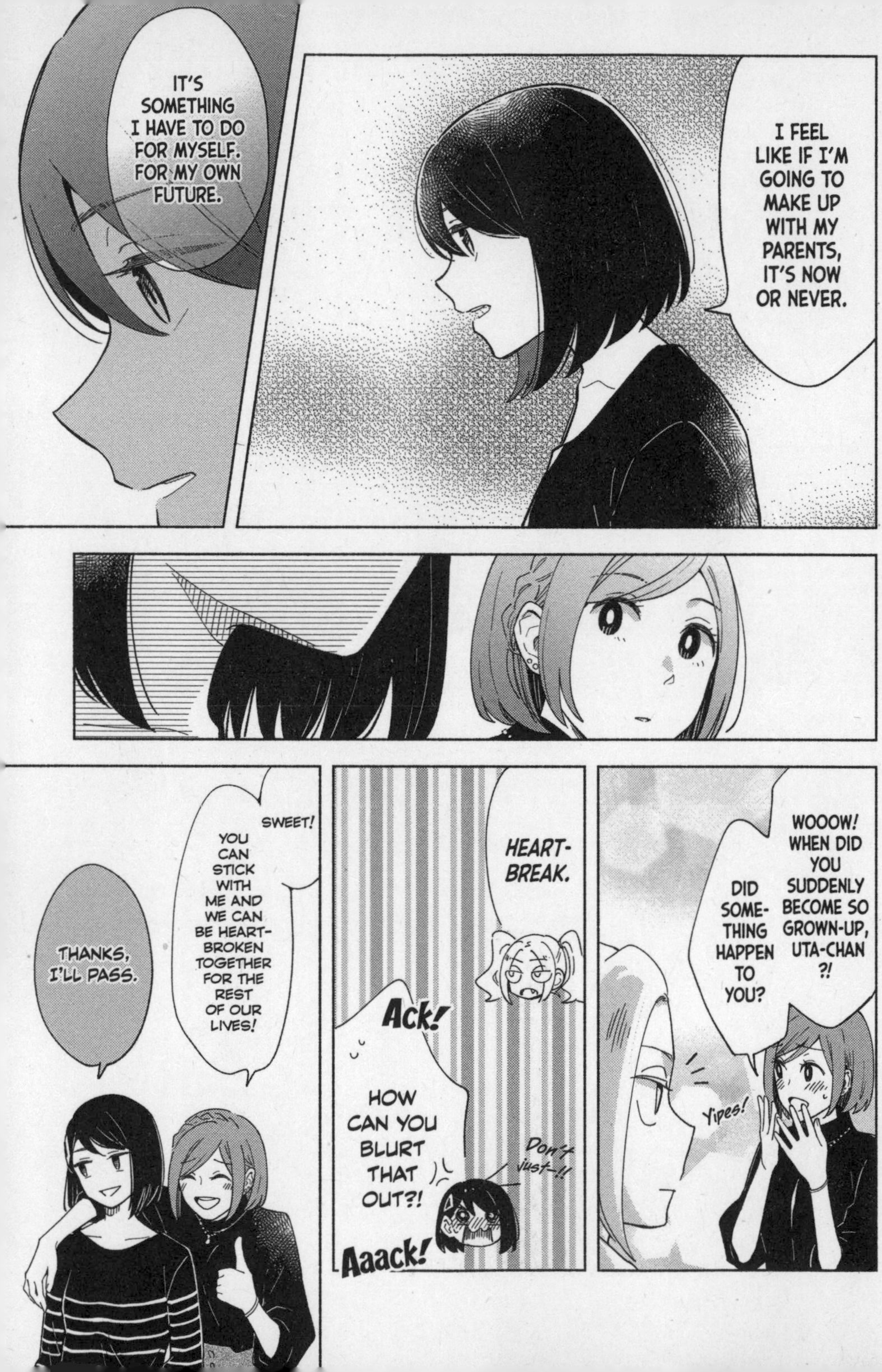
I FEEL LIKE IF I'M GOING TO MAKE UP WITH MY PARENTS, IT'S NOW OR NEVER.
IT'S SOMETHING I HAVE TO DO FOR MYSELF. FOR MY OWN FUTURE.
WOOOW! WHEN DID YOU SUDDENLY BECOME SO GROWN-UP, UTA-CHAN?!
DID SOMETHING HAPPEN TO YOU?
Yipes!
HEART-BREAK.
Ack!
HOW CAN YOU BLURT THAT OUT?!
Don't just--!!
Aaack!
YOU CAN STICK WITH ME AND WE CAN BE HEART-BROKEN TOGETHER FOR THE REST OF OUR LIVES!
SWEET!
THANKS, I'LL PASS.

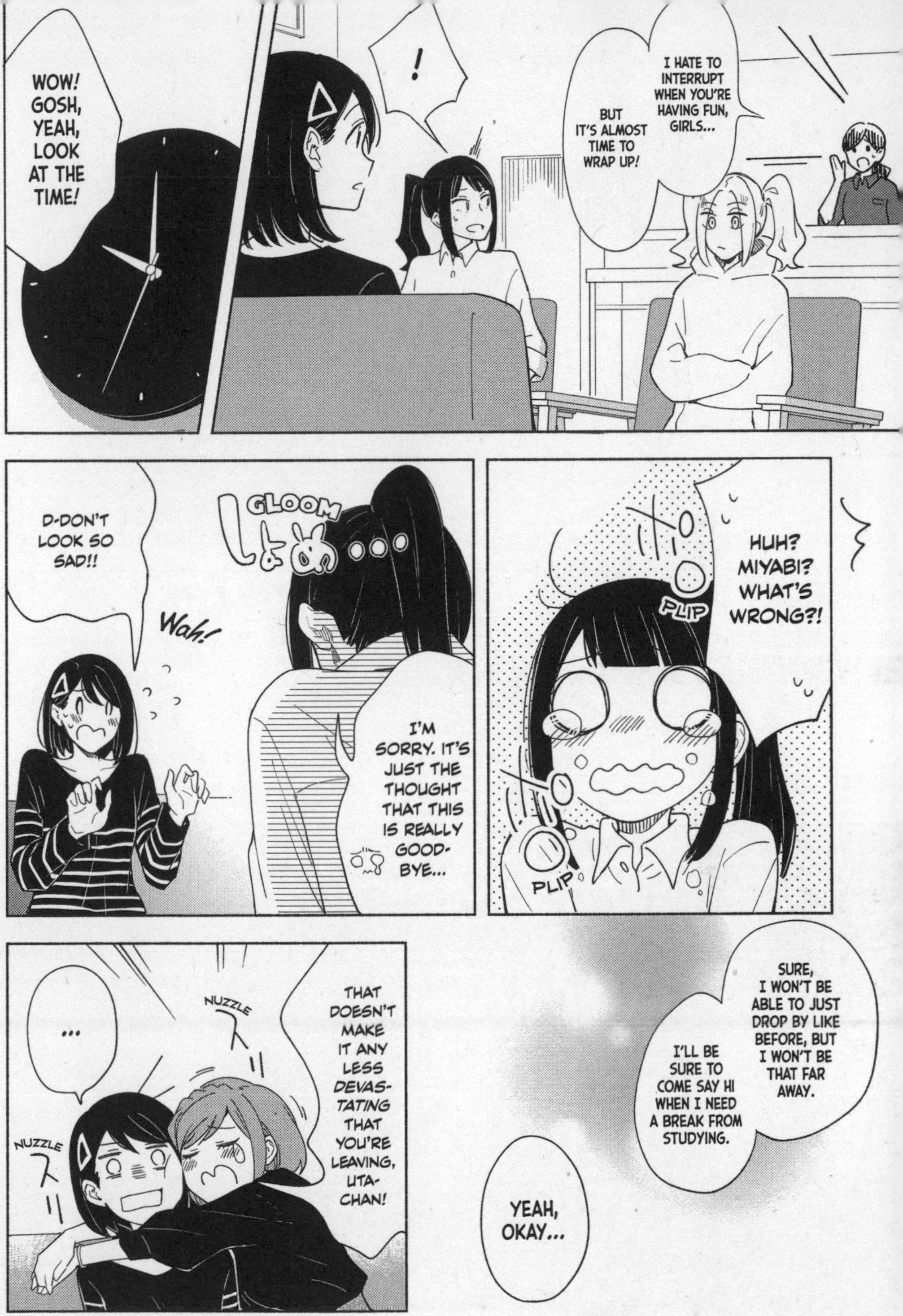
I HATE TO INTERRUPT WHEN YOU'RE HAVING FUN, GIRLS...
BUT IT'S ALMOST TIME TO WRAP UP!
!
WOW! GOSH, YEAH, LOOK AT THE TIME!
HUH? MIYABI? WHAT'S WRONG?!
PLIP
PLIP
GLOOM
I'M SORRY. IT'S JUST THE THOUGHT THAT THIS IS REALLY GOOD-BYE...
D-DON'T LOOK SO SAD!!
Wah!
SURE, I WON'T BE ABLE TO JUST DROP BY LIKE BEFORE, BUT I WON'T BE THAT FAR AWAY.
I'LL BE SURE TO COME SAY HI WHEN I NEED A BREAK FROM STUDYING.
YEAH, OKAY...
THAT DOESN'T MAKE IT ANY LESS *DEVASTATING* THAT YOU'RE LEAVING, UTA-CHAN!
NUZZLE
...
NUZZLE

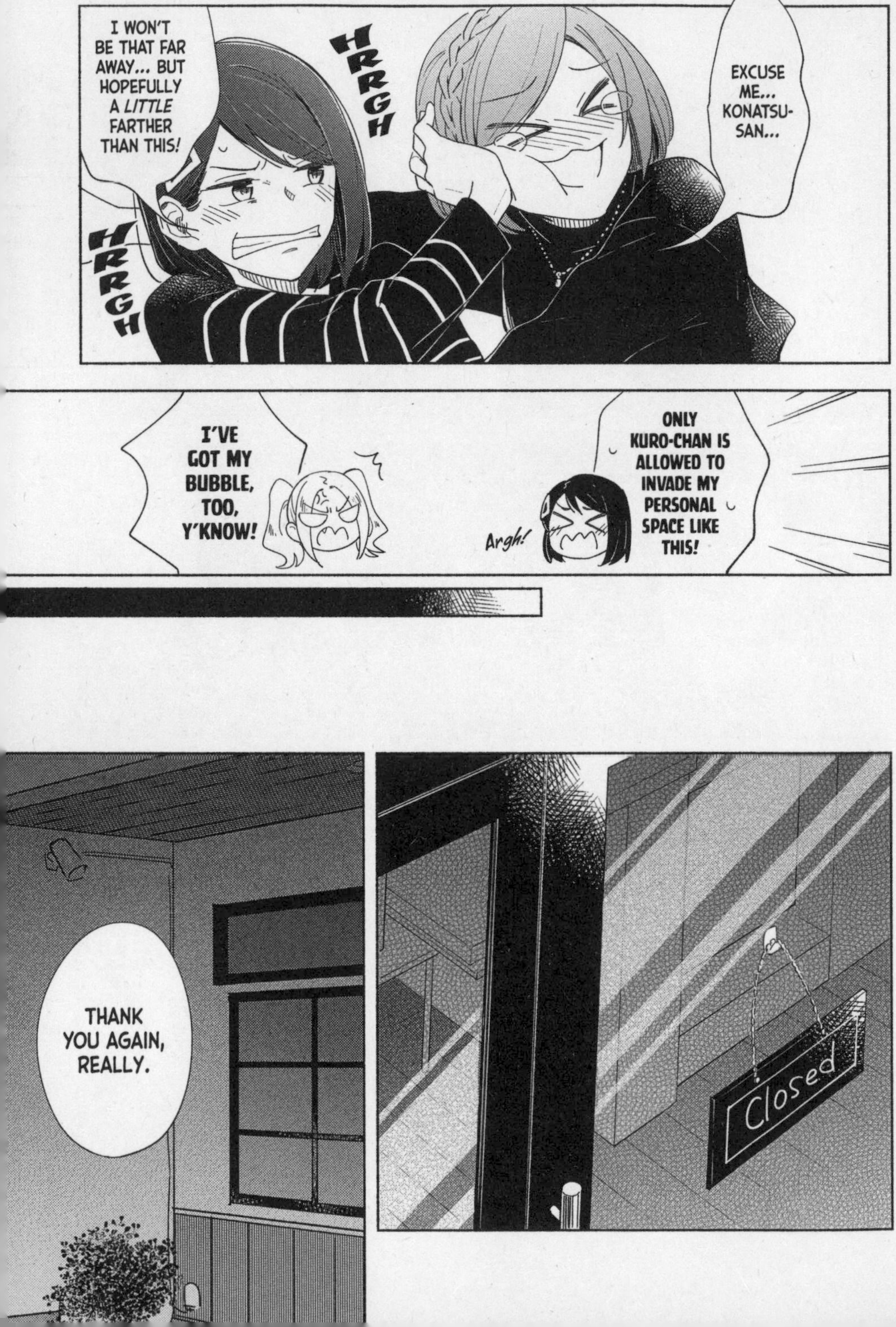
EXCUSE ME... KONATSU-SAN...
HRRGH
I WON'T BE THAT FAR AWAY... BUT HOPEFULLY A *LITTLE* FARTHER THAN THIS!
HRRGH
ONLY KURO-CHAN IS ALLOWED TO INVADE MY PERSONAL SPACE LIKE THIS!
Argh!
I'VE GOT MY BUBBLE, TOO, Y'KNOW!
Closed
THANK YOU AGAIN, REALLY.

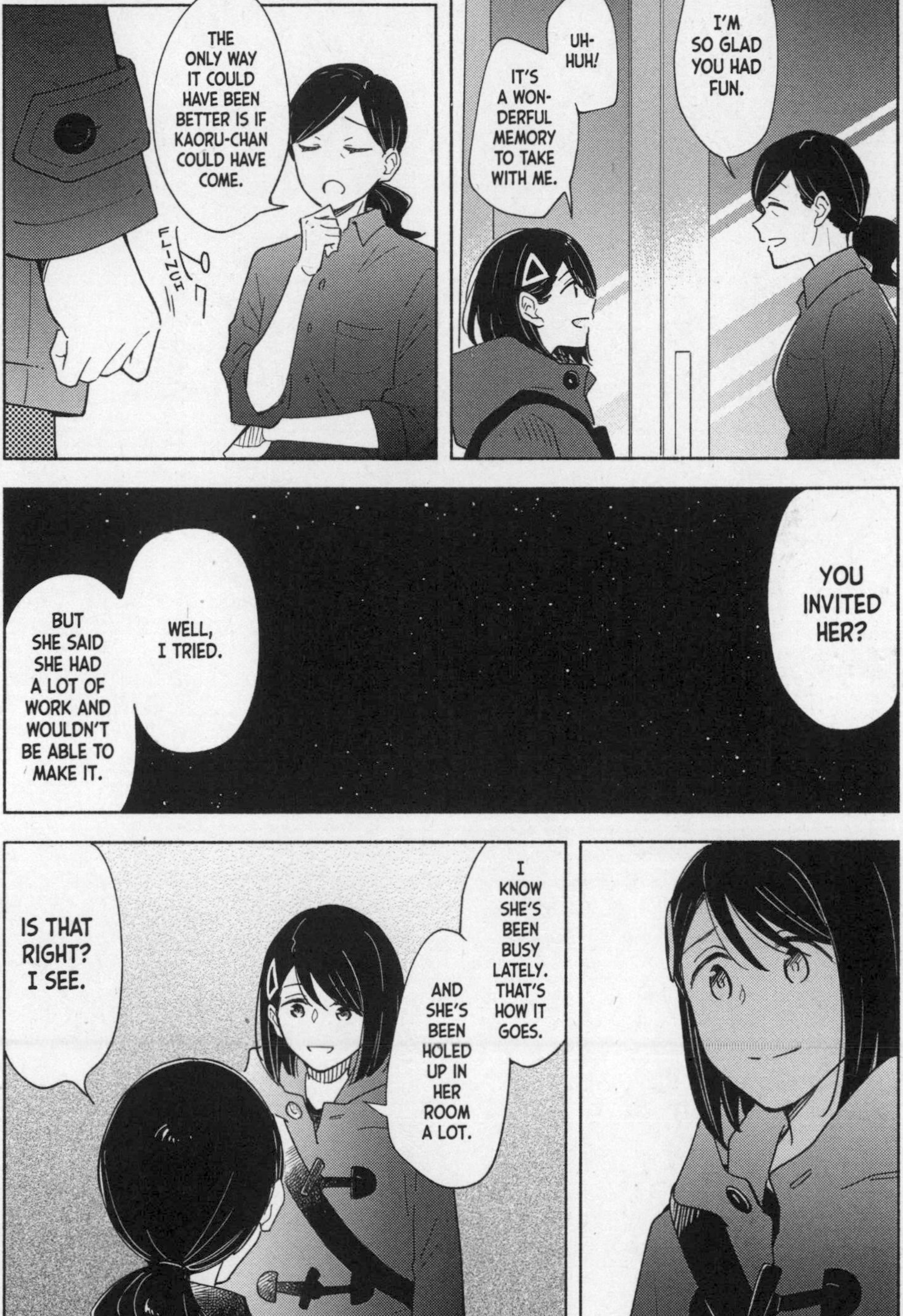
I'M SO GLAD YOU HAD FUN.
UH-HUH! IT'S A WON-DERFUL MEMORY TO TAKE WITH ME.
THE ONLY WAY IT COULD HAVE BEEN BETTER IS IF KAORU-CHAN COULD HAVE COME.
FLINCH
YOU INVITED HER?
WELL, I TRIED.
BUT SHE SAID SHE HAD A LOT OF WORK AND WOULDN'T BE ABLE TO MAKE IT.
I KNOW SHE'S BEEN BUSY LATELY. THAT'S HOW IT GOES.
AND SHE'S BEEN HOLED UP IN HER ROOM A LOT.
IS THAT RIGHT? I SEE.

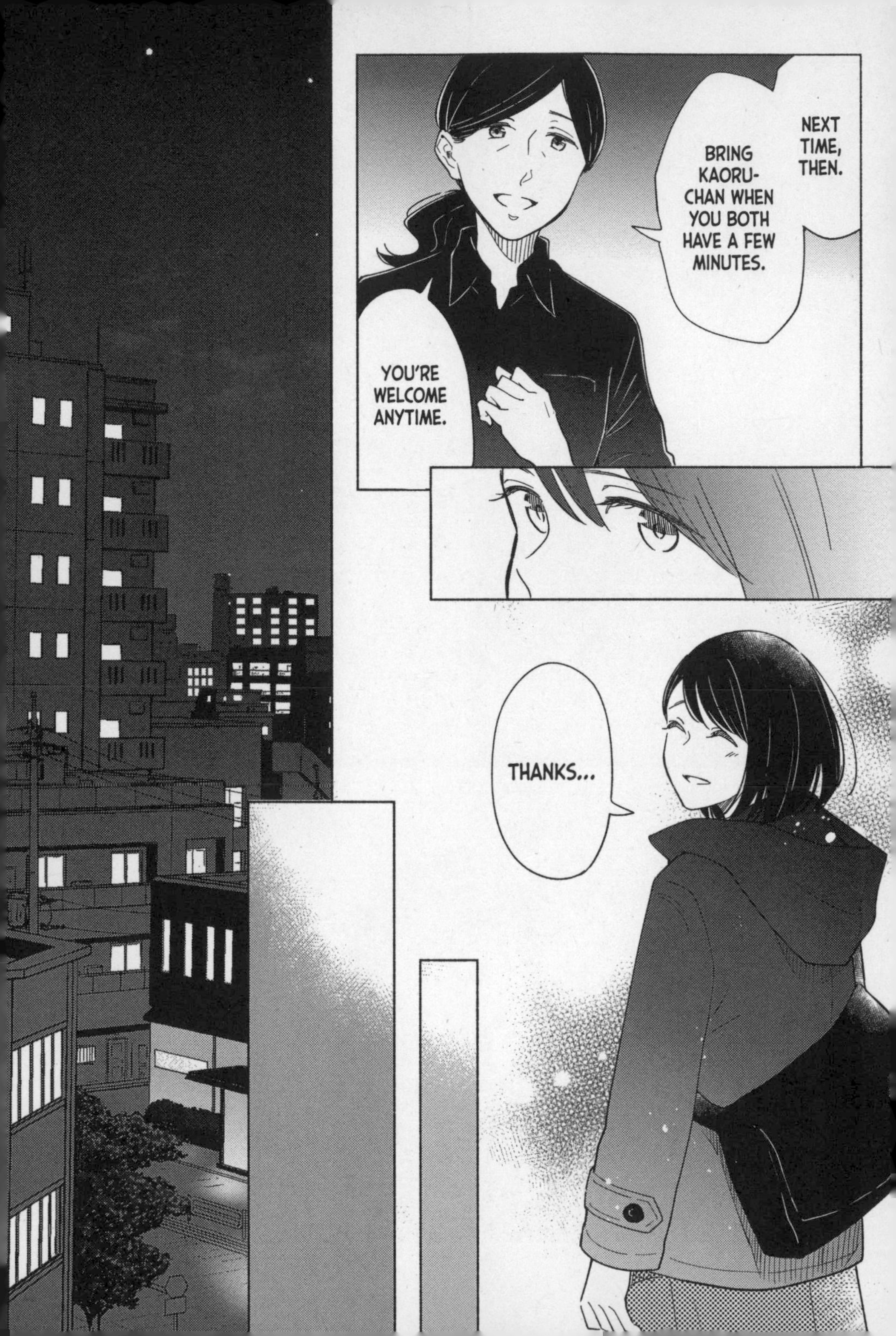
NEXT TIME, THEN.
BRING KAORU-CHAN WHEN YOU BOTH HAVE A FEW MINUTES.
YOU'RE WELCOME ANYTIME.
THANKS...

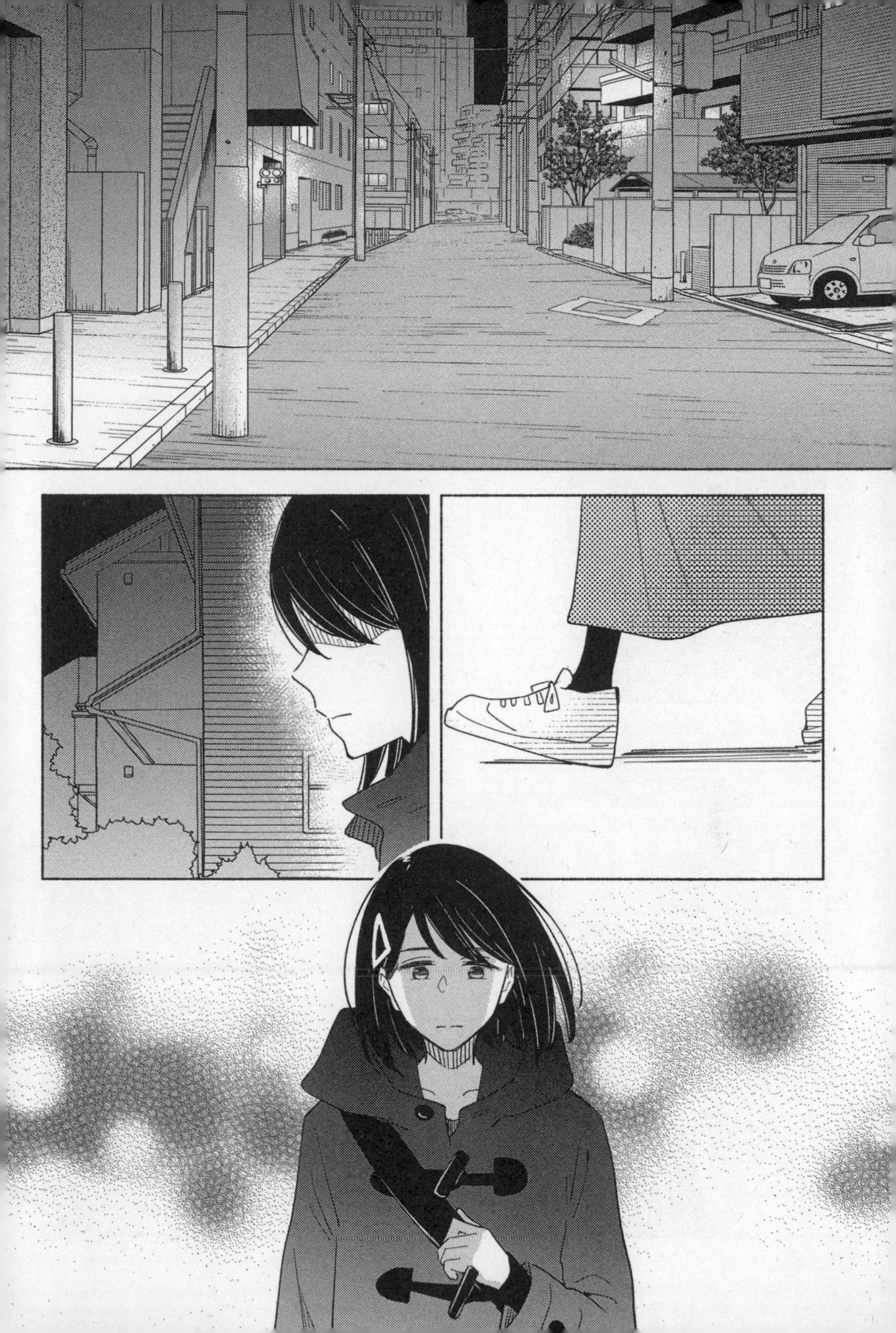

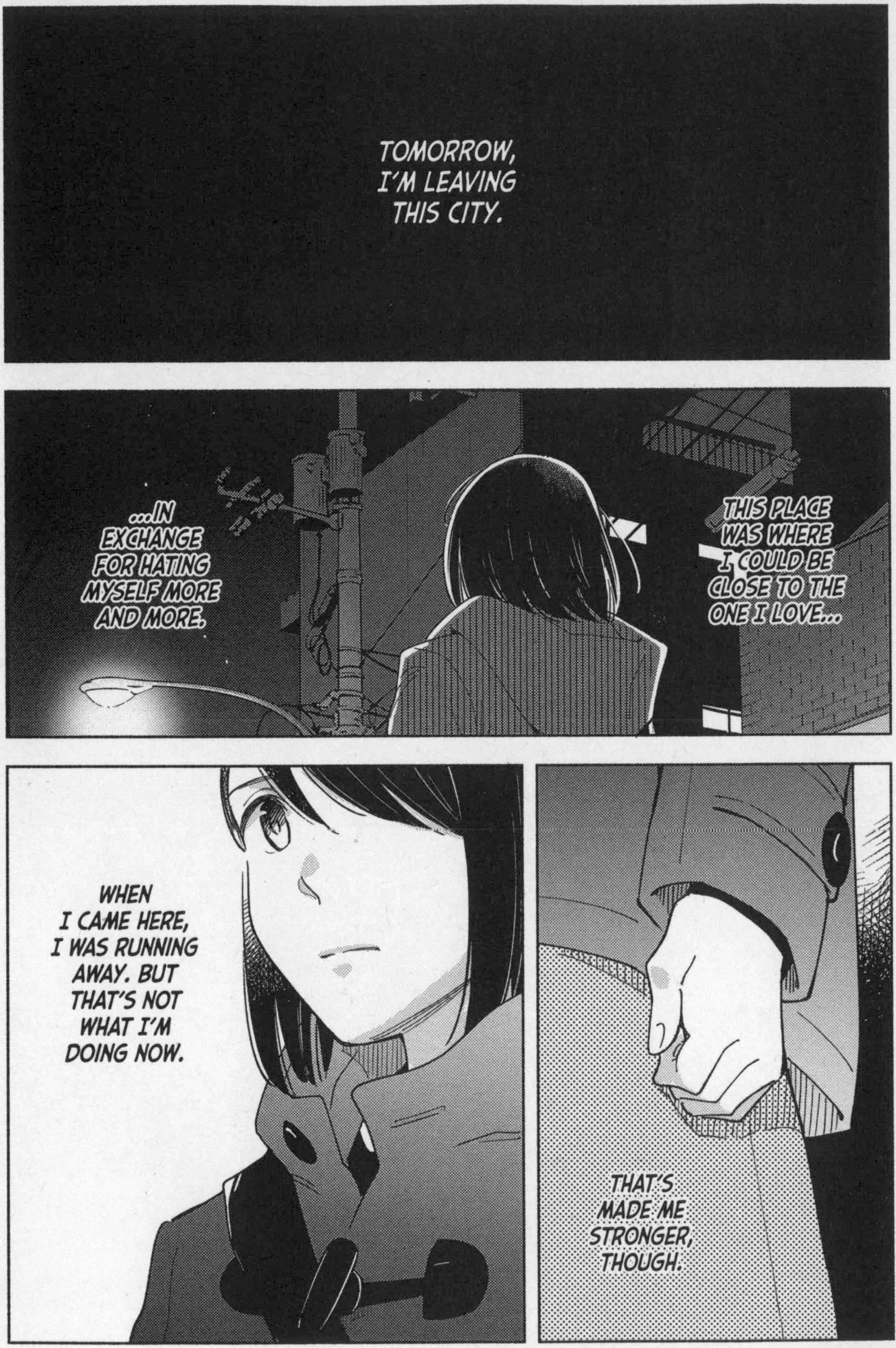
TOMORROW, I'M LEAVING THIS CITY.
THIS PLACE WAS WHERE I COULD BE CLOSE TO THE ONE I LOVE...
...IN EXCHANGE FOR HATING MYSELF MORE AND MORE.
THAT'S MADE ME STRONGER, THOUGH.
WHEN I CAME HERE, I WAS RUNNING AWAY. BUT THAT'S NOT WHAT I'M DOING NOW.

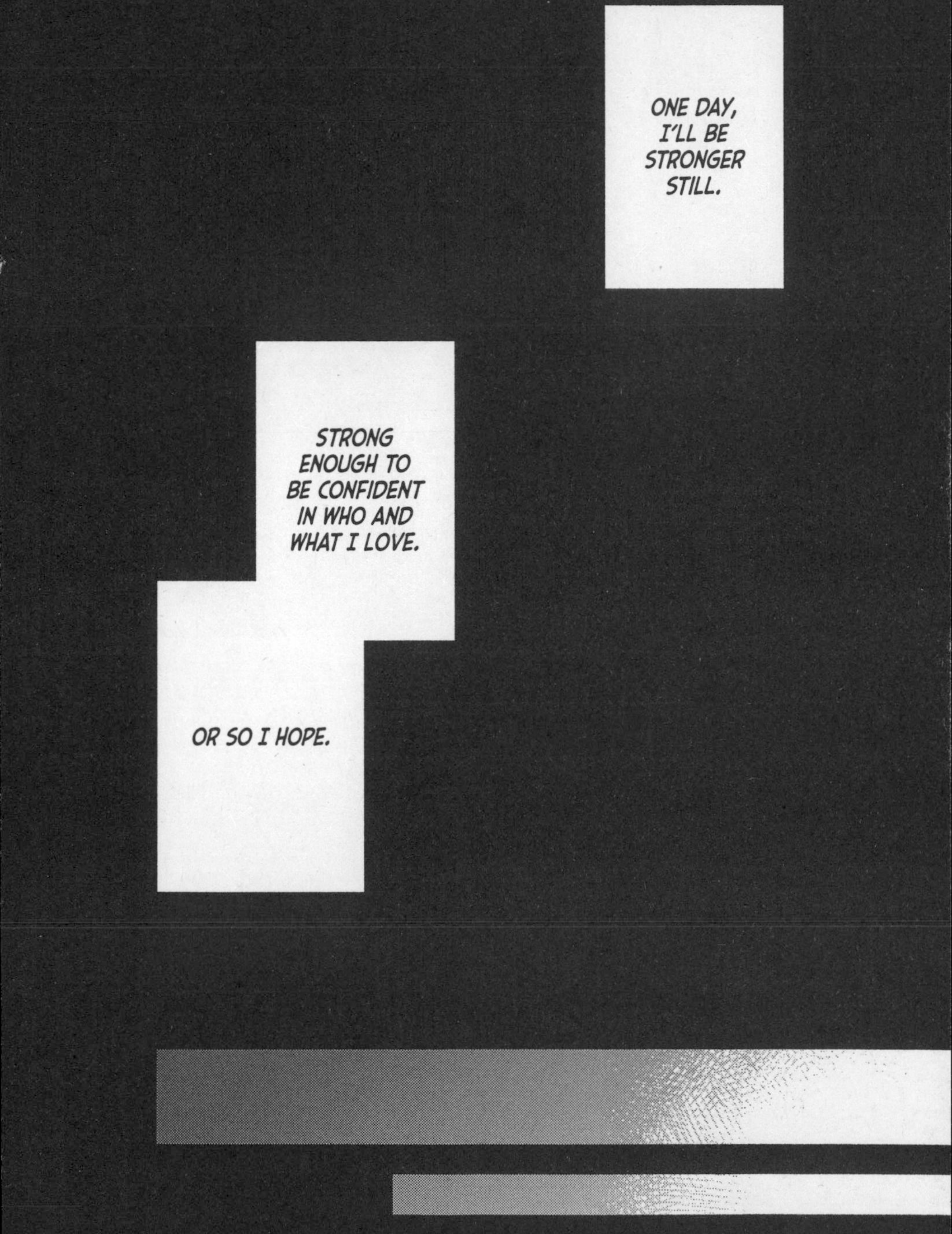
ONE DAY, I'LL BE STRONGER STILL.
STRONG ENOUGH TO BE CONFIDENT IN WHO AND WHAT I LOVE.
OR SO I HOPE.

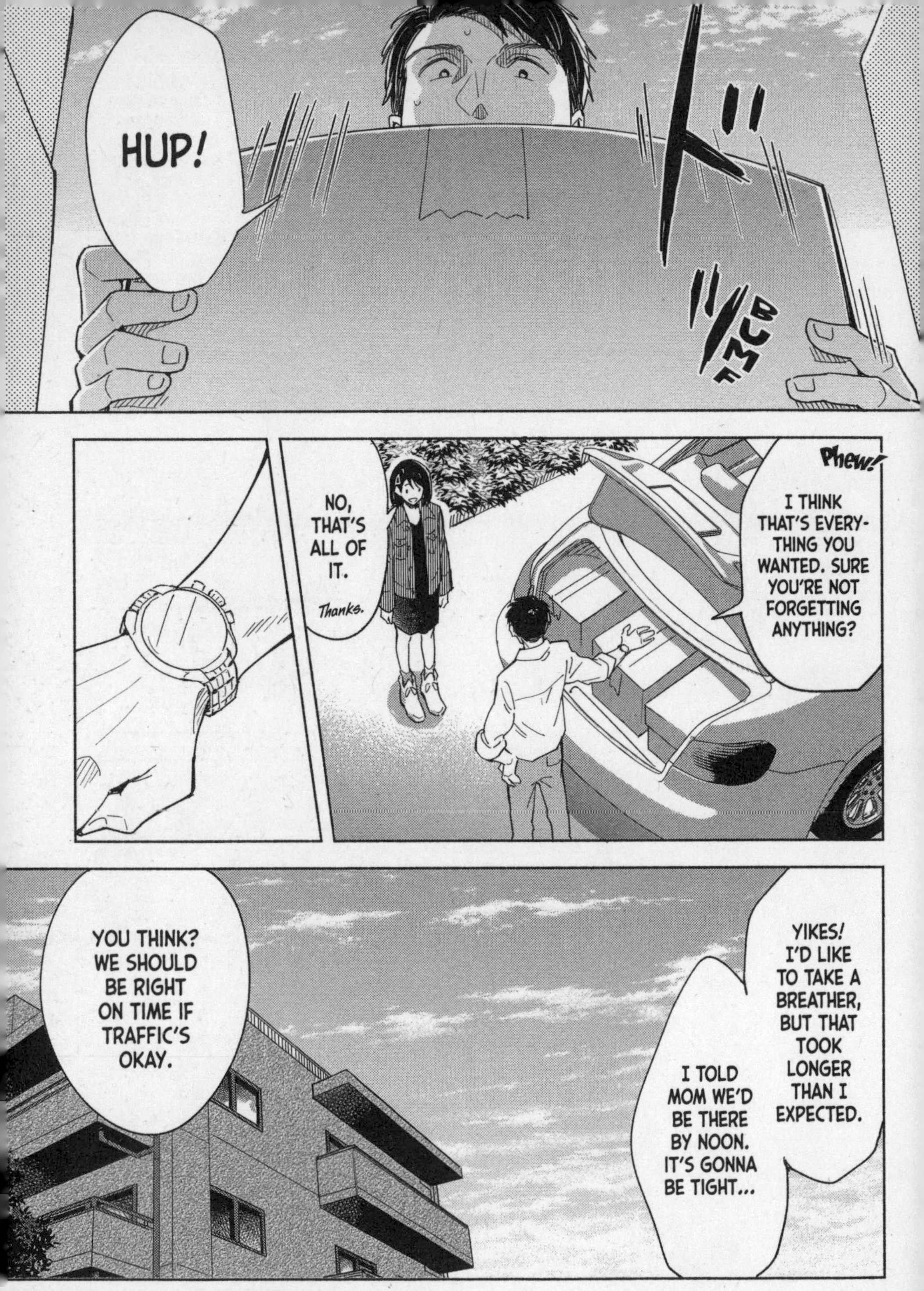
HUP!
BUMF
Phew!
I THINK THAT'S EVERY-THING YOU WANTED. SURE YOU'RE NOT FORGETTING ANYTHING?
NO, THAT'S ALL OF IT.
Thanks.
YIKES! I'D LIKE TO TAKE A BREATHER, BUT THAT TOOK LONGER THAN I EXPECTED.
I TOLD MOM WE'D BE THERE BY NOON. IT'S GONNA BE TIGHT...
YOU THINK? WE SHOULD BE RIGHT ON TIME IF TRAFFIC'S OKAY.

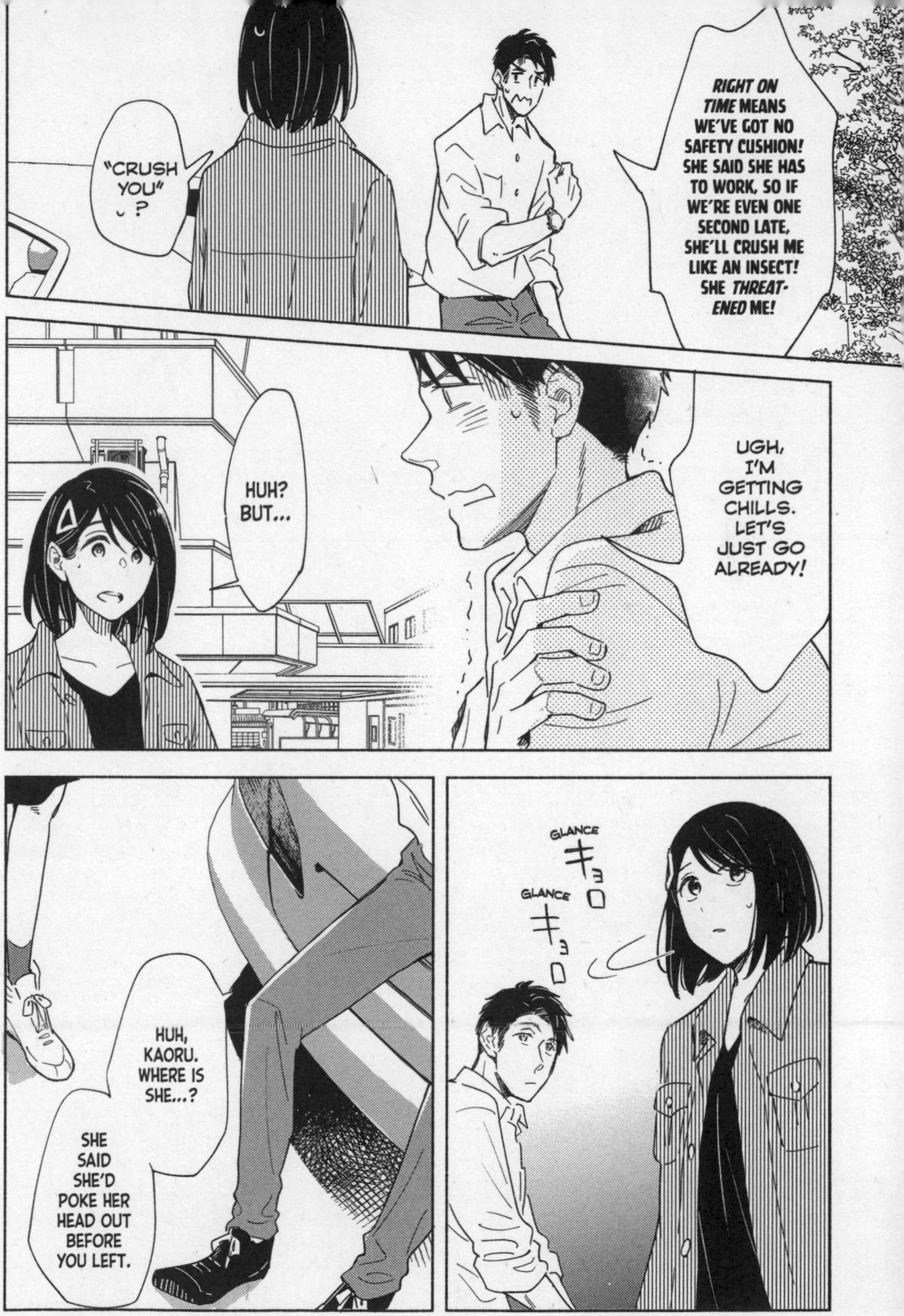
RIGHT ON TIME MEANS WE'VE GOT NO SAFETY CUSHION! SHE SAID SHE HAS TO WORK, SO IF WE'RE EVEN ONE SECOND LATE, SHE'LL CRUSH ME LIKE AN INSECT! SHE *THREAT-ENED* ME!
"CRUSH YOU"...?
UGH, I'M GETTING CHILLS. LET'S JUST GO ALREADY!
HUH? BUT...
GLANCE
キョロ
GLANCE
キョロ
HUH, KAORU. WHERE IS SHE...?
SHE SAID SHE'D POKE HER HEAD OUT BEFORE YOU LEFT.

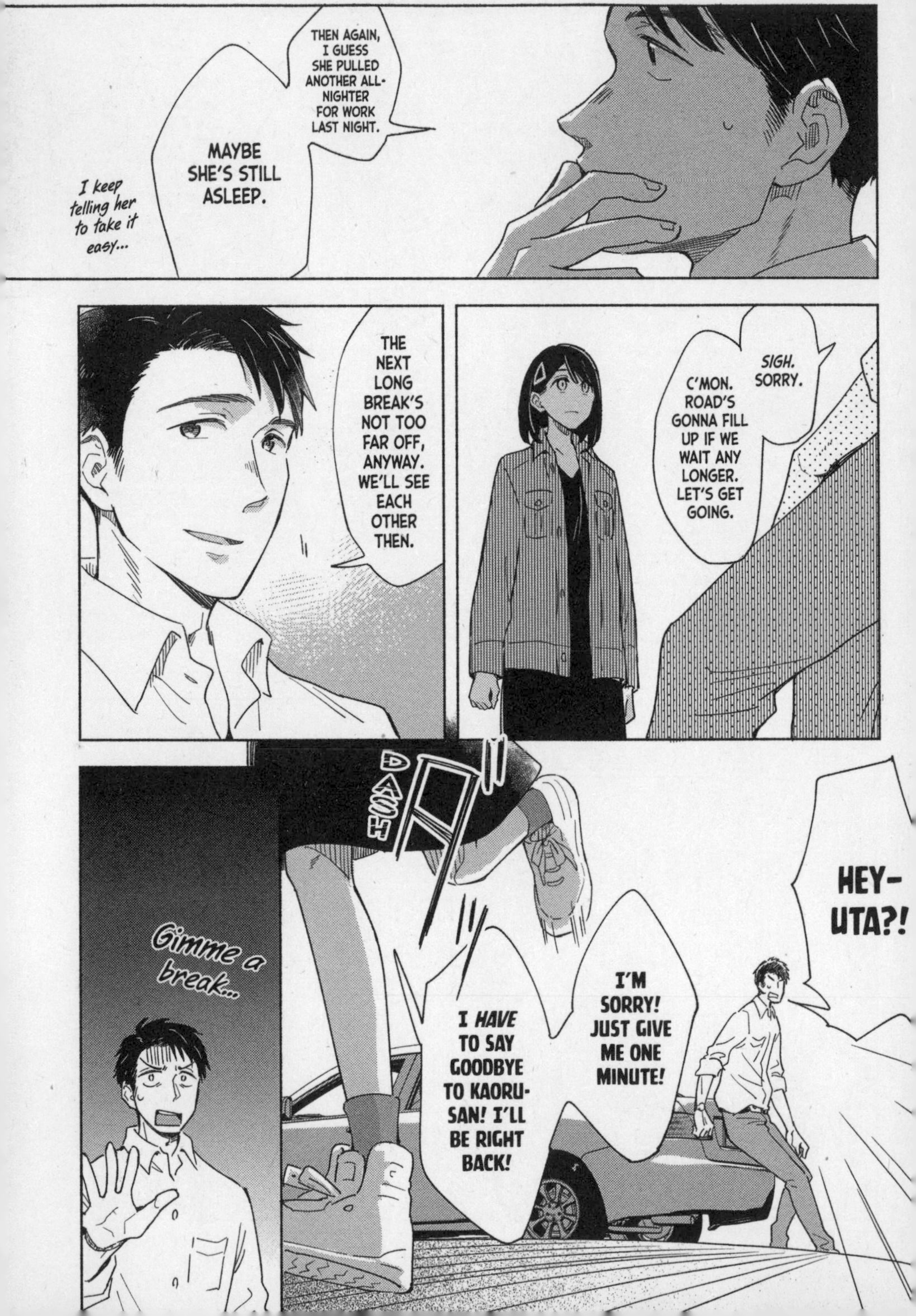
THEN AGAIN, I GUESS SHE PULLED ANOTHER ALL-NIGHTER FOR WORK LAST NIGHT.
MAYBE SHE'S STILL ASLEEP.
I keep telling her to take it easy...
SIGH. SORRY.
C'MON. ROAD'S GONNA FILL UP IF WE WAIT ANY LONGER. LET'S GET GOING.
THE NEXT LONG BREAK'S NOT TOO FAR OFF, ANYWAY. WE'LL SEE EACH OTHER THEN.
HEY- UTA?!
I'M SORRY! JUST GIVE ME ONE MINUTE!
I *HAVE* TO SAY GOODBYE TO KAORU-SAN! I'LL BE RIGHT BACK!
DASH
Gimme a break...

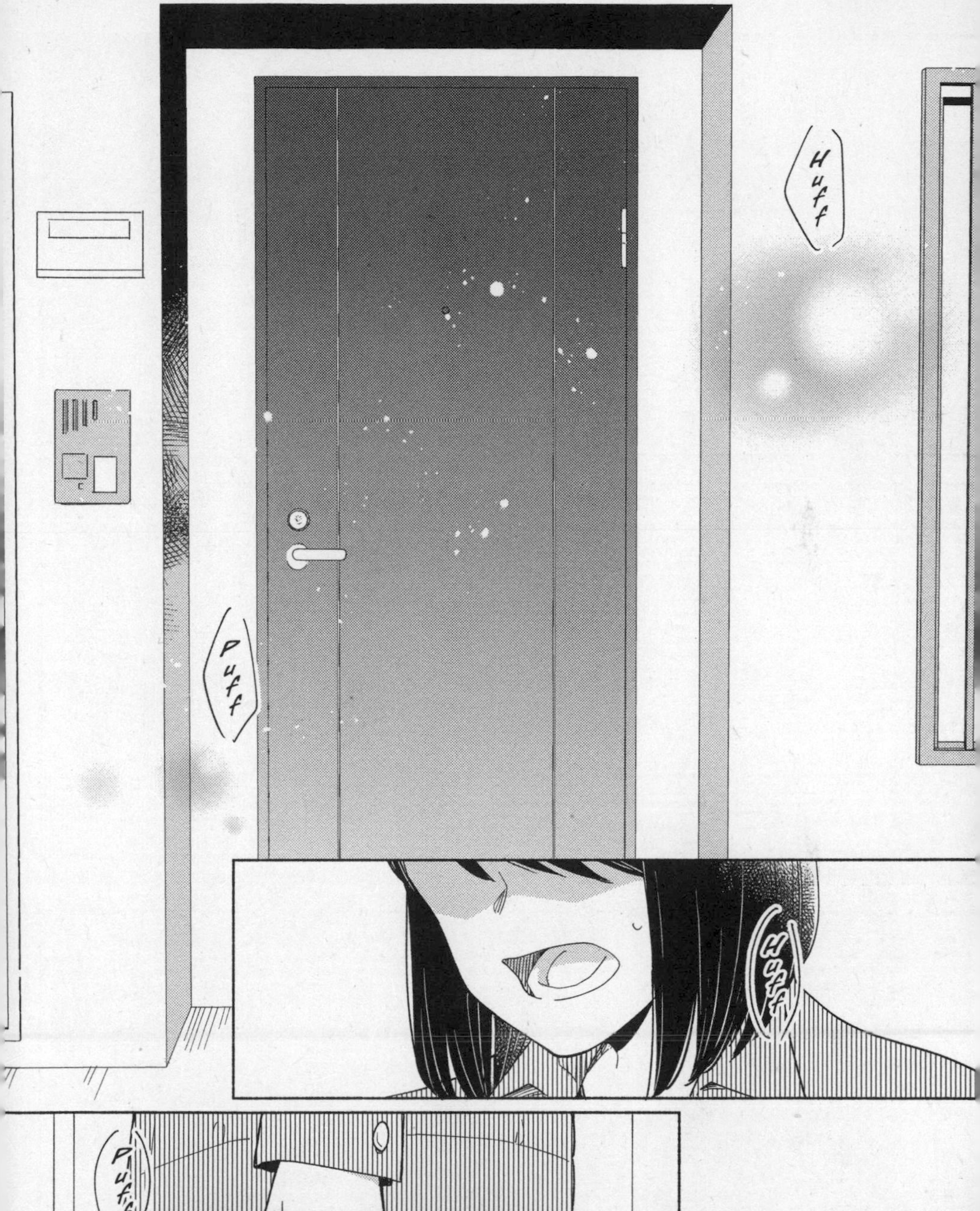
Huff
Puff
Huff
Puff

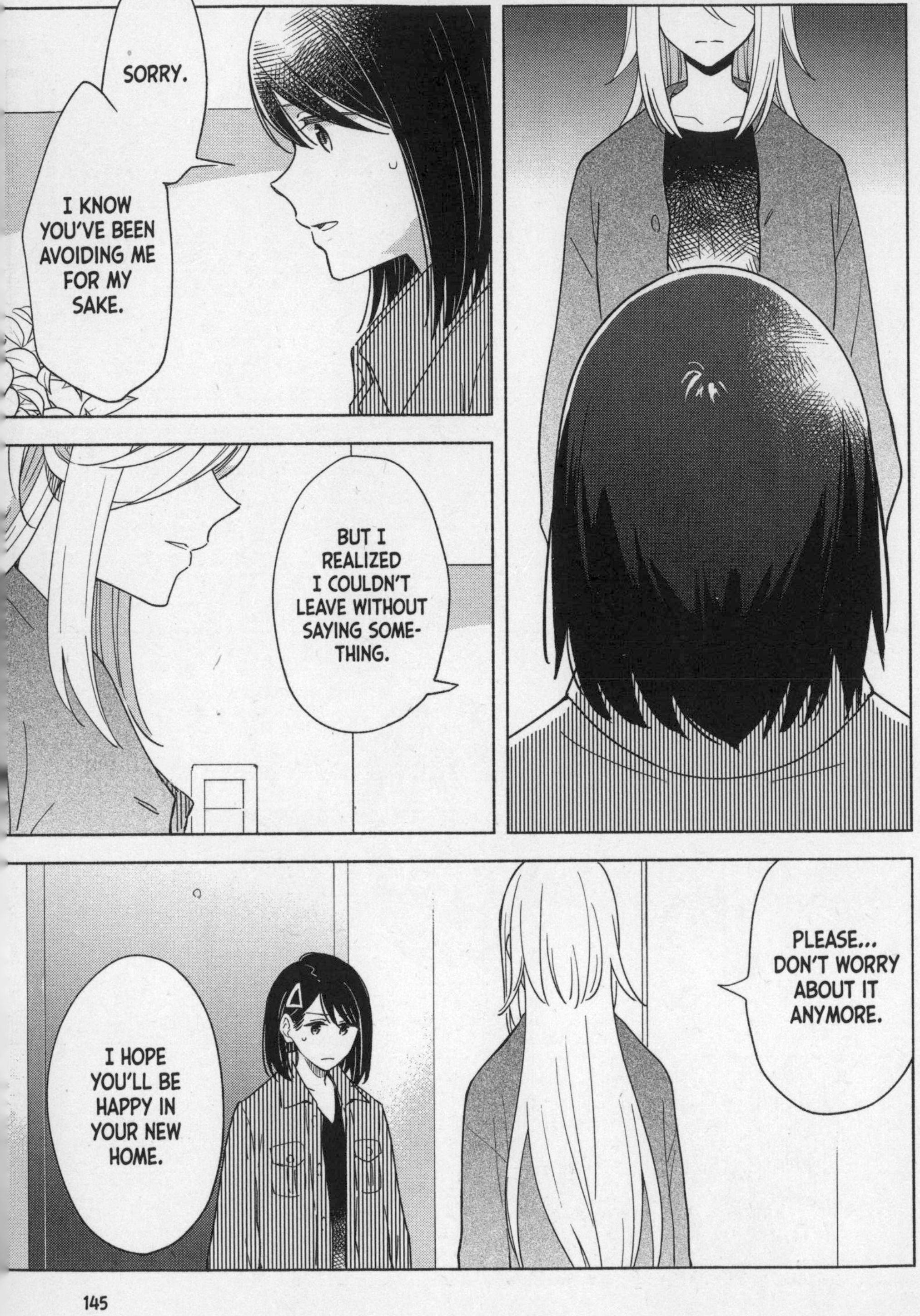
SORRY.
I KNOW YOU'VE BEEN AVOIDING ME FOR MY SAKE.
BUT I REALIZED I COULDN'T LEAVE WITHOUT SAYING SOME-THING.
PLEASE... DON'T WORRY ABOUT IT ANYMORE.
I HOPE YOU'LL BE HAPPY IN YOUR NEW HOME.

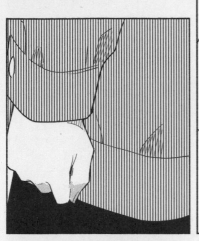
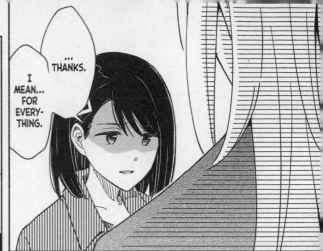

...THANKS.

I MEAN... FOR EVERY-THING.

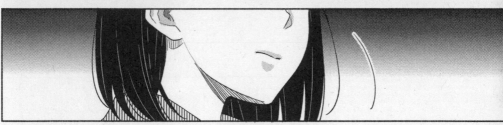

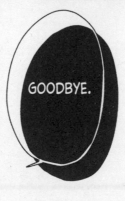

GOODBYE.

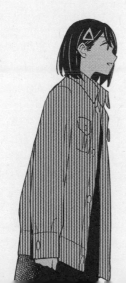

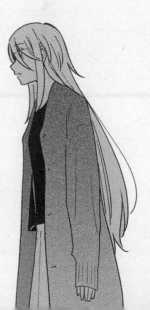

カチャ
CHAK

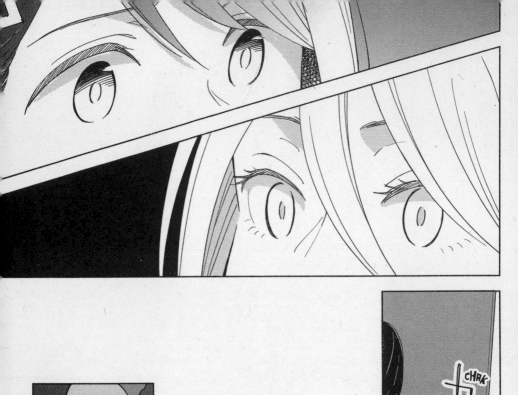

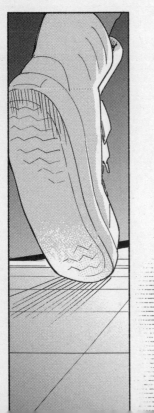

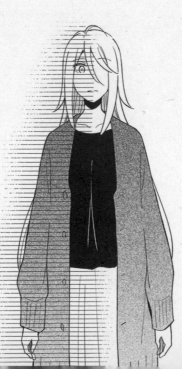

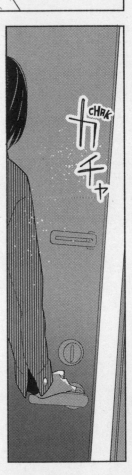

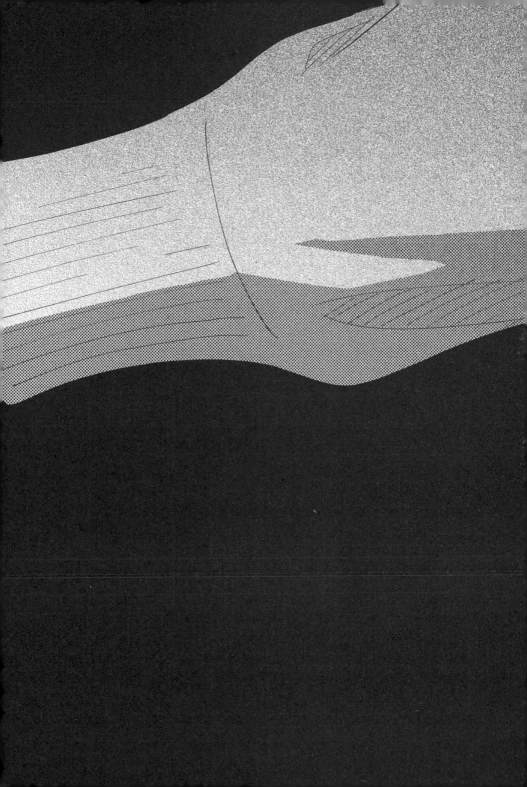

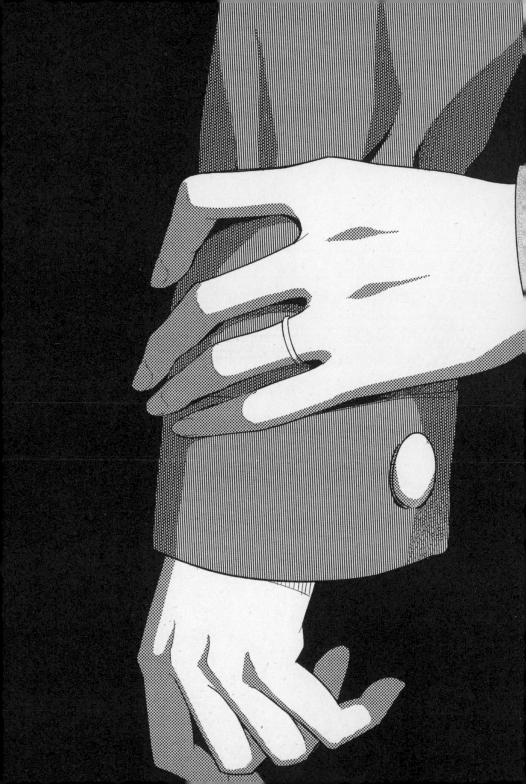

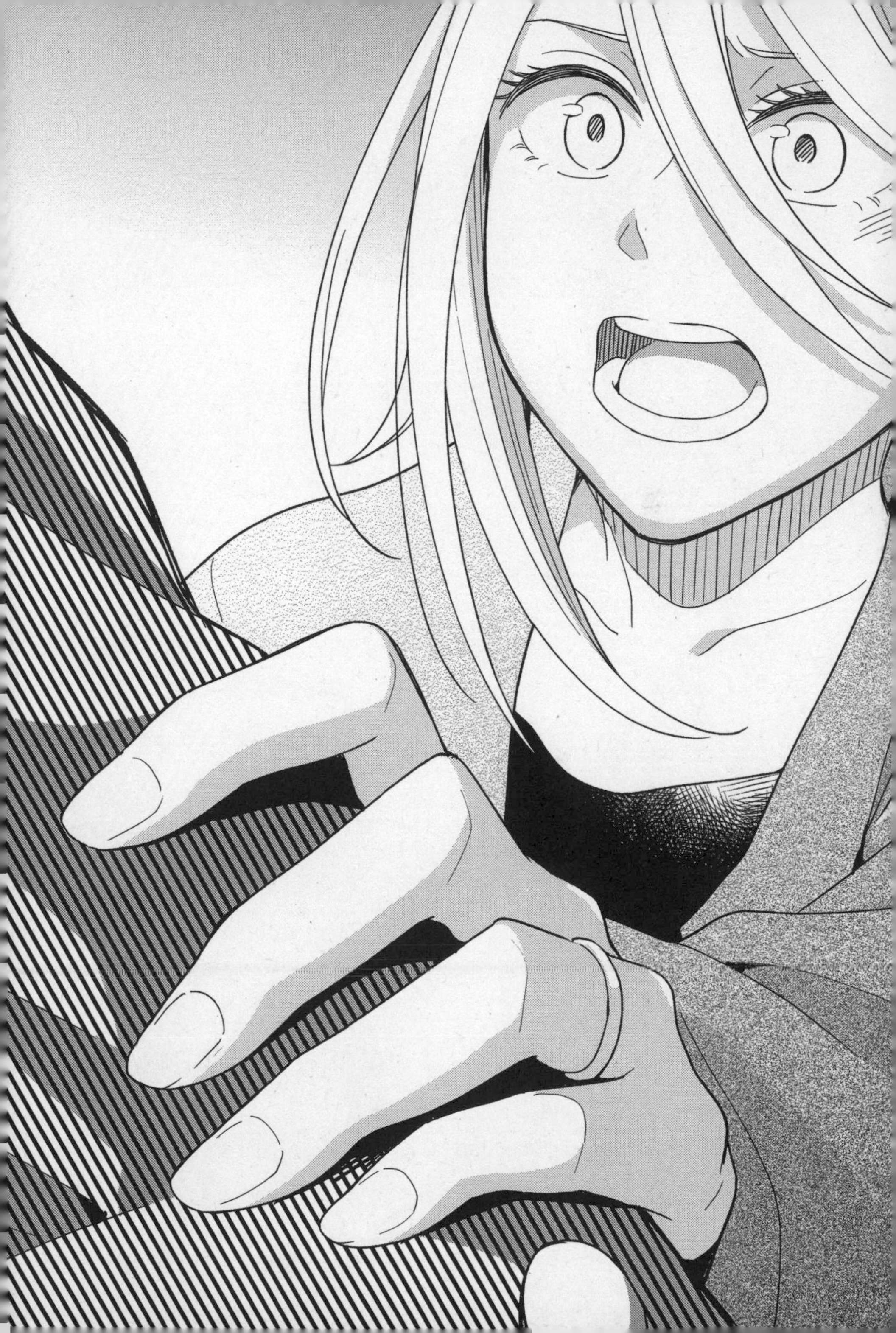

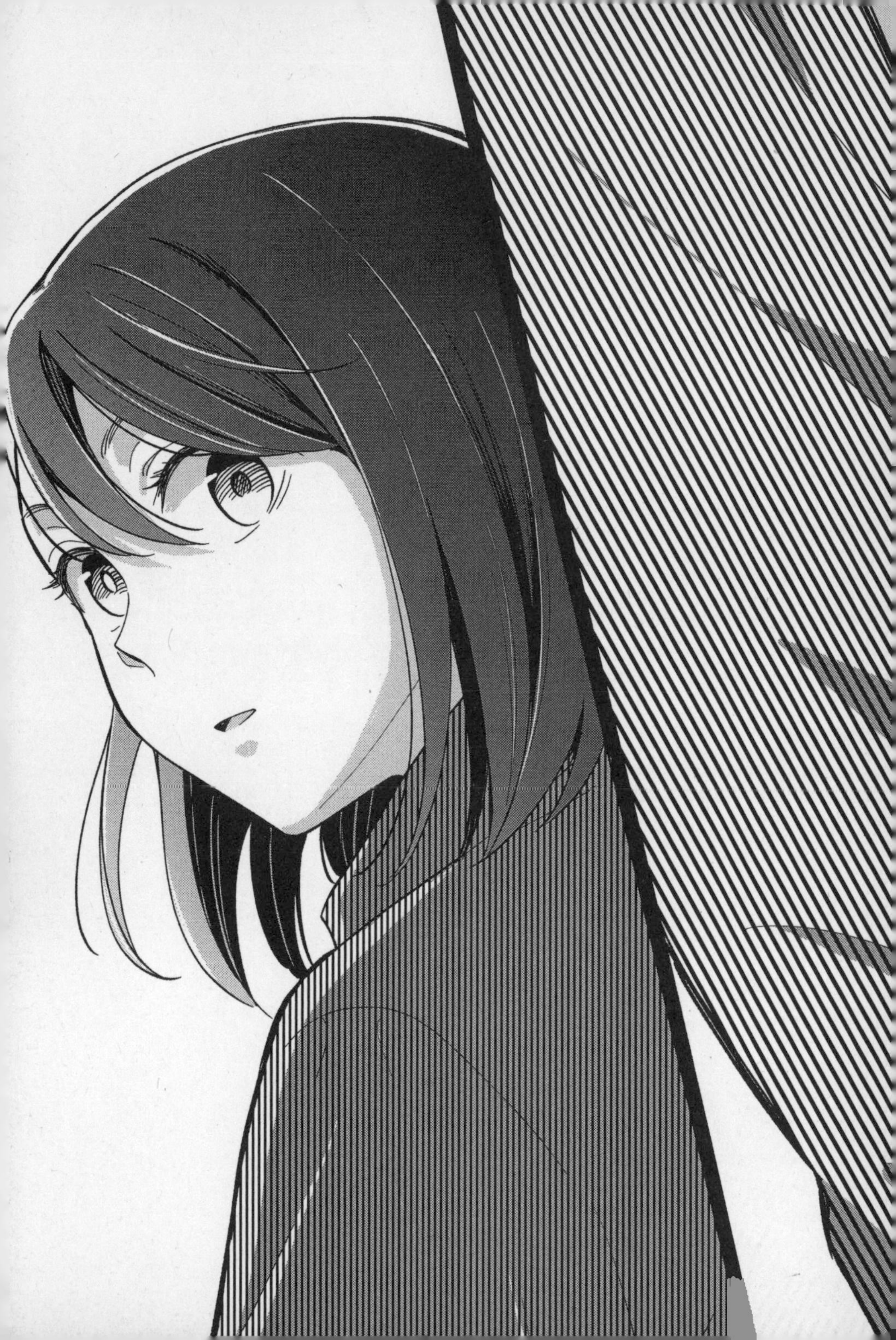

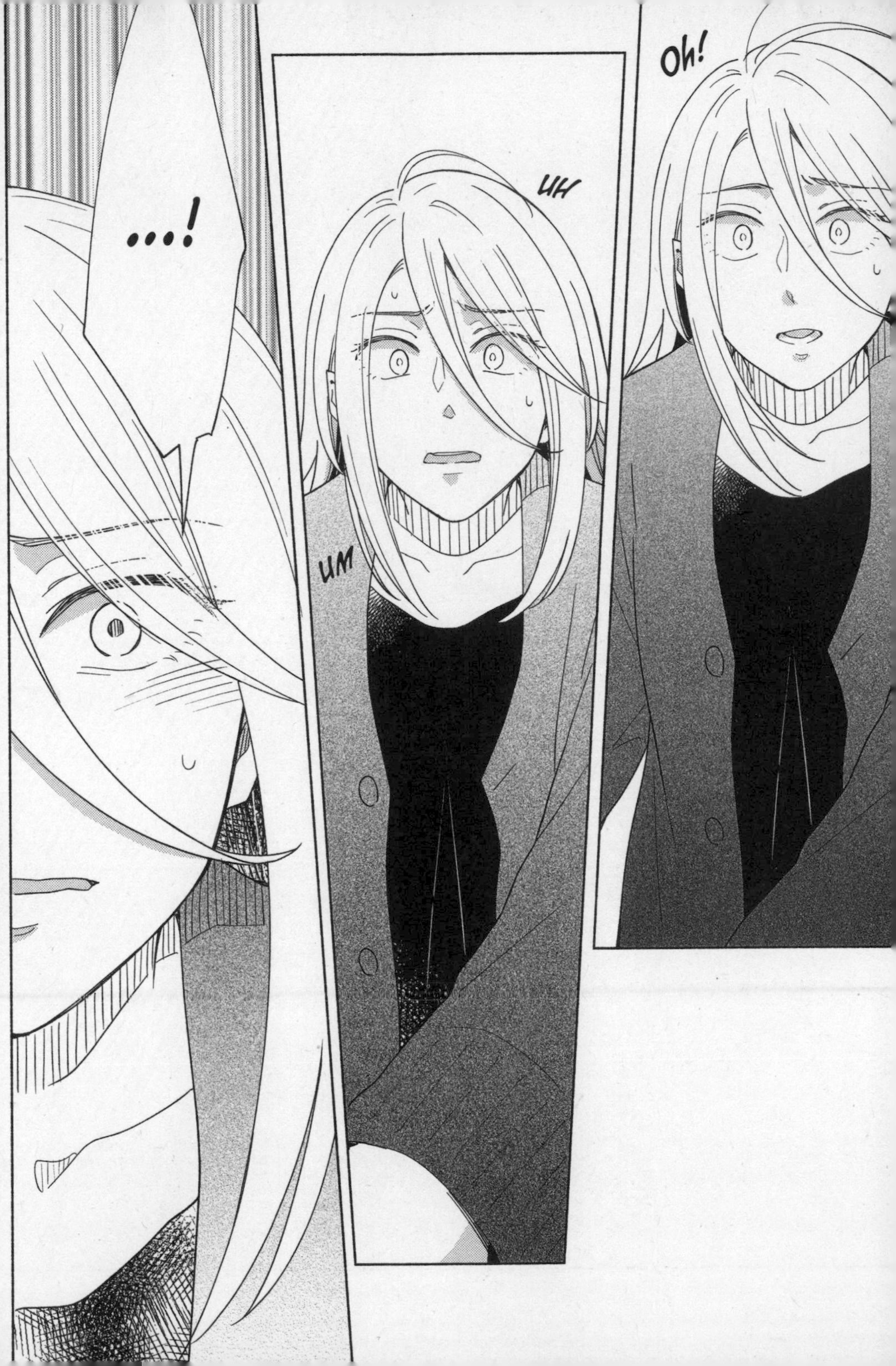

Oh!
UH
UM
...!

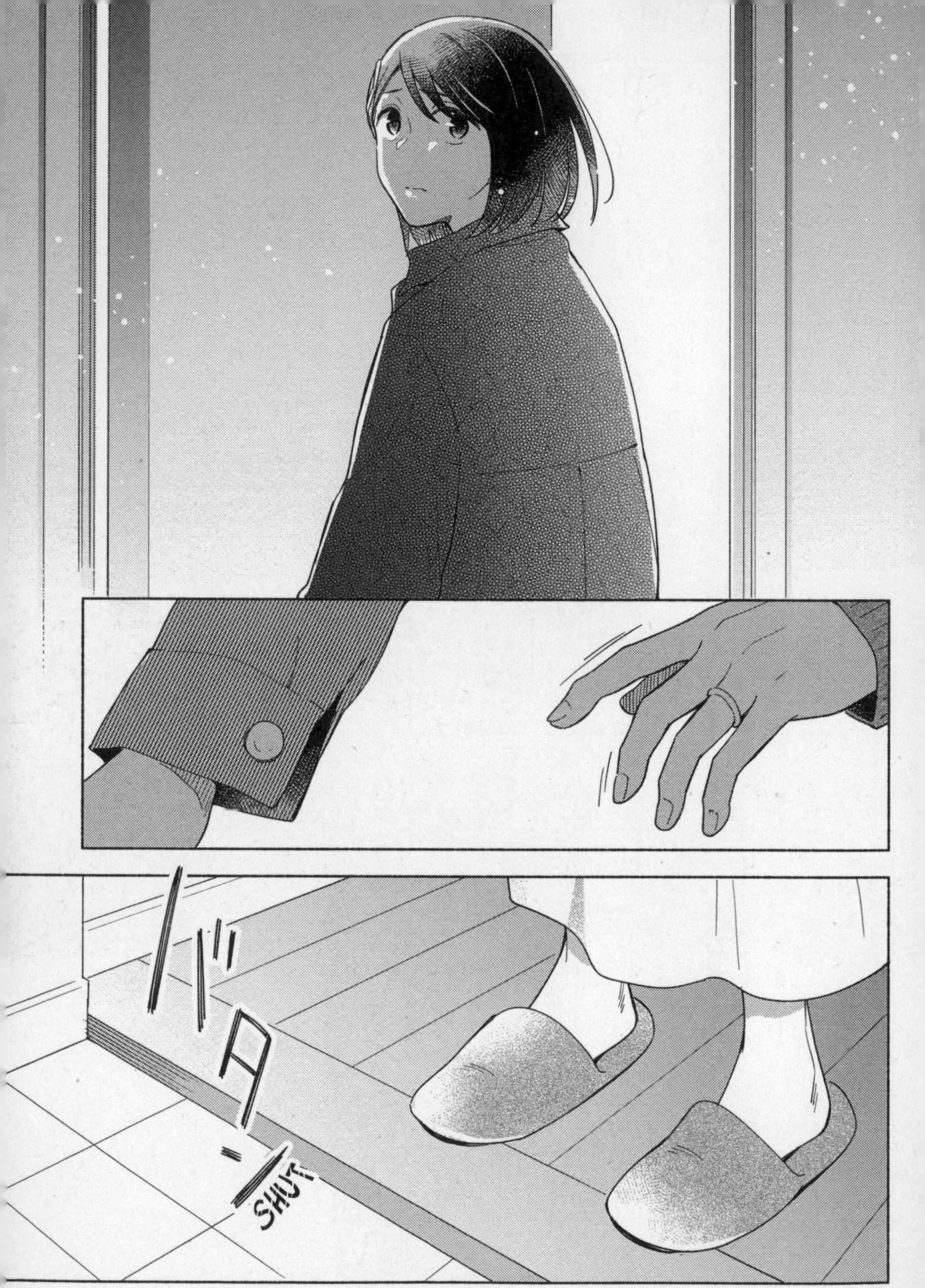
バタン
SHUT

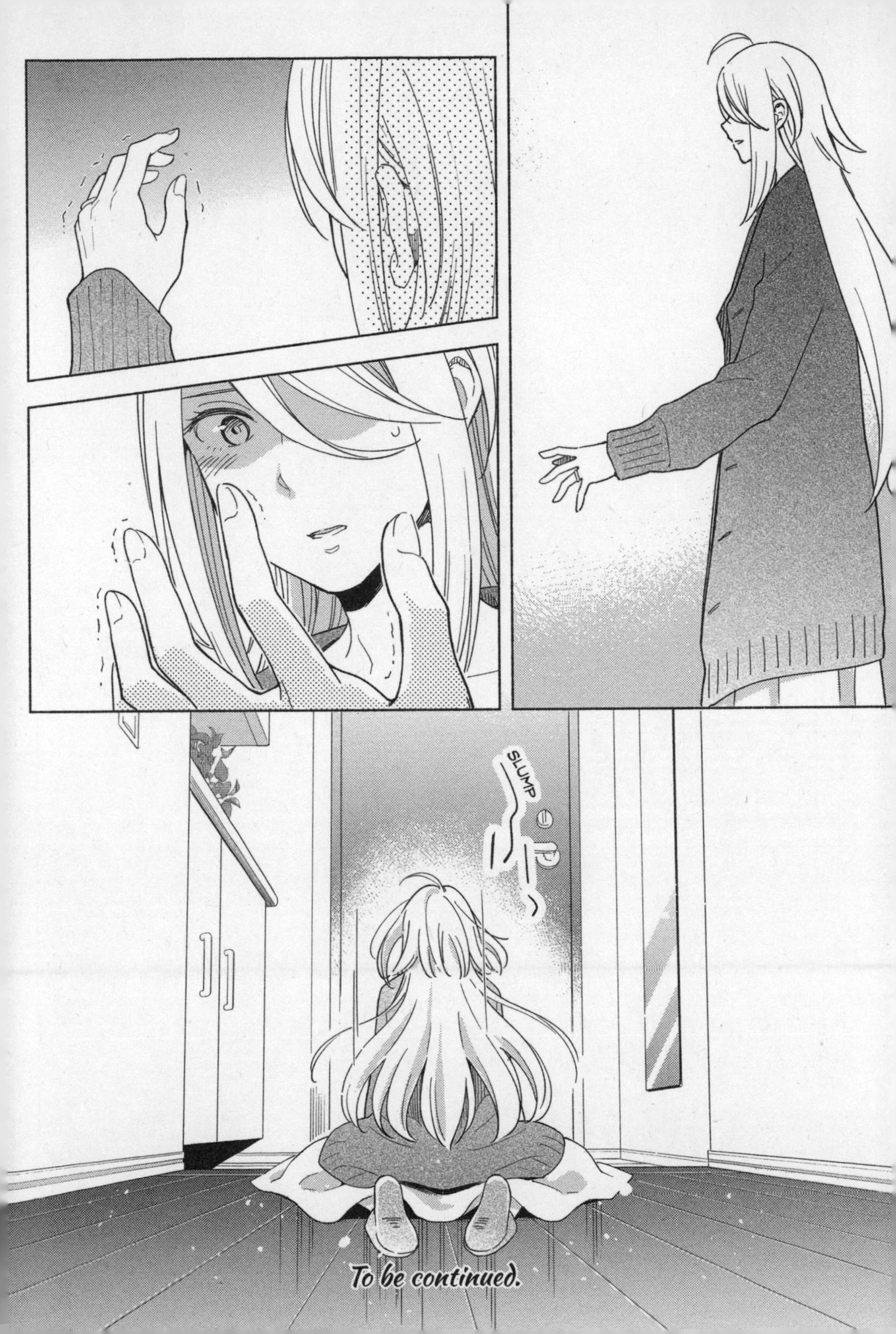
SLUMP
To be continued.

If I Could Reach You

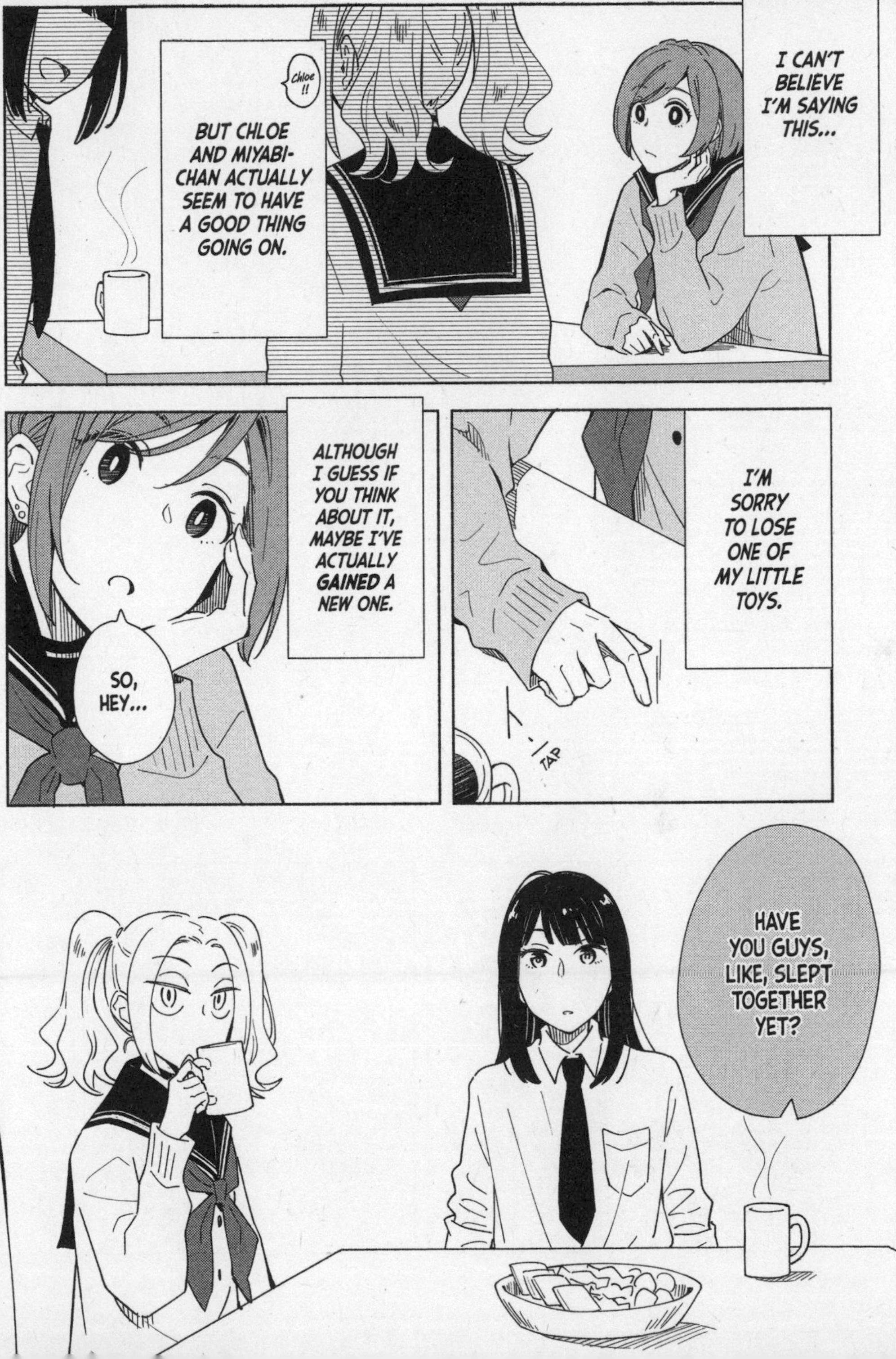
I CAN'T BELIEVE I'M SAYING THIS...
Chloe !!
BUT CHLOE AND MIYABI-CHAN ACTUALLY SEEM TO HAVE A GOOD THING GOING ON.
I'M SORRY TO LOSE ONE OF MY LITTLE TOYS.
TAP
ALTHOUGH I GUESS IF YOU THINK ABOUT IT, MAYBE I'VE ACTUALLY GAINED A NEW ONE.
SO, HEY...
HAVE YOU GUYS, LIKE, SLEPT TOGETHER YET?

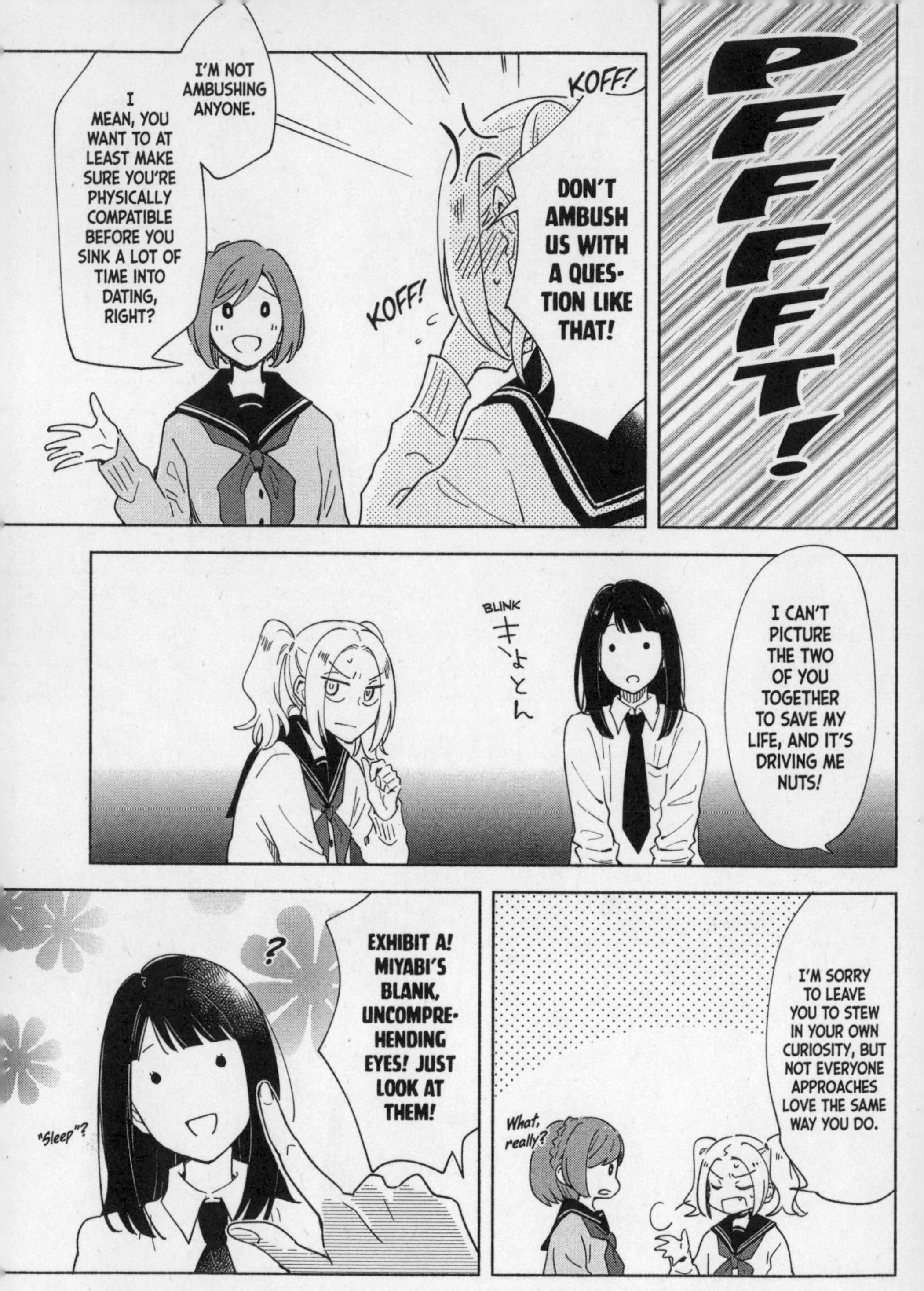
PFFFT!
KOFF!
DON'T AMBUSH US WITH A QUESTION LIKE THAT!
I'M NOT AMBUSHING ANYONE.
I MEAN, YOU WANT TO AT LEAST MAKE SURE YOU'RE PHYSICALLY COMPATIBLE BEFORE YOU SINK A LOT OF TIME INTO DATING, RIGHT?
KOFF!
I CAN'T PICTURE THE TWO OF YOU TOGETHER TO SAVE MY LIFE, AND IT'S DRIVING ME NUTS!
BLINK
I'M SORRY TO LEAVE YOU TO STEW IN YOUR OWN CURIOSITY, BUT NOT EVERYONE APPROACHES LOVE THE SAME WAY YOU DO.
What, really?
EXHIBIT A! MIYABI'S BLANK, UNCOMPREHENDING EYES! JUST LOOK AT THEM!
?
"Sleep"?

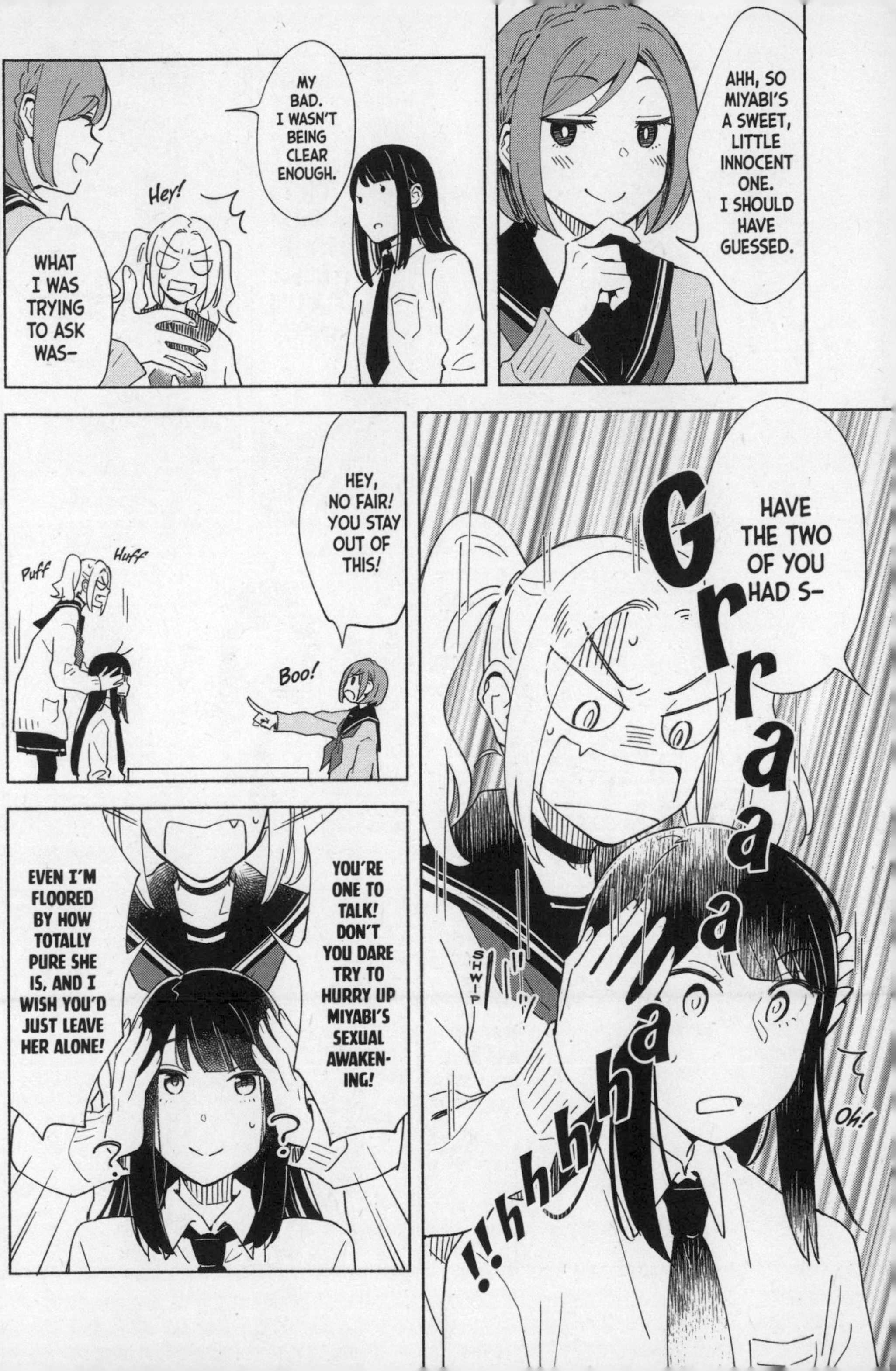

AHH, SO MIYABI'S A SWEET, LITTLE INNOCENT ONE. I SHOULD HAVE GUESSED.
MY BAD. I WASN'T BEING CLEAR ENOUGH.
Hey!
WHAT I WAS TRYING TO ASK WAS–
HAVE THE TWO OF YOU HAD S–
Grraaaaahhhhh!!
SHWIP
Oh!
HEY, NO FAIR! YOU STAY OUT OF THIS!
Huff
Puff
Boo!
YOU'RE ONE TO TALK! DON'T YOU DARE TRY TO HURRY UP MIYABI'S SEXUAL AWAKEN-ING!
EVEN I'M FLOORED BY HOW TOTALLY PURE SHE IS, AND I WISH YOU'D JUST LEAVE HER ALONE!

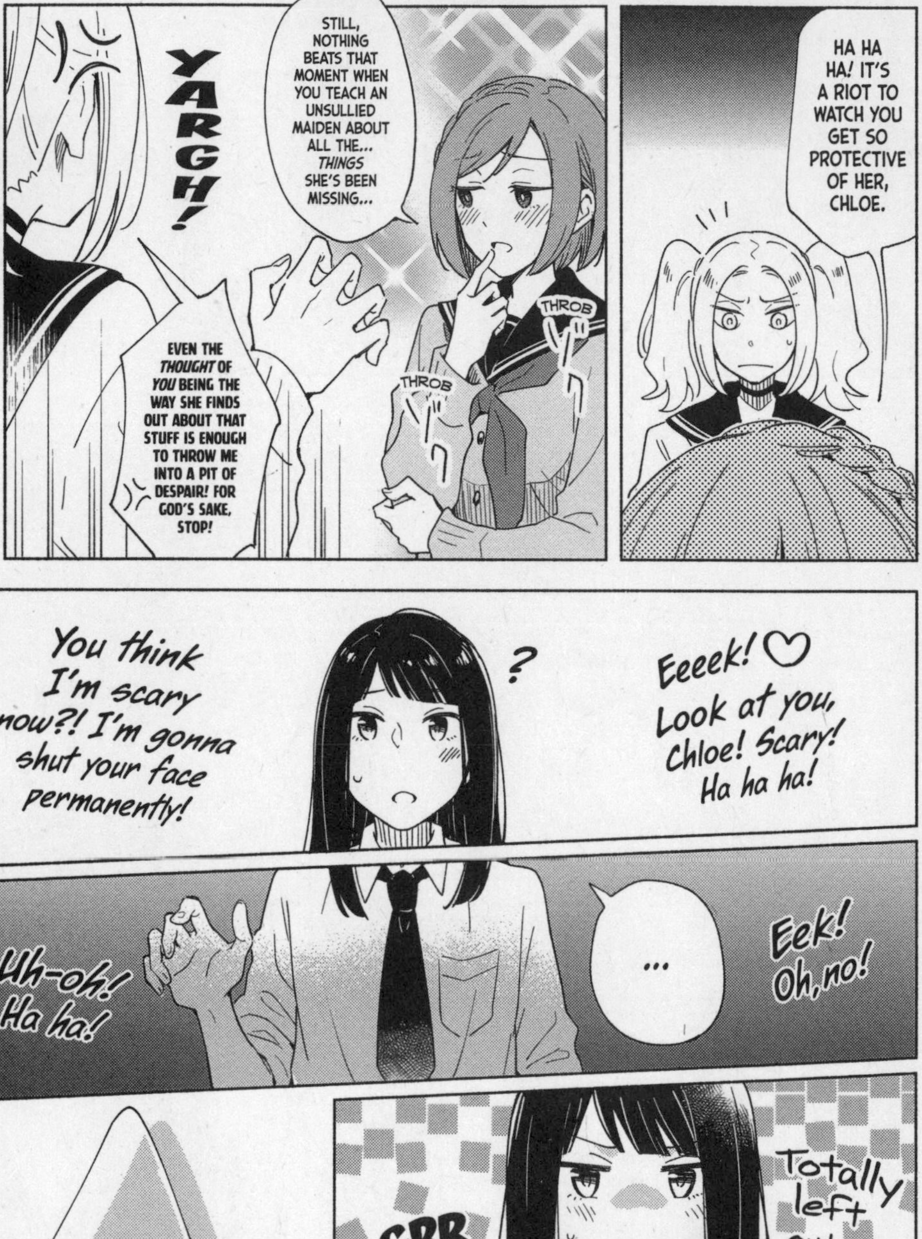
HA HA HA! IT'S A RIOT TO WATCH YOU GET SO PROTECTIVE OF HER, CHLOE.
STILL, NOTHING BEATS THAT MOMENT WHEN YOU TEACH AN UNSULLIED MAIDEN ABOUT ALL THE... *THINGS* SHE'S BEEN MISSING...
THROB
THROB
YARGH!
EVEN THE *THOUGHT* OF *YOU* BEING THE WAY SHE FINDS OUT ABOUT THAT STUFF IS ENOUGH TO THROW ME INTO A PIT OF DESPAIR! FOR GOD'S SAKE, STOP!
Eeeek! ♡ Look at you, Chloe! Scary! Ha ha ha!
?
You think I'm scary now?! I'm gonna shut your face permanently!
Eek! Oh, no!
...
Uh-oh! Ha ha!
Totally left out...
GRR
EXCUSE ME!

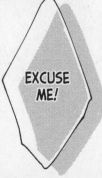

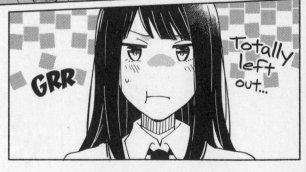

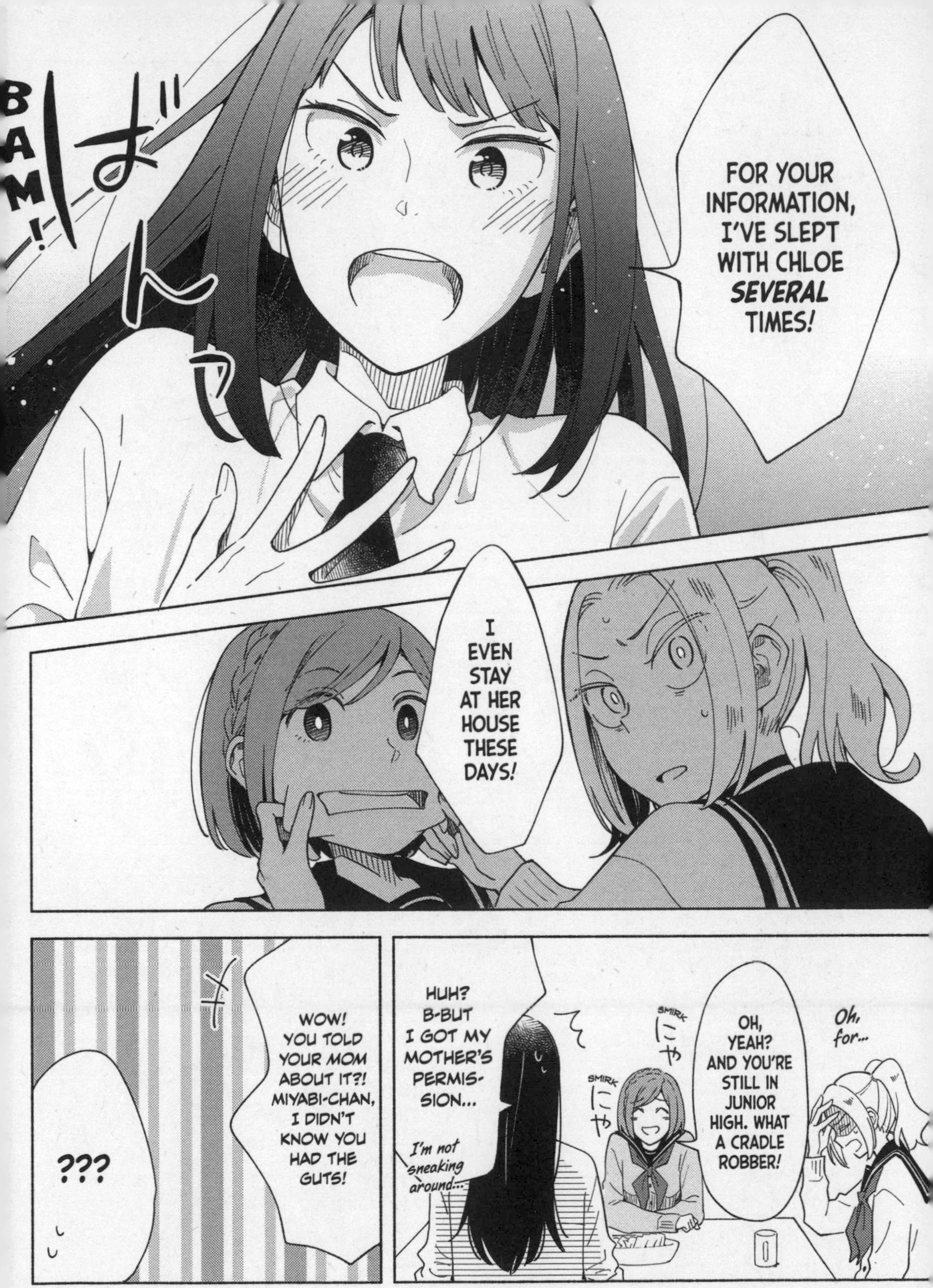
BAM!
ばんっ
FOR YOUR INFORMATION, I'VE SLEPT WITH CHLOE *SEVERAL* TIMES!
I EVEN STAY AT HER HOUSE THESE DAYS!
Oh, for...
OH, YEAH? AND YOU'RE STILL IN JUNIOR HIGH. WHAT A CRADLE ROBBER!
SMIRK にや
SMIRK にや
HUH? B-BUT I GOT MY MOTHER'S PERMIS-SION...
I'm not sneaking around...
WOW! YOU TOLD YOUR MOM ABOUT IT?! MIYABI-CHAN, I DIDN'T KNOW YOU HAD THE GUTS!
???

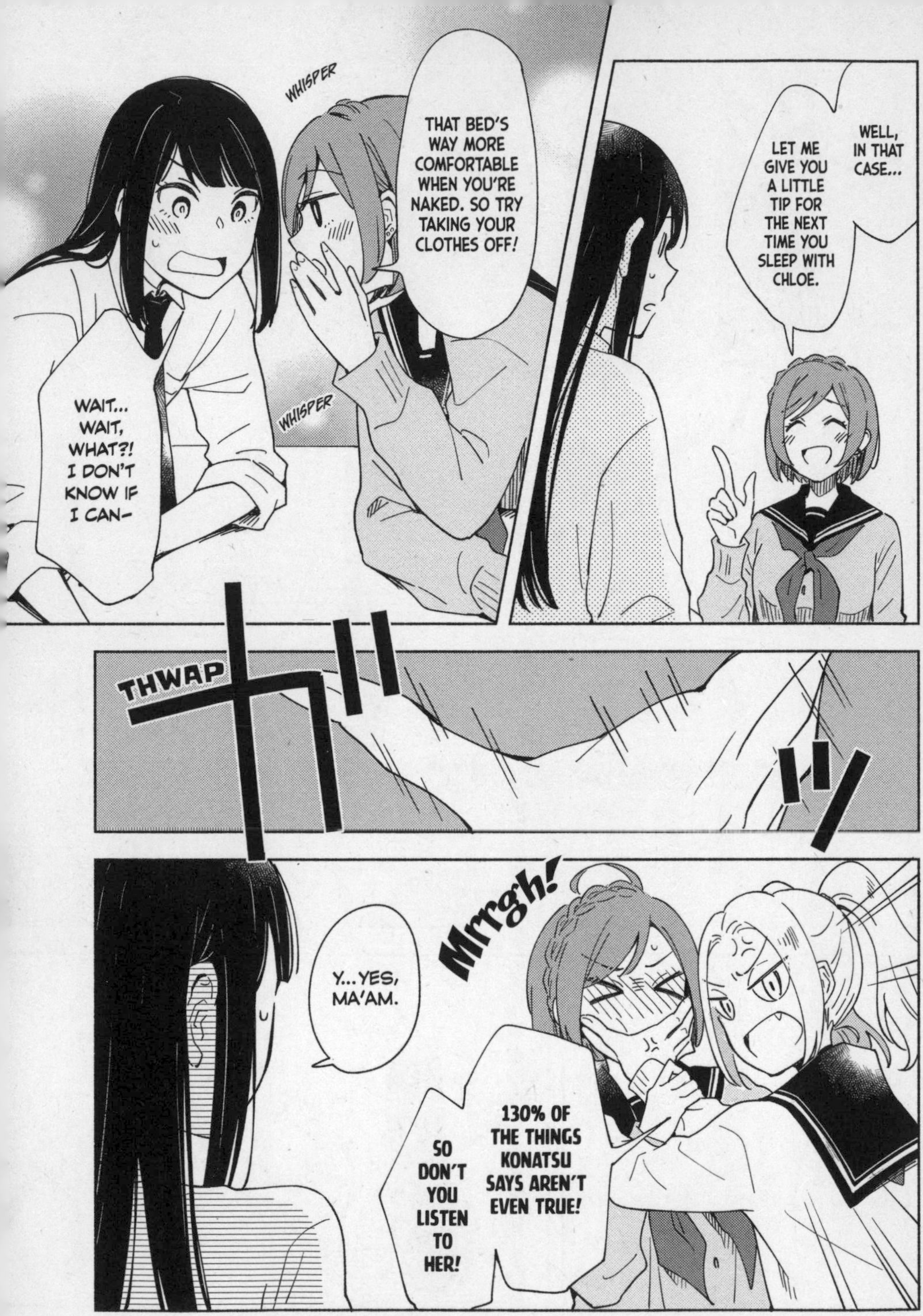
WELL, IN THAT CASE...
LET ME GIVE YOU A LITTLE TIP FOR THE NEXT TIME YOU SLEEP WITH CHLOE.
WHISPER
THAT BED'S WAY MORE COMFORTABLE WHEN YOU'RE NAKED. SO TRY TAKING YOUR CLOTHES OFF!
WHISPER
WAIT... WAIT, WHAT?! I DON'T KNOW IF I CAN-
THWAP
Mrrgh!
130% OF THE THINGS KONATSU SAYS AREN'T EVEN TRUE!
SO DON'T YOU LISTEN TO HER!
Y...YES, MA'AM.

Afterword

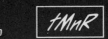

tMnR

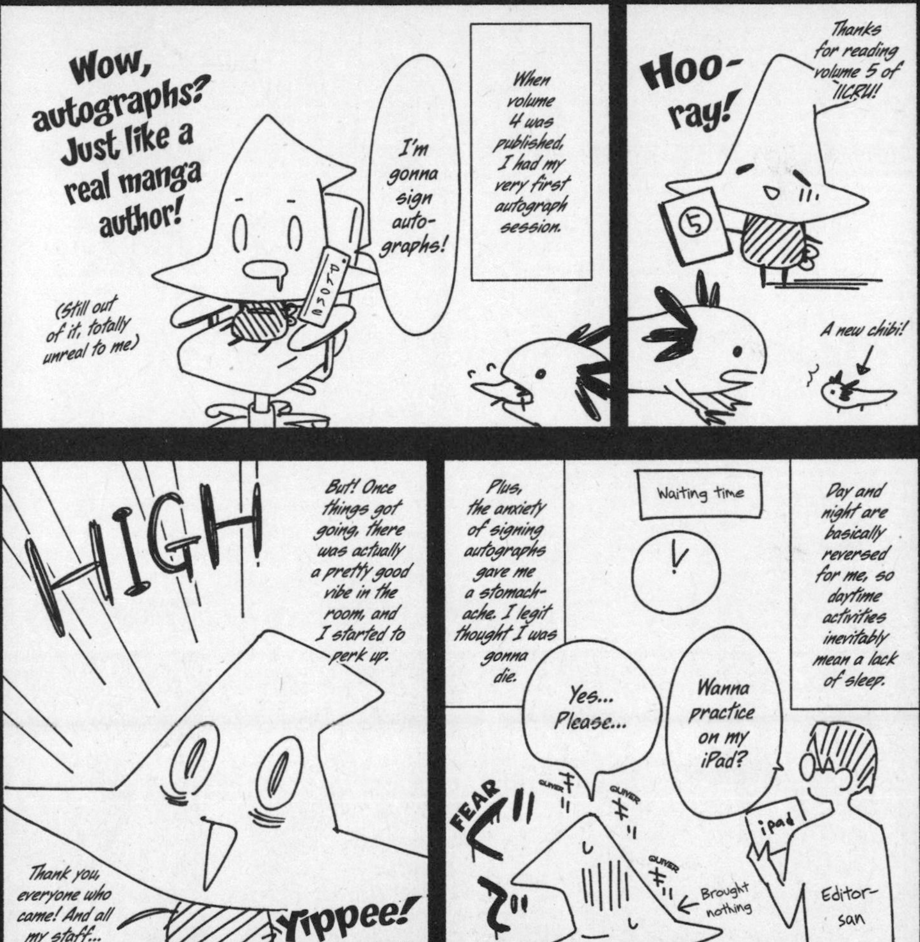

Thanks for reading volume 5 of IICRU!
Hoo-ray!
5
A new chibi!
When volume 4 was published, I had my very first autograph session.
I'm gonna sign auto-graphs!
Wow, autographs? Just like a real manga author!
phone
(Still out of it, totally unreal to me)
Day and night are basically reversed for me, so daytime activities inevitably mean a lack of sleep.
Waiting time
Plus, the anxiety of signing autographs gave me a stomach-ache. I legit thought I was gonna die.
Wanna practice on my iPad?
Yes... Please...
iPad
Editor-san
QUIVER
QUIVER
QUIVER
Brought nothing
FEAR
But! Once things got going, there was actually a pretty good vibe in the room, and I started to perk up.
HIGH
Yippee! Here we goooo!!
Thank you, everyone who came! And all my staff...

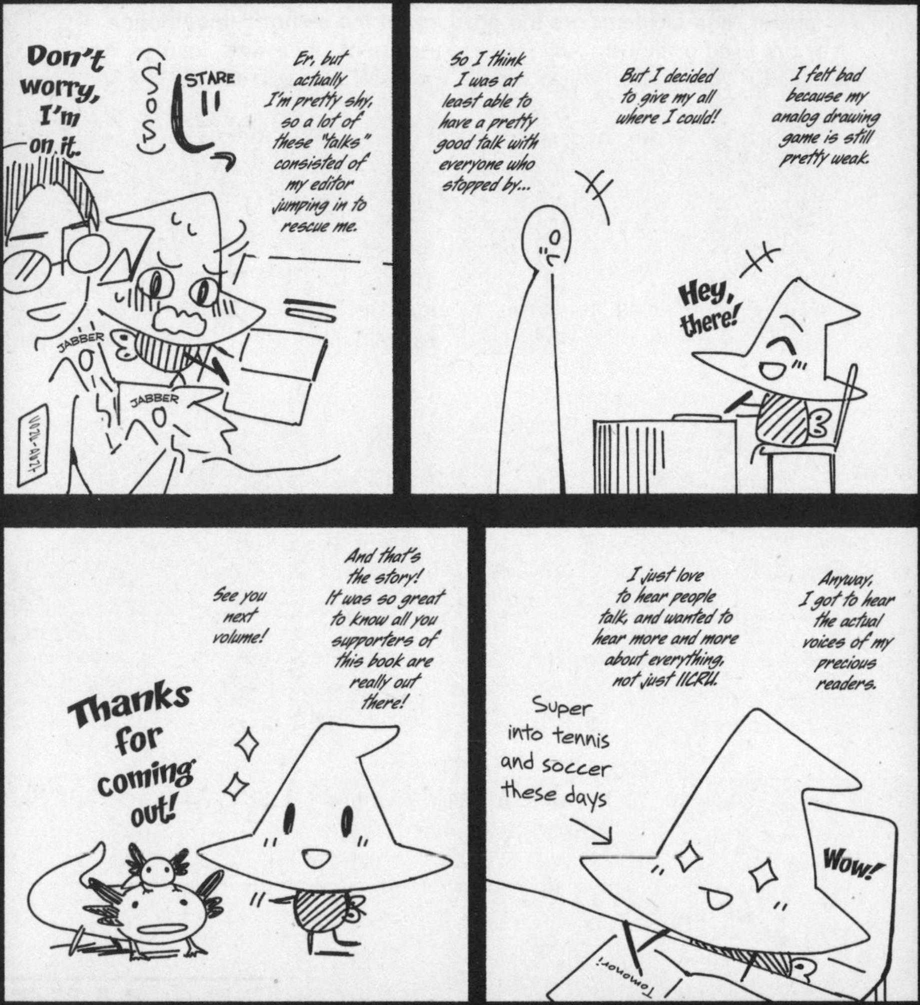
I felt bad because my analog drawing game is still pretty weak.
But I decided to give my all where I could!
So I think I was at least able to have a pretty good talk with everyone who stopped by...
Hey, there!
Er, but actually I'm pretty shy, so a lot of these "talks" consisted of my editor jumping in to rescue me.
STARE
SOS
Don't worry, I'm on it.
JABBER
JABBER
Anyway, I got to hear the actual voices of my precious readers.
I just love to hear people talk, and wanted to hear more and more about everything, not just IICRU.
Wow!
Super into tennis and soccer these days
And that's the story! It was so great to know all you supporters of this book are really out there!
See you next volume!
Thanks for coming out!

☆ Special Thanks ☆

Satou-san (Editor)
Kawatani Design
A-chan, K-kun, and Upa

and my readers!

A Kodansha Comics Trade Paperback Original
If I Could Reach You 5 copyright © 2019 tMnR
English translation copyright © 2020 tMnR

Published in the United States by Kodansha Comics, an imprint of Kodansha USA Publishing, LLC, New York.

Publication rights for this English edition arranged through Kodansha Ltd, Tokyo.

First published in Japan in 2019 by Ichijinsha Inc., Tokyo as *Tatoe Todokanu Itodatoshitemo*, volume 5.

ISBN 978-1-64651-047-4

Printed in the United States of America.

www.kodanshacomics.com

9 8 7 6 5 4 3 2 1
Translation: Kevin Steinbach
Lettering: Jennifer Skarupa
Editing: Haruko Hashimoto
Kodansha Comics edition cover design by Matthew Akuginow
Kodansha Comics edition logo design by Phil Balsman

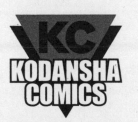

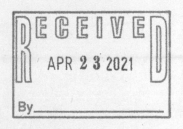

Publisher: Kiichiro Sugawara

Director of publishing services: Ben Applegate
Associate director of operations: Stephen Pakula
Publishing services managing editor: Noelle Webster
Assistant production manager: Emi Lotto, Angela Zurlo

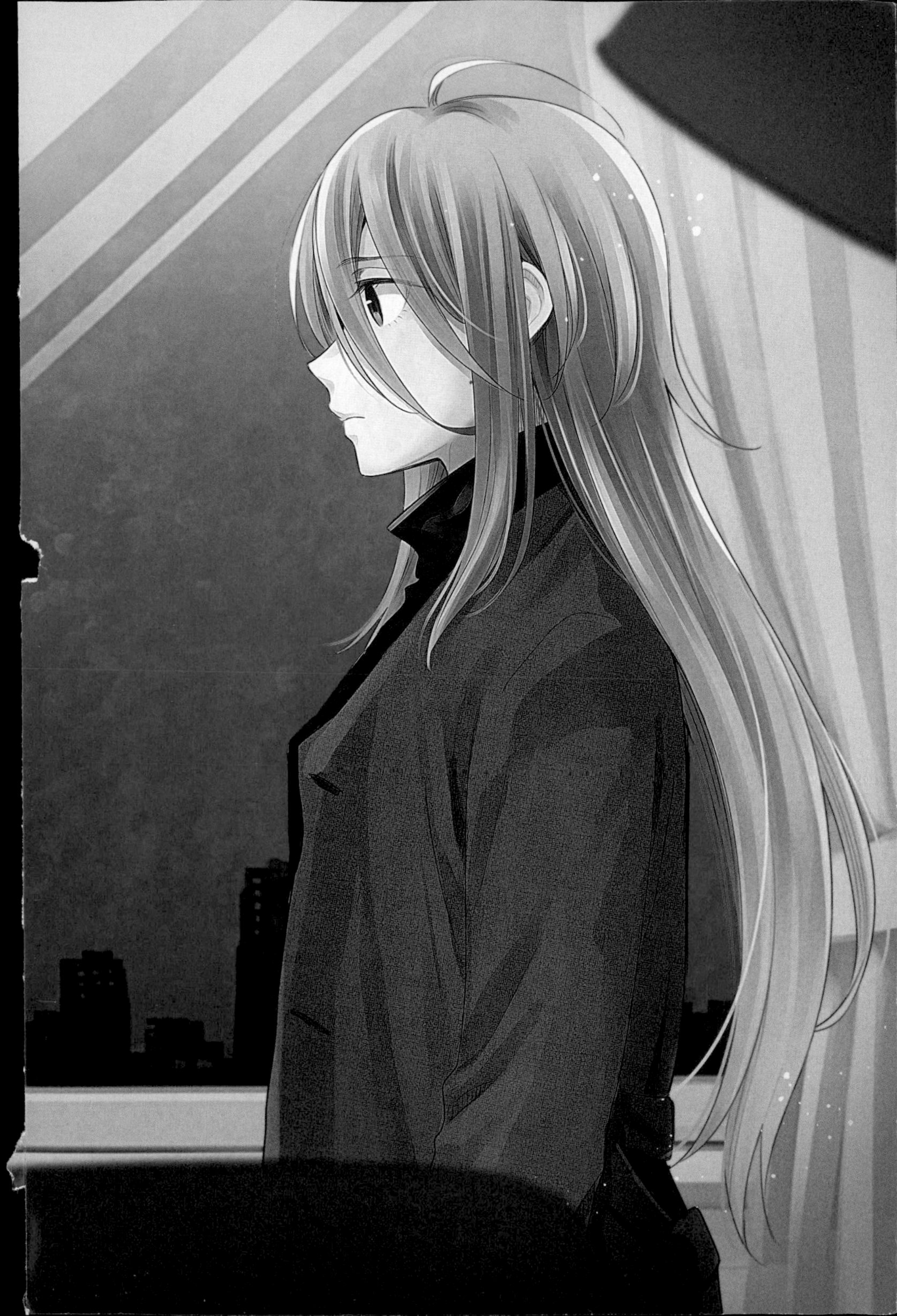